Praise for "Where's th

"Well-written, engaging, friendly, informative, and laugh-out-loud in places – I really enjoyed it."

> – **FIONA GILES** (Author of *Fresh Milk: The Secret Life of Breasts* and *Dick for a Day: What Would You do if You Had One?*)

"Wonderful and eye-opening ... Doula Trainings International will be adding *Where's the Mother?* to our required reading list for certifying doulas."

> – **DOULA TRAININGS INTERNATIONAL**

"Trevor's story is about a man breastfeeding his child, which is certainly unique, but it is also about a parent striving to give a baby the best possible nourishment, love and care – which is something every parent understands. Despite the challenges, Trevor doesn't take himself too seriously: he always keeps his sense of humor and his humility. You can't help but be drawn into his story."

> – **TERESA PITMAN** (co-author, *The Ultimate Book of Breast-feeding Answers* and *The Womanly Art of Breastfeeding, 8th edition*)

"I read this book more voraciously than I have read anything in a long time. As a pregnant trans person I greatly appreciated his story, being shared in his own words. It is woven beautifully with the stories of those he encountered along the way and helpful information about pregnancy, birthing and chestfeeding all written in language that felt relevant and accessible to me."

> – **KORI DOTY**, community educator and host of KCR radio's *Sex, Drugs, and How We Roll,* www.koridoty.com

Where's the MOTHER?

Stories from a Transgender Dad

Trevor MacDonald

Trans
Canada
Press

Winnipeg

This book is a work of nonfiction. Certain names and identifying details in the introduction and book have been changed. URLs accurate as of 24 March 2016.

Cover: Helping to poke fun at gender roles is Jacob's milk donor Tara, an ivy-league PhD candidate. Photo: Rahim Ruda.

Published by Trans Canada Press • Box 17, Group 16, RR1 • Dugald, MB R0E 0K0
For interviews, personal appearances, and permissions: info@transcanadapress.com
Educational and bulk discounts are available. Contact sales@transcanadapress.com
Visit facebook.com/wheresthemother • Visit Trevor's blog at www.milkjunkies.net

Library and Archives Canada Cataloguing in Publication

MacDonald, Trevor, 1985-, author
      Where's the mother : stories from a transgender dad / Trevor MacDonald.

Issued in print and electronic formats.
ISBN 978-0-9919645-1-2 (hardback).--ISBN 978-0-9919645-0-5 (paperback).--
ISBN 978-0-9919645-2-9 (ebook)

      1. MacDonald, Trevor, 1985-. 2. Transgender parents--Manitoba--
Winnipeg--Biography. 3. Gay parents--Manitoba--Winnipeg--Biography.
4. Pregnancy. 5. Breast milk--Collection and preservation--Anecdotes.
6. Breastfeeding. I. Title.

HQ77.8.M33A3 2016   306.76'8092   C2016-901677-3
                                                                     C2016-901678-1

Dedicated to my husband and children, who provided the basis for the subject material in the first place, and then made it nearly impossible to write it down;

to you, the ally who has come to read, learn, and laugh with me;

and to all the trans and genderqueer folks who live their beautiful lives in this difficult world.

Acknowledgements

I offer my deepest thanks to Fiona Giles for contributing her thought-provoking introduction that situates the book's narrative in terms of human rights and social justice. I am forever grateful to her, and to authors Diana West and Terry Jordan, who believed in me from the beginning and have taught me so much. Sincere, humble thanks to Meran Currie-Roberts, Sion Jesse, Mary Lynne Biener, Aimee Ouellette, Melissa Kent, Candice Fisk, Nitsa Ortchuk, Charlie Primeau, Kameron Logan and countless others who have provided encouragement and insights along the way. Finally, I extend my most heartfelt appreciation to the milk donors who helped to feed my babies and who were the inspiration for writing this book.

Going With the Flow

Foreword by Fiona Giles

"People are different from each other. It's astonishing how few respectable tools we have for dealing with this fact."

Eve Kokofsky Sedgwick, *Epistemology of the Closet,* 1990

Last week one of my teenagers came home from school and said, "Something interesting happened today."

"What?" I asked.

"We had a school assembly and the Deputy Principal Miss Lawrence said that one of the kids from my year, Kimberly, is now Tom."

"Did it create a stir?"

"No, not really. Miss just said they'd changed all his documents and he'd like to be treated the same as everyone else."

Around the same time that this conversation with my teenager took place, celebrated United States Olympic athlete and television personality, Caitlyn Jenner—formerly Bruce Jenner—was featured on the cover of the July 2015 issue of *Vanity Fair*, photographed by Annie Leibowitz. In the context of media history, this was reminiscent of an earlier *Vanity Fair* cover by Annie Leibowitz, in August 1991, which featured the actress Demi Moore, naked, and in her seventh month of pregnancy. A socio-political milestone had been reached.

Soon after the Jenner edition of *Vanity Fair* was released, celebrated African-American transgender actress and blogger, Laverne Cox, was also making news, quoted as saying that, unlike Jenner, she'd decided against facial surgery because she prefers to keep her nose the way it is. "This is my black nose," she said, "and it's gorgeous." [1] The conversation in the media had moved on from the spectacle of difference-made-glamorous to a discussion of mundane aesthetics about body size and shape. It was interesting to see how the transgender debate was being absorbed into the familiar compare-and-contrast exercises between celebrities that are found every week in celebrity magazines the world over. Representations of transgender people had moved, just slightly, from freakishness to fabulosity. And in the realm of body modification—from botox to breast surgery and beyond—what's a little nose job, or gender confirmation surgery?

In the same period, still in the middle of 2015, the United States made international news when it joined seventeen other countries in legalising same-sex marriage. With similar laws in several other countries, such as Ireland and Finland, soon to be enforced, and popular support in others such as Australia, marriage equality is on its way to broader acceptance, at least in some Western countries. Another milestone in the journey toward equality is moving closer, adding this much-needed judicial stamp of approval to the symbolic achievements represented by the media in recognizing sexual difference. Battles for marriage equality and for transgender rights have in many ways been conducted separately; and at times these marginalized groups have been in conflict. Thus the timing of these advances provides a real sense of progress, as both the law and mainstream media support the rights of formerly persecuted individuals. There is of course considerable work still to be done to recognize the rights of transgender citizens, particularly in being granted adequate legal documentation,

---

[1] Laverne Cox, "Now I have the money to feminize my face I don't want to," *Guardian*, 15 June 2015, http://goo.gl/aFw6lU

and equal access to health care. But gradual advances are being made in order to free all of us just that little bit more from the constraints of heteronormativity. Although transgender individuals need priority in this regard, it's important to remember that their achievements will loosen the ties that bind all of us into uniformly gendered expectations. Progress in so-called minority rights benefits everyone.

How odd then, that also around this time, the June 2015 issue of Australian *Elle* magazine featured the fashion model Nicole Trunfio breastfeeding her four-month-old son Zion on its cover, but declined to release this version on its newsstands. Instead the editor chose to release the image on the subscriber edition only, calling it an opportunity to "say thank you" to its regular readership.[2] The edition available on newsstands showed the same model fully clothed, and holding her baby, naked and sleeping. While the editor, Justin Cullen, called this a "commercial decision" and a "beautiful bonus" for loyal readers, Trunfio was keen to distance herself from this line of argument, tweeting that the unplanned image taken while breastfeeding during the photo shoot deserved a wider release in the interests of normalizing breastfeeding.[3]

In the context of the increasing acceptance of transgender rights and marriage equality, and for body modification and the diversity of sexualities, breastfeeding stands out as an issue that remains stuck in the past. In particular, any images of breastfeeding in public are tightly regulated, so that mainstream social media has been late to accept that breastfeeding parents might feel free to post online photos of themselves while feeding their babies. Beyond Facebook controversies, with breastfeeding photos removed for "nudity violations" as late as January

---

[2] Mary Ward, "Nicole Trunfio didn't think 'Elle' breastfeeding cover would be a 'big deal'," *Sydney Morning Herald*, 27 May 2015, http://goo.gl/dIumpi

[3] Maybelle Morgan, "'Elle' under fire after refusing to sell controversial cover of supermodel breastfeeding her young son in shops," *Daily Mail*, 22 May 2015, http://goo.gl/1OxlUK

2015,[4] other more artistically framed breastfeeding selfies have also made the news, with Sky Boucher's image on Tumblr, "Tea for Two," showing her tandem nursing her twins, going viral, and attracting "a barrage of both criticism and acclaim".[5] #Brelfies is now a dedicated Twitter feed for parents to protest image restrictions by uploading more pictures.

The furore surrounding the controversial *Time* magazine cover of 21 May 2012, which showed a three-year-old boy standing on a chair to breastfeed, while he and his mother met the viewer's gaze, indicates the unease many people continue to feel concerning the use of human breasts as a source of food. As long as parents breastfeed under strictly normative circumstances, they are revered for being dutiful, virtuous, "good mothers." This ideal breastfeeding is conducted in private, domestic spaces; and if it occurs in public, then it's preferably a low-traffic area, with breast and baby covered by scarves or clothing. Departures from this protocol, with breasts or breast milk visible, or an older child breastfeeding, can incite ejection from premises, social harassment and shaming, despite women being protected by law in many countries to breastfeed in public.[6] Even cautiously breastfeeding parents, who have taken their baby to a secluded position in, for example, a public swimming pool, and where it's normal to be scantily clad, have been targeted.[7]

As Petra Bueskens notes, it's as if breastfeeding in public triggers

---

[4] Rachel Moss, "Facebook clarifies nudity policy," *Huffington Post UK*, 16 March 2015, http://goo.gl/xFCOf3

[5] Sonja Boon and Beth Pentney, "Virtual Lactivism: Breastfeeding Selfies and the Performance of Motherhood," *International Journal of Communication,* 9 (2015): 1760.

[6] Legislation in many areas specifically names breastfeeding women, and it is unclear whether or not men and genderfluid individuals have the same legal protections.

[7] Nor are these isolated cases, with frequent reports in recent years from UK and Australia in the news, for example: http://goo.gl/TKRd6o; http://goo.gl/Jg6697; http://goo.gl/vsuO7l

the last form of veiling for women in Western secular cultures; and lactating breasts represent one of the final bastions of modesty to be observed in order for mothers to qualify as public citizens.[8] If a mother can conduct herself in public while mothering, then her mothering body must remain concealed. Given that attention to decorum is rarely applied so intensely to other activities that entail the sharing of food, it appears to be the lactating body that is yet to be fully accepted.

Such difficulties might seem trivial compared to the many other challenges faced by working, single, or inadequately supported parents to produce enough milk to exclusively or even partly breastfeed their children. Yet the public rejection of breastfeeding taking place when and where the child needs to be fed represents a significant obstacle to the acceptance and success of breastfeeding overall. As Dowling, Naidoo, and Pontin write in their essay on "Breastfeeding in Public," "The crux of our argument is that for women to be successful in breastfeeding, they have to be able to breastfeed in public." Furthermore, they add, even though the "public spaces where women are most likely to breastfeed are spaces of consumption (shops and cafes); paradoxically, these are the very places where women find it most difficult to breastfeed."[9] Again, it is the role of the mother's body as a producer (not consumer) of milk, that causes alarm.

So what might happen when a transgender man chooses to breastfeed his baby? What happens when he seeks help through friends, neighbours, online postings, and his local La Leche League group? How might he locate the people who are in a position to help, and are willing to accept him? What happens when a transgender, gay

---

[8] Bueskens, P. "Breastfeeding in public: A personal and political memoir," in *Mothers at the Margins,* ed. M. J. Jones Porter, and L. Raith, (Newcastle upon Tyne: Cambridge Scholars Press, 2015), 204-224.

[9] Dowling, Naidoo and Pontin, "Breastfeeding in Public," in *Beyond Health, Beyond Choice: Breastfeeding Constraints and Realities,* ed. Paige Hall Smith, Bernice Hausman and Miriam Labbok (New Brunswick: Rutgers University Press, 2012), 250.

man seeks breast milk donors online? What happens when his interest in and passion for breastfeeding results in him wishing to become a volunteer with La Leche League? And what might happen when he writes about his experiences?

Here is a marginalized individual, who struggled with his gender identity throughout childhood, and into his twenties, who is in an openly gay relationship, and who finds that the most daring act he has committed to date is to use his own chest to feed his baby.

* * *

Mainstream media profiles of transgender celebrities have been published since the mid 20th century, beginning with Christine Jorgensen's memoir in 1952.[10] In 1974, celebrated Welsh travel writer, Jan Morris, wrote *Conundrum,* the story of her transition to womanhood and her travels to Morocco for surgery. Since the '90s, with the explosion in popularity of the memoir genre, which continues unabated today, a subgenre of transgender memoirs has also emerged, with numerous autobiographical narratives such as *The Testosterone Files: My Hormonal and Social Transformation from Female to Male,* by Max Wolf Valerio (2006), Aleisha Brevard's *The Woman I Was Not Born to Be: A Transsexual Journey* (2001), and *Crossing: A Memoir* by Deirdre McCloskey (1999), to name just a few.

Given this history, it's perhaps unsurprising that a transgender

---

[10] Jorgensen was not the first person to undergo this surgery, merely the first to have a high profile memoir published. For example, Lile Elbe had surgery in stages beginning in 1930; and there may be others before her, as yet unknown.

memoir might now focus on just one aspect of the transitional body, by exploring the experience of pregnancy, birth, and breastfeeding from a trans perspective. As we have seen from the challenges that women encounter, this is a courageous project. By focusing specifically on the role of breasts in parenting and the importance of human milk in childcare, Trevor's memoir not only goes into the delicate terrain of transgender experience, it also explores the delicate terrain of breastfeeding. So what if the maternal body might also be a male body? How might this shift the discussion about breastfeeding more generally? Could it help to identify the source of our cultural anxiety about breastfeeding as one that is attached to our oppressive views of feminine sexuality? Or could it suggest uneasiness with the human body — regardless of gender or sex — as a source of food? If one man breastfeeds, leading the way for others, might our culture's approach become more supportive? And what might this have to say about our definitions of maternity, mothering, and parenting? How might this deepen our understanding of the inter-subjective and trans-subjective nature of these embodied, nurturing roles?

In 1978 Gloria Steinem famously wrote a cover story for *Ms Magazine* titled "If Men Could Menstruate." Playing with the idea that social status is conferred on the activities of the powerful, and that work done by women, whether by their bodies or intellects, is therefore devalued, Steinem listed the possibilities for cultural change if men had periods. "The answer is clear," wrote Steinem, "menstruation would become an enviable, boast-worthy, masculine event: Men would brag about how long and how much."[11]

In my book, *Fresh Milk: The Secret Life of Breasts* (2003), I also touched on the idea that cisgender men can lactate, if they put in the work and really want to. They have breasts, nipples, and mammary

---

[11] Gloria Steinem, "If Men Could Menstruate," *Ms Magazine,* October 1978. Reprinted in Gloria Steinem, *Outrageous Acts and Everyday Rebellions,* (New York: Holt, 1995). 1986. www.mylittleredbook.net/imcm_orig.pdf

ducts; and prolactin is produced by the pituitary gland, which sits at the base of the brain. Delivery of the child, and the accompanying hormones from the uterus, make it easier for women to produce milk, but there are examples of women (as well as cisgender men) who have never given birth, but have successfully nursed their adopted children, or someone else's.[12] The prostate gland is also a source of prolactin in men; and fathers of young children experience elevated levels of the hormone, regardless of their intention to breastfeed. Anthropologist Helen Marieskind, who studied a Zulu Chief in Africa who helped his many wives breastfeed his children, noted that three conditions need to be fulfilled for successful male lactation: the desire to breastfeed, the opportunity to breastfeed (to achieve nipple stimulation by putting a baby to the breast) and the high cultural status of breastfeeding.[13] Although it can make the task easier, you certainly don't have to be female. Nor does a female need to have just given birth: she can be a grandmother, or just a woman who desires to lactate and has the time and resources to apply herself to the task.[14]

Marge Piercy's second-wave feminist science fiction novel *Woman on the Edge of Time* (1976) has been interpreted as condemning the idea that men might breastfeed, as though she considered it yet one more instance of men colonizing women's power. Her protagonist Connie objects to men giving birth and breastfeeding, saying, "These women thought they had won, but they had abandoned to men the last refuge of women [...] They had given it all up, they had let men steal from them the last remnants of ancient power, those sealed in blood and in milk." But Connie later concedes that this is a pro-social change, since it means men and women are required to

---

[12] Janet Golden, *A Social History of Wet Nursing in America,* (Cambridge: Cambridge University Press, 1996).

[13] Helen Marieskind, "Abnormal Lactation," *Journal of Tropical Pediatrics,* 19, 2 (1973): 127.

[14] Ibid., 123.

share the labour of mothering more equally.[15] Additionally, every child has three mothers in Piercy's utopia, there is ambiguity regarding gender overall, and the children are let loose in the woods to find their own name, with the implication that gender identities are also self-applied.

The thought experiment of men breastfeeding, or menstruating, is also useful to show how differently we value the physique of the male and female body. We are taught to revere masculine strength and cohesiveness, the streamlined consistency of flesh that produces muscle more readily than fat, that doesn't seep, or swell or change on a disturbingly regular basis. The female body is not far from monstrous in the imagination of many, who recoil at the thought of the blood and mucus signifying fertility, and the birthing process itself, not to mention lactation.[16] In practice then, the man who does take on feminine tasks is less likely to raise them to the status of maleness, and is instead more likely to be reduced to the feminine, to have been diminished — to be, in short, a failure or a freak. Perhaps this is another reason transgender women are so often subject to violence and discrimination. Even though they don't menstruate or give birth, the association is enough, together with a perceived betrayal of their masculinist, ideal body. But it might not be too long before the gender of parents becomes somewhat insignificant, just as Piercy envisaged. As Susan Stryker notes in *Transgender History*, "As these and other biomedical developments continue to coalesce, it appears that we are on the verge of completely separating biological reproduction (the functional reason for sexual difference) from the status of one's social and psychological gender. That is a future radically different from the whole of past human experience. Contemporary transgender issues

---

[15] Yigit Simbul, "Marge Piercy's Conception of a Feminist Utopia in *Woman on the Edge of Time,*" *Journal of Language and Literature Education,* 10 (2014): 180.

[16]Jane Ussher, Managing the Monstrous Feminine: Regulating the Reproductive Body, (New York: Routledge, 2006).

offer a window onto that coming world."[17]

The media interest in Thomas Beatie, the so-called "Pregnant Man," which peaked in 2008 with a one-hour Barbara Walters special on United States ABC television, may have been useful to raise community awareness of the way that people formerly regarded as different, disabled, or inferior, can also be outstanding, and make extraordinary contributions — whether in sport, fashion, film, or other areas. Media coverage of this kind sets an agenda for discussion, which can result in critical reform.

But what of the people who are quietly attending to their daily lives, and who, perhaps above all, seek merely to be ordinary? Having grown up as gender ambiguous, living with dysphoria, ostracism, and bullying, perhaps it isn't surprising that feeling normal, loved, and happy is the number one ambition of many transgender individuals. Fitting in, not just socially, but to their own sense of embodied normalcy, will have been a lifelong struggle for many. The gender of the transitioning individual might also play a role in the extent to which visibility is desired. As Jonathan Ames notes in his "Introduction" to *Sexual Metamorphosis: An Anthology of Transsexual Memoirs*, there are differences in the ways trans women (male to female) and trans men (female to male) have narrativised their journeys. Female to male memoirs, he writes, "are often in the shadow, publicity-wise, to their male to female counterparts." [18] Ames wonders if the latter seem glamorous and sexy, and perhaps more theatrical and performative, or "more of an affront to nature." It's also the case that trans women are more easily identified than trans men; and as men who appear to have "chosen" to become women, are perhaps expected to justify themselves through narrative. Nearly all memoirs belie a desire to blend in, though of course that might be an

---

[17] Susan Stryker, *Transgender History* (Berkerley, CA: Seal Press, 2008): 39.

[18] Jonathan Ames, "Introduction" to *Sexual Metamorphoses: An Anthology of Transsexual Memoirs* (New York: Vintage, 2005): xv.

important objective for individuals of both sexes. But the historical record offered by memoirs is of social value in addition to the possible therapeutic benefits to the subject who writes the story. And certainly their political importance is undeniable.

It's for this reason perhaps, of trans men unobtrusively going about their business, that I was surprised to learn of a study reported in *Obstetrics and Gynecology*, in which researchers interviewed forty-one transgender males who had given birth "after transitioning from female to male gender."[19] Similarly in Barbara Walters' interview with Beatie, who has given birth to three children, Californian midwife Stephanie Brill reported that she is aware of at least forty cases, and the number is increasing.[20] In Australia, transgender Melbourne man AJ Kearns featured in a documentary about giving birth, choosing to become pregnant before taking testosterone and having chest surgery. His wife had suffered complications giving birth to their first child, so they agreed he should carry their second child.[21]

Numbers of this kind suggest that underlying the television specials and magazine cover stories, there exists a quiet groundswell of social change, which has mostly been hidden from view. Such is demand from this new demographic of transgender men who would like to give birth, The American College of Nurse Midwives has issued a Position Statement on Transgender/Transsexual/Gender Variant Health Care; and the Association of Ontario Midwives has developed a "Tip Sheet – Providing Care to Trans Men and All 'Trans Masculine Spectrum' Clients".

---

[19] "Transgender Men Who Experienced Pregnancy After Female-to-Male Gender Transitioning," *Obstetrics and Gynecology* 124, 6 (December 2014)

[20] Alan B. Goldberg and Joneil Adriano, "Transgender Couples: Changing the Face of Family," *ABC News*, 24 November 2008, http://goo.gl/ycLDdg

[21] Janine Cohen, "Melbourne transgender man AJ Kearns says he is 'blessed' to have become pregnant and given birth," *Australian Story*, ABC News, 10 August 2015, http://goo.gl/qeIlnc

This accommodation to transgender reproduction has happened rapidly, which is surprising given that, as of 2015, in some European countries and Canadian provinces, sterilization, or permanent infertility, is still a requirement before an individual can have documents such as passports and driver's licenses altered to reflect their gender. Due to widespread discrimination that continues in the community and workplace, transgender people still report mental illness, self-harm and suicidal thoughts, at up to three times the rate of the general population.[22] However, after decades of being denied adequate health care, or being pressured to accept sterilization, it seems that transgender individuals are gradually being supported and accepted.

Information regarding the capacity of trans women to breastfeed is also a barely explored area, and Trevor's blog, Milk Junkies, is one of the few places to record this happening. Interviewing Sarah for his blog, Trevor reports that a same-sex female couple succeeded in creating their own biological child using Sarah's gametes, despite her having been on estrogen therapy for over five years; and she then went on to successfully share the breastfeeding of their son.[23] Breastfeeding men are therefore only one part of this story. Intersex people, gender nonconforming individuals, or trans women might also breastfeed, and multiple parents might share the breastfeeding of their children. Such changes will further dismantle the relationship between sex, gender, reproduction, and—perhaps most politically enabling of all—the parenting roles we have traditionally attached to these categories.

With the relaxing of attitudes toward the gender of the birthing parent, and the sharing of breastfeeding between parents, we might also begin to see a shift in understandings of maternity itself. Transgender parenting is opening out the meanings of mothering and

---

[22] Wendy Bostwick, "Mental Health Issues Among Gay, Lesbian, Bisexual and Transgender (GLBT) People," National Alliance on Mental Illness (Arlington, VA: 2007). See also: http://goo.gl/8IuWkV

[23] Trevor MacDonald, "Milk Junkies," http://goo.gl/9PMEMq

motherhood, and disentangling them from gender boundaries in interesting and positive ways.

* * *

In the history of sexual liberation—from women's suffrage in the 19th century to the Second Wave of the 1970s, the gay and lesbian rights movements of the late 20th century and the transgender battles of today—a common thread has been the desire to view the world from outside the traditional boxes of patriarchal thinking. In addition to removing legal and judicial constraints, and reforming conditions in the workplace, encouraging different ways of thinking has also been a focus of the feminist project. One of the most important means to achieve this has been through undermining the habits of phallogocentrism. This term was adopted from Jacques Derrida by Helene Cixous in the 1970s to describe the philosophical under-pinnings of Western thought that values male over female, adult over child, reason over emotion, the phallus over the vagina, solids over fluids, and countless other "binaries" that we habitually use to order and evaluate our world.

Another box of traditional thinking is heteronormativity, a term adopted by queer theorist Michael Warner from Adrienne Rich's insights about "compulsory heterosexuality."[24] Heteronormativity is used to describe the worldview of patriarchy in relation to sexual

---

[24] Michael Warner, "Introduction: Fear of A Queer Planet," *Social Text*, 9, 4 (1991); and Adrienne Rich, "Compulsory Heterosexuality and Lesbian Experience," *Signs: Journal of Women in Culture and Society*, 5 (1980).

preference, identity, and other expectations based on gender. As such, through the growing influence of queer theory, which initially focused on the interests of homosexuality, the term soon extended beyond a critique of the normative insistence on the moral superiority of heterosexuality and reproductive sex, and offered alternatives to the assumptions that accompany it, such as the nuclear family, fixed gender identities, traditional gender roles for parents, and the norms attached to myriad other gendered behaviours.

These two terms have in common the enactment of queering, by looking sideways at a subject, and by moving away from an insistence on stable relations between sex, gender, and desire. Because queer theorists reject the standard ways of understanding ourselves, they open up discussion to the possibility that alternative approaches are equal if not better than those we've inherited. Hence the queering process can offer critiques of both heteronormativity and phallogocentrism. These tools can then be applied to aspects of gendered behaviour that need not be specifically related to sex, sexual identity, or sexual preference. As Eve Kokofsky Sedgwick put it, "'queer' spins the term outward along dimensions that can't be subsumed under gender and sexuality at all...'Queer' seems to hinge much more radically and explicitly on a person's undertaking particular, performative acts of experimental self-perception and filiation." [25] By revisiting our assumptions about parenting and gender, and breastfeeding and parenting, we can extend the potential for filiation itself, through relations of embodiment, both to self and other, and ideas of what constitutes care.

In writing *Fresh Milk*, I began to discover that the stories being told to me were queering breastfeeding in a similar way, since this part of maternal sexuality (if it's admitted as such) has been strictly constrained by phallogocentricism and heteronormativity, in ways that we were only beginning to learn about. Added to this conservatism

---

[25] Eve Kokofsky Sedgwick, *Tendencies* (Durham, NC: Duke University Press, 1995): 9.

around the maternal body, the many decades in the 20th century when very few Western mothers were supported or encouraged to breast-feed, means that a cultural archive of memories, practices, and skills was lost. Out of this space a more medicalised version of breastfeeding has emerged, as scientific evidence of the benefits of breast milk became the foundation for the renewal of the practice. Normative breastfeeding now prescribes an ideal female mother, supported by her husband, breastfeeding her baby for between six months and two years, and doing so discreetly and preferably in private so as not to be viewed by others or to impinge on a sense of decorum established through decades of bottle feeding. Yet in recording the stories for *Fresh Milk,* I came across a range of breastfeeding behaviours, such as nursing older children, adults nursing each other, nursing the children of friends, eroticizing lactation as foreplay, using breast milk in cooking, donating to milk banks or posting offers online, feeding breast milk to animals or suckling them directly, performing lactation as part of a stage act, and exhibiting breast milk-based artworks, or including it in installlations. In addition to this impressive list, one of the most radical potentials of queering breastfeeding is to show how it queries (or queers) our definition of individuals themselves, and their stake in identities of any kind, since it softens our corporeal boundaries, and insists on the importance of embodied connection and interdependence for survival.

One of the loveliest elements of Trevor's story is the way that he encounters generosity and hospitality in his efforts to find milk donors. Public health scholar Julie Roberts coined the term "embodied philanthropy" to describe the trend which encourages people to make changes to their behaviour in order to raise money, such as Dry July (promoting lower drinking rates), or Movember (which has raised hundreds of millions of dollars for men's health initiatives through sponsoring men to grow a moustache). Another use for this term might also be applied in a more direct way, such as through donating blood, or organs, or other human tissues, including eggs and sperm, trading in which has become highly commercialised, if not yet adequately regulated. Yet there is another layer of embodied philanthropy that occurs through the donation of breast milk, whether expressed and stored for transportation, or through cross-nursing. (Or even dry nursing where a non-lactating breast or chest can comfort a child.) It seems to me that Trevor has discovered a rich vein of embodied philanthropy, which testifies to the willingness of humans to help out with their bodies, perhaps even more readily than they might with money, time, or labour. And by sharing breast milk, the parents in Trevor's life not only donate *with* their bodies but *of* their bodies. As Roslyn Diprose writes, "corporeal generosity" describes the "carnal and affective" nature of our "openness to otherness."[26]

The gradual acceptance of sharing breast milk also invites a revision of the ideal of exclusive breastfeeding. Although it's exclusive in that no solids are included, and ideally no formula is used, shared breastfeeding and use of donor breast milk might more generously be called inclusive, since it includes others' milk, and encourages further connections within a community of parents. On a San Diego Breastfeeding site, "The Sanity Spot," Aran Tavakoli writes of packing away her pump after nine months of breastfeeding and pumping, and notes the way the term exclusive breastfeeding can lead to an unnecessary tension between mothers who have enough of their own milk to feed their babies, and mothers who supplement their supply, whether with formula or donated breast milk. Aran admits that she hasn't exclusively breastfed her baby according to the limited definition, but that "I do exclusively give my baby all the breast milk that I have." She writes, "Honestly, I am so tired of the 'low supply' conversation, I wish there was a different word for how I feed my baby. A word that matches the pride of the mamas who do exclusively breastfeed their little ones all that they produce." Noting that one of the definitions of "exclusive" is "not shared," she decides that the opposite of exclusive—

---

[26] Roslyn Diprose, *Corporeal Generosity: On Giving with Nietzsche, Merleau-Ponty, and Levinas* (Albany: State University of New York Press, 2002): 8.

inclusive—might be not only a friendlier term but also more accurate, as it means "open to everyone: not limited to certain people."[27]

This is intriguingly similar to Trevor's experience, and must ring true for the majority of breastfeeding parents, including me, who supplemented their breast milk while also focusing on maximizing their own supply and maintaining a long-lasting breastfeeding relationship. As Aran writes: "Saying that, 'I inclusively breastfeed' is so much more positive and empowering than saying, 'I have low supply and need to supplement.' My lactation consultant, Ashley, always said to me, 'He is getting your milk.' That has become my motto. He's getting my milk, the amount doesn't matter, and he is getting my milk."[28]

The inclusive breastfeeding concept that Tavakoli has proposed includes the option to supplement with formula—which some parents would reject. But it also allows for the option of many people contributing to the nurturing of babies, opening out the breastfeeding relationship in ways that could benefit everyone. With the chests of fathers, the breasts of close friends, whether lactating or not, could we make our bodies, our resources, our affection, more freely available? And in so doing, could we also accommodate the differences those bodies might encompass, whether they be of male, female, or genderfluid? As long as the primary carer consents and has the opportunity and support to give the best care they possibly can, could this kind of sharing, and inclusivity, be feasible for some?

* * *

_____

[27] Aran Tavakoli, "Sanity Spot" 2 June 2014,
http://www.sdbfc.com/blog/
[28] Ibid.

By bringing breastfeeding out of the nursery and disentangling it from gendered maternity, we can learn more about the nature and meaning of our capacity to produce food, and the implications of this for who we are as human mammals. In Sarah Blaffer Hrdy's view, lactation provides the origins of empathy in primates, and is the source of our sociality as humans.[29] Canadian anthropologist Penny Van Esterik takes this further, writing about the special quality that breastfeeding has in anchoring the commensality of our species. She writes that, "breastfeeding is at the conceptual core of human commensality, and models food sharing for all humans. Without being fed by someone, a newborn dies; but the act of feeding a newborn sets up a social relationship that can last a lifetime. The commensal relation created by the first paradigmatic act of food sharing involves reciprocity, intimacy and nurturance, and can be analyzed by reference to commensal circles. The commensal circle is a space where people share food, eat together and feed each other."[30] In other words, by breastfeeding more inclusively, we could broaden our commensal circle, our kinship, and community.

Additionally, the producing, interdependent citizen is more self-sufficiently sustained within a mutually supportive community than the consuming, atomized one, who is idealized as autonomous and independent. Sharing breast milk has the same countercultural implications as other acts promoted within locavist, slow food, and food security movements. The fluid subject who engages in corporeal generosity is more likely to uphold communitarian values over neo-liberal, consumer-oriented ideals encouraging traditional economic growth.

With the interdependence that maternity insists on, together

---

[29] Sarah Blaffer Hrdy, *Mother Nature: Maternal Instincts and How They Shape the Human Species,* (New York: Ballantine, 2000).

[30] Penny Van Esterik, "Commensal Circles and the Common Pot." Rpt. in *Commensality: From Everyday Food to Feast*. Ed. Susanne Kerner et al. (New York: Bloomsbury, 2015): Chapter 3.

with its enactment of commensality, shared breastfeeding undermines neo-liberal assumptions about the incontestable status of the individual, and his or her self-reliance. Is it the blurring of subject boundaries that transgender experience can imply which is unsettling to some? It could be argued, for example, that the gay rights campaign, as opposed to the transgender movement, fits more easily into the individualist paradigm than do the shifting, inter-subjective and trans-subjective qualities of those bodies moving between genders. Just as breastfeeding destabilizes a clear distinction between corporeal boundaries, the queering of gender destabilizes a clear distinction between the categories of man and woman. In both, the concept of the individualist subject may be called into doubt. Perhaps it's this taxonomic fluidity that troubles us.

Citing Irigaray's work on the ontology of fluids and fluidity, New Zealand feminist Robyn Longhurst writes of the way in which masculinity is traditionally understood as solid, and femininity as fluid. If a masculine, solid body is encouraged to produce milk through lactation, how does this undermine its claims to superiority? Longhurst draws on Sarah Walker's views to see this as positive for both sexes when she writes, "Male lactation recodes men's bodies as fluid, nurturing and maternal."[31] By allowing the possibility that fluidity could also be associated with masculinity, the breastfeeding male deepens our understanding of parenting, and broadens our possibilities for doing this together, whatever our gender or circumstances. As Barbara Johnson wrote in her classic study, *Critical Difference* (1980), to maintain polarized differences between entities, such as categories of male and female or father and mother, there must exist "a repression of differences within [them]."[32]

---

[31] Robyn Longhurst quotes Sarah Walker in *Maternities: Gender, Bodies and Space*, (New York: Routledge, 2008): 114.

[32] Barbara Johnson, *A Critical Difference: Essays in the Contemporary Rhetoric of Reading*, (Baltimore: Johns Hopkins University Press, 1980): x-xi.

The interest in Caitlyn Jenner following the *Vanity Fair* magazine cover has since been modulated by Jenner's attempts to be viewed as "normal," perhaps to distance herself from what she perceives as more radical elements of transgender politics. As Johnson suggests, the differences *within* political groupings can be as significant, particularly in relation to race and class, as differences between them. The transgender movement is no less diverse than any other political force, encompassing various ages, sexual preferences, ethnicities, race, class, and so on. These sometimes lead to conflicting interests—as the women's movement, which has birthed many feminisms, readily demonstrates. But pluralities can result in a strategic repertoire that could be useful—from acceptance in mainstream media, to campaigns for legal reform, to calls for a post-gender alternative that acknowledges a range of human interests and identities across a spectrum of bodiliness.[33]

And so, from moment to moment, we might celebrate our differences within a framework of common interests, and take pleasure in continuing to change.

Fiona Giles
Sydney, 2015

Fiona Giles is Senior Lecturer in Media and Communications, University of Sydney, Australia.

---

[33] David Hester, "Intersexes and the End of Gender: Corporeal Ethics and Postgender Bodies," *Journal of Gender Studies*, 13, 3 (2004).

Part One: Transition

March 24, 2008

Dear Mom and Dad,

I am writing this to you because I want to explain it carefully and completely, something I am not sure I could do in person or over the phone. I have felt ever since I was very young that there was something different about me, but for a long time I didn't know what this was. Starting around puberty, I became aware that it had something to do with gender. I have never felt like a woman, yet at the same time I know that my body is not that of a man, and this mismatch makes me very uncomfortable. I am transsexual. I feel as though things are backwards for me in terms of gender – my body is female when it should be male, everyone treats me as a woman when they should treat me as a man, and I am expected to dress and behave as a woman even though I am male in my mind.

This situation is not my fault or yours or anyone else's – this is just the way I am. Although I don't know the reason for my problem, I am doing something about it, and the steps I have taken so far have been encouraging. I have seen a clinical psychologist specializing in gender dysphoria. She assessed me as transsexual and believes I have the necessary maturity and self-awareness to make this type of decision. She wrote me a letter of referral to an endocrinologist who will be able to prescribe hormones and monitor my health so that I can begin to transition safely and effectively from female to male. I would eventually like to have top surgery and possibly other procedures as well to become closer to being a complete man.

At work, I have explained my situation and my plans to the personnel manager, who has been understanding and helpful. He said that although some people might be uncomfortable at first, he is certain that every single employee will support me in this. Together with him and a few other friends, I am preparing a plan to come out fully at work.

Friends outside the company have been nothing but positive as they've shared their curiosity and confusion in conversations we've had. I am happy with my life in Winnipeg, and with my relationships with friends and family. However, I am often extremely frustrated and I think this will only become much worse if I do not transition. The knowledge that I can and will do something soon about my situation keeps me going. I recently cut my hair short in a masculine style and bought new glasses that are helping me start to look more male. These changes, though still far from getting me where I want to be, are beginning to allow me to feel truly good about how I present myself physically.

I have chosen to go by Trevor. I found it difficult to think about changing my name – I know that my current name is undeniably feminine, but I had never thought of it that way when it was applied to me; it was simply my name. Trev for short sounds relatively close, and I am comfortable and happy with it. I hope that you will eventually feel that way as well. I am sure that you will have many questions, and I'll respond to them the best that I can. Phone when you're ready to talk.

Love, T

Neither I, nor my parents I'm sure, thought that just over three years after writing this letter I'd be breastfeeding a baby. As a man. It has been a challenging, rewarding journey, with little that I would do differently if I had a chance to do it all again. My husband says that I am like the platypus. Unclassifiable. European naturalists were mystified when they saw this mammal that is duck-billed and egg-laying, and has a beaver tail. There is nothing wrong with the platypus itself; it just doesn't fit into our system of classification. I will begin from the beginning, and try to explain to you how this is my normal.

Since teenage-hood, I've always imagined myself having a masculine voice, a square jaw, short, messy hair, a beard and moustache, a muscular chest, square hips... and then I have trouble visualizing the rest. I don't like to think about it. When I look in the mirror, most of what I see today matches what I envisioned. Taking testosterone for a few years and having chest surgery diminished my gender dysphoria, my sense of incongruity between the sex of my body and the gender of my mind, to a bearable degree. I like small mirrors the best so that I only see my head and shoulders. I recognize those parts.

About the down-there bits. When I was born, some doctor looked at them and said simply, "It's a girl!" In that moment, it was decided that I'd need to have a girly name, complete with two different French accents, a rolled "r", a silent "h" and a silent "e." I would be dressed in pink and purple and given dolls to play with. I would have braids, bobby pins, and barrettes. I'd use figure skates, not hockey skates. I would not be allowed to play-fight like the boys always did at school. My bicycle would have V-shaped bars instead of a horizontal one. I'd be told not to stick my hands in my pockets or wear a baseball cap. When sitting, I would have to cross my legs or keep them close together – all this, because of what was between them.

My mother insists that when I was a child, I used to love wearing a particular red dress. She says I wore it so much she had trouble finding time to wash it.

A friend recently saw a photo of me at around age five, done up in pig tails – he gasped, looked at me, and then examined the photo once more. "I think I sometimes forget," he said. "You grew up as a girl."

I guess I did.

Being a musical kid, I regularly took part in recitals and festivals, and had to contend with formal clothing at each event. I felt the usual nervousness that most people experience when called upon to perform in front of others, plus another layer of intense discomfort: instead of the casual, formless t-shirts and baggy pants that I preferred, I had to put on clothing that highlighted my presumed female gender. I never said so, but I felt anguish beyond measure, every time.

One day, when I was maybe eight years old, a teacher at the music school complimented me on my performance and then added, "In a few years you'll get to wear a slinky, spaghetti strap dress while you play. Won't that be so fancy?"

I was horrified.

My inner conviction that I was a boy was so strong that from time to time I entertained a conspiracy theory to explain it. Perhaps I'd been injured in a routine circumcision and then my parents had opted to raise me as a girl. This got tricky when I hit puberty. What had they done to me to make breasts grow? Mom could be slipping hormone drops into my breakfast cereal.

I felt utterly betrayed by my periods. Nobody could make that happen if I was really a boy. My body was growing up without my brain, leaving me behind.

Rather than try to grapple with the overwhelming dysphoria I felt, I ignored it, doing homework, and practicing violin and piano. I wore dresses when I had to, and waited for a day when I could make a different choice.

At school, I became lost among my classmates. My best friend virtually forgot about me one day – she was now interested in boys. I liked boys, too – the fast ones, the strong ones, the smart ones, the tough ones – and I wanted to be like them. The boys didn't seem into me, or when they did, they were most keen on parts of me that I hated, and I was dismayed. School became a swirling mess of hormonal energy with each kid choosing a side and then jockeying for position. I couldn't just hang around with whomever I liked anymore.

I was saved by honours classes in high school and a small group of high achievers. I kept my head down, in my books. When I ventured out of my safety zone, others immediately caught scent and went on the hunt. A girl named Maya used to leave her post at the smokers' corner beyond the school fence, coming over to mock-flirt with me. She smacked her lips in loud kisses and lifted her skirt up high to show her legs, pressing her body into mine until I got away to a class that she couldn't keep up with.

I had one friend, Emma, who was beautiful, feminine, and sensual but accepted that I wasn't any of those things. One evening we were working together at her house on a photography project for our social studies class, and she gave me some clothes to wear for a portrait. After she left the room, I tried to put on the tank top she'd picked out. I didn't own one. I put it on over my head and pulled it down from where it bunched around my shoulders. The material stretched over my upper half, into the shape of two breasts I'd never seen before in daylight. I couldn't breathe. I peeled the tank top right off without modeling it for Emma. No one could see me like that. I felt shocked, angry, betrayed. Where had those lumps come from? The innocent-looking fabric had created boobs and left me wanting to crawl out of my skin.

"I can't wear that. I can't wear something that tight."

"Ah, okay. I'll find you a t-shirt that we can use instead."

Emma understood. I started to talk to her about feeling different. I didn't have the words or awareness to say that I was transgender, but I told her that when I closed my eyes and just imagined myself, I was a gay guy.

"I wish one of *my* kids was gay!" said Emma's mom. "I mean, how awful that some people reject their kids over this. I think it's a waste – I would be so good at raising a gay kid."

"Thanks, Mom," said Emma, with the sarcastic tone a teenager can muster so perfectly.

I had found a safe haven.

When I was an older teen, I became serious about violin playing, and I lived in awe of the teacher who mentored me at the time. She had studied with some of the eminent masters of the twentieth century, the most famous being Jascha Heifetz.

As a young woman, my teacher was big, self-conscious, and talented. You had to be good to study with Heifetz. His time was precious and any word out of his mouth was to be acknowledged as a pearl of wisdom from one of the greatest musicians who ever lived.

Each week at the beginning of my teacher's lesson, Heifetz made her stand on a weigh scale. He expected her to have practiced her etudes, learned a concerto, and lost a few pounds.

"Do you want people to feel sorry for you when you walk out on stage?" Heifetz asked. He told my teacher she must be thinner to make it as a violinist.

She obeyed, and later carried on his tradition of taking a keen interest in every aspect of students' lives, especially the ultra-personal. One day I came to my lesson, dressed as always in respectable but gender-neutral clothes, my hair cut unisex style. I played the first movement of Mozart's Fourth Violin Concerto. My teacher stopped me just before the cadenza.

"*You look like an it,*" she said. She made me stand in front of the mirror, and started discussing my features. She brushed my shortish hair forward from behind my ears so that it came to fall around my face, creating a softer, more feminine look. I instinctively moved it back to where I liked it. She laughed in a strange, angry way, and pulled my hair forward again.

"When people see you, they don't know whether you are a man or a woman. You confuse people, make them uncomfortable. You need to get one of the other girls in the studio to pluck and shape your eyebrows. You should learn how to put on makeup. You need to look sexy. Okay? It doesn't take much to be a little feminine."

As if she had merely suggested a few alternate fingerings or a change in dynamic markings, she said, "Let's hear the cadenza."

I shook all through the intricate, showy passages, my face burning red. I wondered, while I played, if I could just explain to her how I felt, that I did not *feel* female, maybe she would let me be. By this age, I'd started to read and learn about transsexual people. I was sure that most adults, especially artists, had heard about them, too.

"I don't feel female," was all I could get out.

"What?!" She exploded.

She knew exactly what I was talking about.

"Do you want a penis and testicles?" She was yelling now. Aloud, her question sounded utterly preposterous to me. *Was that what I wanted?* I thought about the next student sitting outside the door waiting for her lesson, hearing everything. I couldn't speak. I put my instrument away and left to cry in a practice room. A day later I begged my teacher not to tell my parents about any of it, and she agreed.

I spent the next six months trying to do what I'd been told. I plucked my eyebrows and bought girly clothes that showed off my "shape". At my college auditions, I was uncontrollably nervous. My arms and fingers didn't seem to have any connection to my brain or one another. I fell apart almost every time.

Somehow, I was accepted by McGill University's excellent music faculty, although nowhere else. I'd reluctantly followed my parents' advice to apply to the general arts programs at a few other schools, "just in case." When it came time to enroll, I found that I dreaded the thought of spending the next four years going to violin lessons, no matter that it would be a different teacher. I quit music and went to university to study political science.

Vancouver, 1967

An adoption agency notified Judith and Timothy in early summer that a young college student was expected to give up her baby, my future husband, for adoption. When the baby was born, the couple was invited to view him in the nursery from behind glass. They restated their enthusiastic interest in the child and went home to wait for the completion of the necessary paperwork. They were not to touch the baby until the decision was finalized.

Six days later, Timothy picked up the family telephone, hoping to hear a dial tone. Instead, it was their neighbor, Mrs. Rathegaber, on the shared party line, still talking to her friend in nearby Surrey. "I thought she'd have learned her lesson the first time she wore that in public."

Timothy cleared his throat loudly into the phone and then hung up.

"She's been yakking away all afternoon. Again."

"It's been so long," said Judith. "I just can't believe they wouldn't have tried to call. Maybe she's changed her mind. But wouldn't they call to tell us that, too?"

"I can't stand it anymore. I have to say something."

"Oh, no. We shouldn't be pushy. They know we are waiting. I don't want anyone at the agency to..."

"No," he cut her off. "I mean to Mrs. Chatterbox next door."

Timothy picked up the phone, hearing this time, "The children rule the show at their house..."

"Mrs. Rathegaber, we're expecting a very important call. Could you keep the line clear?"

He slammed the phone hard into its receiver.

Daniel, their toddler, roared around the small house as his parents waited. For days, Judith had limited her outings to those times when her husband was not at work so that someone would be home to answer the phone.

Finally, they received good news. They collected their newborn, whom they named Ian, from the nursery of the Salvation Army Hospital. He was ten days old. Sitting in the family's Rambler station wagon, Judith held and comforted their cherished boy on her lap for the short ride home.

University of British Columbia, Vancouver, 2003

In my first class on the opening day of university, I sat next to a nervous, excited teenager with a pimpled face and a pronounced Adam's apple. While we waited for our introduction to Political Science lecture to begin, we shared personal trivia, each of us trying hard to get to know *someone* on the campus of nearly 50,000 students. His name was Lloyd and he was from a small town in the interior. Along with Political Science, he was taking English, French, History, and Psychology, and, like me, he would be living in residence. We listened to the lecture together and took copious notes, trying to write down every word as freshmen are liable to do. We left class together and then lost each other in the crowd.

The following week, I decided to go to Pride UBC's discussion group, "On-the-QT." I was finally part of an institution that was progressive and large enough to have an active queer community. I had heard of gay/straight alliances before, but my suburban high school certainly didn't boast one.

When I walked into the meeting room, the first person I saw gulping down a slice of pizza was Lloyd. We were thrilled yet terrified to recognize each other. We had each imagined that we could visit this group without meeting anyone we already knew, nor see any of the participants again over the next four years. UBC was huge, wasn't it? Aside from the greasy, free food, I had been attracted to the group by the promise of anonymity among some like-minded peers.

Lloyd and I awkwardly avoided each other that evening, but

subsequently realized we were in the same history class, too. We ended up getting along well, regularly sharing bland cafeteria food and lecture notes. I didn't ask, but assumed Lloyd was gay or bi and I guessed he thought I was lesbian.

In my second year, I ventured to date a guy I met at the university badminton club. He was kind, smart, and funny and we enjoyed each other's company. Tall and lean, he had an expressive, beautiful face that collected small beads of sweat as he ran and jumped across the court, focused on the bird. We spent late nights kissing, walking in the rain, and talking about science, politics, and literature.

After a few weeks of seeing each other, he tried to touch me, *down there,* for the first time. He said he'd make me feel better than I ever had in my life, but instead I felt ill. I hated the look in his eyes when he was affectionate towards me. I liked *him,* but he wasn't seeing the boy I was. He was intent on something he thought he saw in me that I didn't own. Feeling this boy being drawn to the female aspects of my body and my "femininity" made it impossible to do what I usually did, which was to ignore those parts of me. I stopped returning his calls. Then I told him I was done, and he was sad but not surprised. He'd known that something wasn't right.

Although I didn't tell people at the time, I preferred using the word "gay" to identify myself. Usually no one asked, but when they did, I became tongue-tied. Despite hoping I was straight, and trying to see if I could be, I knew I wasn't. I couldn't seem to use the word "lesbian" to describe myself, either. I sometimes wondered if I had a case of internalized homophobia and just needed to get over it.

After a year of taking space, I tried to date a girl for a few weeks. She, too, was kind, smart, and funny and we got along well. I was flattered that someone like her was attracted to me. I had to try a relationship with this girl, who was incredibly intelligent and sensitive. There was no reason not to like her. I played music for her and she, a philosophy major, wrote me poems.

After a while, when *she* put her hands down my pants for the first time it felt good and I hated it at once. She became more and more devoted to me and I more overwhelmed. What, and who, was she so into? She was a lesbian woman, meaning that as her lover, I, too, must have been a woman. I avoided her for a few days to breathe and gather my thoughts, and then I told her I was done. She yelled and pounded on my dorm room door because she was in love with me. She said she wanted to help me. I hid my body in the baggiest sweater I owned, and drank tea and did homework, refusing to let her in to talk.

Finally, I faced my problem head on and tried to apply myself to it. I knew I had to do something. I was miserable and ashamed of myself in my body and I had to change. When I imagined actually transitioning though, I felt terrified. How would I tell the people that loved me? The whole thing was so embarrassing. I was trapped and could only crumple up into a sobbing mess on the floor. I never knew I could cry so hard or for so long.

Okay, this isn't working. Your sinuses are as full as they can get and you still don't know what to do. You have a paper due tomorrow.

I dried my tears, blew my nose, and got my homework done. I knew now that I couldn't risk dating anyone else until I found a way to solve my dilemma, if I could ever understand what exactly it was. I didn't want to subject any more sweet, sensitive people to the hazardous experience of going out with me.

Lloyd and I kept in touch, and we both still went to the occasional Pride UBC event. One day in an online chat on our computers one dormitory apart, he typed the words, "I hate it when someone calls me a man. I'll take 'boy', but I prefer 'woman'." I was stunned that without ever talking to him about it before, he had described the precise opposite of what I felt about myself. I didn't ever think of myself as a "woman," but could tolerate "girl." I preferred "boy."

"Man" simply felt too unrealistic to me. Trying to imagine myself as a man made me think of my violin teacher shouting at me, "Do you want a penis and testicles?" It seemed too far from my physical reality to use that word, even in my private thoughts.

Lloyd said that he wasn't going to transition. His family would disown him if he did. I knew that I had to change something, but it wasn't time for it yet. I was in the middle of college, and wasn't self-sufficient enough to take a risky course of action as far as my own family was concerned.

I struggled on through the rest of my degree. I went running in the forest daily to cope with my stress. It calmed my nerves deeply to feel the rhythm of my shoulders swinging and my feet hitting the soft, dirt trails as they weaved around pine trees and lush ferns. On one occasion I started lacing up my runners, aching for the respite that I knew a run would bring, when I realized I'd already gone running once that day. I went again anyway. I knew that I was barely holding it together. I always thought it a shame that I didn't have a dog to take with me on all those runs – there must have been a good number of animals waiting at the pound, needing to get out and move as much as I did. I decided that someday, when I was done with apartment living, I would make a canine companion very happy. I pushed my thoughts about my body to the back of my mind and stayed as busy as possible.

Vancouver, 1967

Melissa had come from her home in Ontario to birth at the Sally Ann in Vancouver because it was the only thing to do. She did not want to marry, she knew she would be permanently outcast if she chose to be a single mother, and abortion was criminal. The previous year, Ontario's Chief Coroner, Morton Shulman, had begun a campaign to publicize the disastrous, often lethal effects of abortions that were performed illegally. Melissa hid her pregnancy while finishing the end of the school year, and then told her parents that she would spend the summer as research assistant to a psychology professor at the University of British Columbia. She took the train alone across the country.

In Vancouver, she met with a social worker, Ms. Robinson. "I want you to make sure that my baby goes to a good family. What can you tell me about where he will end up?"

"There's a very nice couple that I've been in touch with," said Ms. Robinson. "The husband is a teacher, and the wife used to be a nurse. They have one child already but want to adopt another. I think they are devoted parents."

"That sounds good. I wish I could..."

Ms. Robinson cut her off, asking, "What about your living situation? How are things going?"

"I'm worried about the baby. The family I'm staying with has got me running around after their kids all day and vacuuming and cooking and sweeping. They are never happy with what I've done and always asking for more. When I'm not working, they want me to stay out of view, in the basement. They don't want me to be seen leaving their front steps. I'm exhausted, and not eating well. I just want to stay healthy for this baby."

Melissa's eyes became watery. Ms. Robinson noticed the young woman's belly jump as the baby gave a few kicks. Melissa put one hand on herself to meet the tiny, vigorous feet.

"You're right," said Ms. Robinson. "That's not good. We'll get you out of there. I have friends that might be able to take you in for the last few months. I'll help you find something."

The new family was marginally better. Melissa was allowed to rest a bit more and eat properly, but she still had to care for three young children all day.

Although the prospect of birthing was terrifying, she looked forward to it happening so that she could go home. After many weeks of teasing Braxton Hicks spasms that came and went, full contractions came on gradually. Melissa took a taxi to the hospital when the contractions started coming about four minutes apart and she had trouble breathing through them.

She was shooed into a small, dilapidated section of the basement reserved for unwed mothers. The nurse examined her and listened to the baby's heartbeat, and then hurried off to attend to another woman. Melissa's labour progressed quickly during the following five hours. The nurse came in briefly once in a while, but a few times she was gone for so long that Melissa wondered if she'd forgotten her. The sensation of the contractions intensified until she was sure she'd split in half during the next wave.

Then the nurse checked her again. "It's time to start pushing," she said. "Wait until I've got the doctor." Melissa wanted to say that she didn't know how to push, but she couldn't form the words. The nurse left the room. Suddenly, she felt herself bearing down. She heard someone counting, and realized that the nurse had returned. More people came into the room, congregating around her legs and midsection.

After the baby was out, she was told it would be better if she didn't hold him for too long. He needed to be weighed, bathed, and fed, and she should rest. She was moved to a recovery room and given an injection of estrogen to dry up her milk. She signed the adoption papers, trying to picture the kind schoolteacher and his wife. A few days later she was ready to pack her things and go back east.

Mr. Swanson, the head of the household that had taken Melissa in, called her into his office, apparently to say goodbye.

"I guess it's too much to expect that you might have learned something," he said with a chuckle.

Melissa swayed noticeably, still weak from pushing out her baby just days before. She put her hand to her belly and then remembered that the baby was gone, the adoption sealed.

He continued, "You're lucky we took you. Most wouldn't want anything to do with" – he gestured toward her trunk – "all this."

She was too shaky to respond. She looked at him, wondering why he bothered.

"That's it," he said.

Melissa carried her bags down the front steps of the house, lowering herself carefully onto each stair and pausing a moment so as not to lose her balance. She took the bus to the train station. She was returning home, the only evidence of her ordeal in her fuller breasts and widened hips.

Vancouver, 2007

The year that I finished my BA, I decided to come out to my parents. I knew on some level that I was transgender but I couldn't yet say that aloud, or even to myself. At the same time, having my family assume that I was a straight woman felt too disingenuous. I tried to have a conversation with my mom, but couldn't seem to speak. I'm not the type to sit everyone down together and make a big pronouncement. My family doesn't do that sort of thing. Moments came and went where I almost said something and then didn't.

One day I was completely determined to do it. I would tell her after lunch when she was lingering over her cup of tea at the kitchen table, as she did every day. I watched her boil the kettle, make her tea, and then leave her drink to cool while she went to throw a load of laundry in the washer.

Well, now of course I can't tell her. She's going to be running back and forth doing laundry the rest of the afternoon. What bad luck.

I decided to give the project a break for a few weeks. Or maybe it was months.

Eventually I mustered some courage again. I was even more resolute this time, right up until mom mentioned that she was going out at some point to get groceries.

Oh, well, I guess today won't be the right day for this, either.

More months went by.

Finally, I just blurted something out. We were in the car. I started telling her about Pride UBC, and that I felt like I'd found my community there. I didn't clearly define my sexual orientation or gender identity, but just said that I appreciated the opportunity to be around people like me.

Mom told my Dad that I'd come out. They assumed I was lesbian. Dad was incredibly supportive, and immediately planned a coming out party for me, which was both touching and bizarre.

At the end of the summer, I moved to Winnipeg to live on my own, and found a job working in the office of a theatre group. Within weeks of starting my new life, I located a regular support meeting for transgender people. Before my first meeting, a Friday evening in September, I waited outside the door to the building for a while, trembling and flushed. I looked around to see if anyone was there to notice me going inside. Eventually, I entered the Rainbow Resource Centre and made it up the stairs into the meeting room.

The evening was informal and friendly – a group of mainly trans women shared their stories and latest updates. People I had never met before described feelings that eerily matched my own. Transgender women who were born with typical male anatomy, the opposite from myself, spoke of experiences that were unique, yet instantly recognizable to me.

Every time I walked into a women's bathroom I felt fraudulent. I silently changed pronouns from "she" to "he" when people referred to me. When filling out an application form, I would automatically start to check off "M" for male, and then catch myself, remembering that I was technically female. I had to purposefully recall my gender, like the spelling of my mother's difficult maiden name. I was f-e-m-a-l-e.

The transgender support meetings served mostly as a place to strategize about the process of transitioning. In order to get a physician to prescribe hormones and a surgeon to agree to perform gender-affirming procedures, you have to first gain approval from a clinical psychologist or a psychiatrist. In Winnipeg, nearly every transgender client went to the same mental health provider, called

Ellen. Like most care providers, Ellen didn't have any special training in transgender issues, but she had developed a reputation in the community for being willing to see trans clients and had gained substantial experience in doing so.

Ellen was often the main subject of our meetings. One woman had already been going to weekly sessions for several years. She was waiting for Ellen to be willing to write the necessary letter of support to her surgeon in Montreal. Another trans woman had only been to see Ellen twice when the psychologist declared that she was prepared to recommend transition, starting with hormone replacement therapy. We spent hours in that group trying to figure out the reasons behind the decisions. We could only guess at Ellen's thinking and compare notes.

Some couldn't afford to see her and bought hormones illegally via the internet. Others tried to convince a general practitioner, whose appointments would be covered by public health, to prescribe the hormones without the support of a psychologist. Any medical doctor may do so legally, but most refuse, citing a lack of expertise and familiarity with the process of transition.

I waited to book an appointment with Ellen until I had no doubt in my mind as to what I wanted to do. I knew that I had been feeling miserable and desperate for a long time, and that I had to try out transitioning. At the same time, it would be horrifying to begin the process, come out to all my family, friends, and colleagues, and then realize I'd been wrong. I still wasn't certain that it would be the right decision for me but I was convinced that I had to go for it. After so much back and forth in my thoughts, and time spent trying to convince myself to feel womanly, I didn't know for sure who my innate self really was, or what was forced. I thought I was extremely certain, but not one hundred percent.

I often wonder about what will happen if I develop Alzheimer's. The disease runs strongly in my family, especially for those born with typical female anatomy. If my brain were to be cleared of every 'should' and 'ought to,' who would the raw person underneath it all be? Maybe one day I'll find out, but there won't be enough of myself left to know what it means.

I told Ellen the things I thought she wanted to hear – that I'd known I was this way since I was a small child, that I played with trucks and never dolls, that I felt I was in the "wrong body." None of it seemed to be this straightforward to me in reality, but I'd made my decision and I didn't want anyone to hold me back.

After one session, Ellen told me she was convinced, and that I had only to write a multiple-choice exam that would screen for a range of mental health problems. I passed. Ellen advised me to find a family doctor so that there would be someone for the endocrinologist to work with. After a few more months, I had a formal letter from Ellen and an appointment scheduled with the hormone doctor.

In my new city, my life was highly compartmentalized. People at work knew me by the legal, female name given to me by my parents, but in other spaces, I asked friends to call me the neutral "T".

I came out to my all-male aikido class early on. This gave me a chance to explore and enjoy being known as a trans guy in a place that carried little risk – if the experience was awful, I could just stop going to class. The teacher and other students accepted my news with relative ease and began to educate themselves about transgender folks. They helped me pick out new clothes and affirmed my identity in other big and small ways.

My yoga class was more difficult. The pool of students was large, ever-changing, and predominantly women. Not yet having come out there, I had to use the crowded women's changeroom, where my presence was inappropriate. I wore loose t-shirts and shorts, and looked away from the skin-tight, sexy, feminine outfits all around me.

Outside the changing room, I loved how the poses made me feel. Like when I was running through the forest, I could concentrate on the animal rhythm of my breath and how my muscles were tightening and relaxing. I could leave my thoughts behind – until I had to get into street clothes again at the end of class.

As I was putting on my shoes to leave my second yoga class in Winnipeg, I saw a vaguely familiar face. I quickly realized it was a man from work, rushing in just in time for the next session, a more advanced level.

I came here to get away from people like you. I came here to do my own thing. I don't want to be seen or remembered.

My yoga compartment was not airtight. Annoyed as I was to find a colleague there (Winnipeg was a smaller town than I thought), I kept going to the classes.

A few months later, a friend from Vancouver came to town on a business trip and suggested that we meet up for drinks with another Winnipeg buddy of his. When I arrived at the bar, my colleague from the yoga studio was sitting there with my visitor. His name was Ian.

That evening was the first time I spoke to him. We hit it off immediately, becoming fast friends. Soon Ian revealed that when he first he saw me, from a distance, he thought I was a guy. I couldn't have been happier. He said, too, he thought I was "kinda cute." Of course, he was unsurprised when I confided in him about my gender struggles.

The next and by far most difficult step of my transition was to come out. Again. Between family, friends, and colleagues, I had over one hundred people to whom I needed to explain my change. I had long discussions about this with Ian, who often simply listened to what I said and then repeated it for me to hear.

"It sounds like you are frustrated that people don't get who you really are."

"Yeah! Isn't it obvious? I'm NOT a woman. I cut my hair short and wear baggy clothes but people still call me 'she' all the time and treat me like a girl."

Ian reminded me, "You're also worried about telling people that you are a guy. You're scared of what they'll think. But isn't that exactly what you want them to know?"

"Well, yeah. I guess so." That was the dilemma, right there. I was desperate for people to know me as a guy and terrified of telling them.

I tortured myself with hypotheticals. If I lived on a tiny island in the middle of nowhere with just a few people around, would I still feel the need to transition medically? Could it ever be enough to explain to my community that I am a guy, and leave it at that? Would I be happy to have people recognize me as male, without actually changing anything about my body? *Would anyone be able to do that?*

A huge part of my discomfort was social – the pronouns, the public bathrooms, the clothing required for work, and conversations in general. Having noticeable breast tissue identified me as female to everyone, all the time. In a mass society where I encountered strangers each day, I couldn't realistically explain to each person I met that although I appeared female, I was actually male between my ears. *I didn't live on a tiny island in a community of mind readers and I never would.* If I wanted to live as a man, then I had to alter my body so that I would "pass" as a guy. To those who knew me as a girl, I had to come out.

Eventually my fear was overcome by my frustration. I came out like jumping into a glacial lake. Once I was sure I wanted to do it, I took that irreversible step fast and blindly. Most often I came out by email, since it was easier and quicker to click "send" than to speak the words.

My parents reacted to my letter with disbelief. Unfamiliar with the efficacy of synthetic testosterone, my dad didn't think any medical treatment could possibly make me look or sound like a man. He laughed at my plans. He seemed to believe I was delusional.

My mom wanted to know why I couldn't just be happy having my hair cut short – medical transition seemed much too unnatural to her.

"There's nothing wrong with your body!" she said.

I agreed with her, in a way. There was a lot about my body to appreciate. I was strong and healthy. I liked the way I could trust my legs to carry me, running over long distances, or climbing mountain paths to see stunning panoramas. The female body, in general, is beautiful and perfect in all the shapes and sizes that it comes in. Parts of my body were wrong *for me* – for my brain, heart, and soul.

My parents knew that I had already made my decision. They tried their best to remember to use my new name and male pronouns, a choice for which I will always be grateful. I made sure to call them a few times every week, even when it was hard and awkward. I wanted them to see that I was going to be essentially the same person, just happier.

Coming out at work was less nerve-wracking. I was thrilled that I was going to let people learn about the genuine me.

When I asked for a meeting with the manager, he said, "Oh, no! Is someone giving you a problem?"

"No, nothing like that."

In his office, I explained my intention, and he was visibly relieved.

"This is really cool. I usually have to deal with endless conflicts, but this is happy news. I'm glad to be part of it. I think you should draft an email of what you'd like to say, I'll read it over, and then you can come to my office and we'll send it together to everyone at once. We could do it when there are a few days off in a row so that people have a chance to check their email and think about the message before the next work day."

This plan seemed perfect until the manager mentioned it to his boss, the day before we were supposed to send the email. I got called in for a meeting first thing the next morning. I lay in bed awake all night, wondering what the issue was, and how I would handle it.

Ian was worried, too. He surreptitiously followed me down to the office and waited outside the meeting room, pretending to try to fix a photocopy machine. He heard the boss's voice getting louder and more intense.

"But I don't think we can make this official! We can't change your name in our documents and website until you are legally male. I don't think we should send out this message."

Every cell in my body wanted to scream to everyone I knew (and everyone I didn't know) that I was a guy, not a woman. I couldn't wait.

I said, "I won't be legally male for years. I will have to have major surgery before I will be legally male. I'm starting testosterone in two months, and that will make me look male. I have applied to change my name, which should take effect within a few months as well."

The boss's voice was getting louder still. He repeated, "But you won't be legally male. We have to do everything correctly here." Ian was ready to burst through the door, but held back for a few more minutes.

The boss came out with another objection. "Bathrooms will be an issue. I am not sure what to do about that. I don't want to ask the other employees which bathroom they think you should use, but some of them might be uncomfortable with you in the men's room."

My manager spoke up this time. "We can't ask other people about that. He can use the ones in the basement if he wants, since people rarely go down there. Or he can just use the men's. None of the guys are going to care. It might be an issue for the women if it was the other way around."

I felt fortunate to be transitioning in the direction I was. Even if I didn't "pass" at first, men at work were not going to feel threatened by me. It was hard for some of my female trans friends to be correctly perceived by others as women, even after taking estrogen for years. Or, more accurately, people *understood* that they were presenting as women, but chose not to accept it. While testosterone would soon help me pass, eliminating the need for me to worry about others believing my stated gender identity, it did just the opposite for trans women who had been through puberty before transitioning medically. Thanks to testosterone, my trans women friends had to contend with large noses and prominent jawbones that outed them immediately. I'd once heard cisgender (meaning non-trans) female colleagues of mine talking hatefully about trans women in a bathroom. They said it was obvious if someone was "really a man," and that these "men" weren't fooling anyone. Disgust oozed out of their words.

The boss agreed that bathrooms would not be a problem for me, but he was still not satisfied. "We need some time to consider this. I want you to work with our communications person to prepare a response in case of media inquiries. We should know ahead of time exactly what we would say about you."

"Okay, I can do that, but I want to send the email today," I said.

I knew there wouldn't be any media requests. Nobody was going to notice this, or care about it if they did. People transition all the time and it rarely makes the papers. The big news of the day, of course, was the pregnant trans guy, Thomas Beatie, who went on *Oprah*. I assured everyone that I had no intention of doing anything like that. I just wanted to transition and keep going to work.

I said, "I really need this. This was as long as I could wait, and it already felt like forever. I am very uncomfortable living the way that I have been..."

I gave the boss Trans 101, describing how I felt as a young child and adolescent, how I had seen the psychologist and what she had said, and what effects testosterone would have on my body. I explained that if I'd been born in Manitoba, I could have my gender designation on my birth certificate changed to male after starting testosterone therapy and having top surgery, but that my birth province, British Columbia, would require a complete ovariohysterectomy (the law in BC finally changed in 2014 to allow trans individuals to correct their gender markers on official documents without requiring sterilizing surgeries). Waiting for me to be legally male would take many years.

Outside the door, Ian started to relax. I was calmly and effectively explaining what I needed and why. I held my ground.

By the end of our conversation, the boss had changed his mind completely. He told me that if we called right away, we could get my new name into the next company newsletter, which was about to be printed. Everything after that was comparatively simple and pleasant. The personnel manager's prediction was correct, and although some employees were overly curious, all were encouraging:

"I just received the email and wanted to tell you how happy I am for you and wish you all the best with all my heart!!"

"Reading between the lines, I guess you've been doing a lot of soul searching lately. Just want you to know that Bob and I support you. I'm pretty sure this can't be easy."

"I wanted to congratulate you on your decision to transition. It sounds like a complicated process, but there's something so wonderful about being able to be comfortable with yourself, and I'm so happy you found a way to do that. This is probably going to sound silly, because I don't even know you that well, but when I saw your new haircut last month I thought it looked great on you and when I read your new name in the e-mail it also seemed exactly right."

One woman, Lauren, and her husband, Dayton, sent their congratulations and invited me to their house for dinner to celebrate, even though I barely knew them. This turned out to be the beginning of an enduring, deep friendship. Lauren would be the officiant at my wedding to Ian two years later.

In the week following my announcement, I had conversations about my transition with every one of my co-workers. A few of the guys said they'd help me shop for some new clothes.

Vancouver, 1970's

Ian's adoptive mother, Judith, once explained to me that when she was a young woman, "There were two choices – a girl could become a teacher or a nurse. That is, if you didn't just get married and be a housewife." Judith became a nurse and married a schoolteacher.

Following the birth of her first son, Daniel, who was six weeks premature, Judith quit her job and decided not to return. She'd had a challenging pregnancy with dangerous hypertension, after which her doctor told her that she shouldn't attempt to carry any more children. She loved being at home with her boy and couldn't stand the thought of dropping him off every day to be looked after by someone else.

When baby Ian came along, Judith and Timothy took turns holding him. If they put him down, he cried endlessly.

As a young child, Ian seemed unsure of himself. At summer camp, the pony he rode was too quick and unruly. The water slipped past his team's rowboat faster than he could keep track of it, filling him with anxiety. He felt overwhelmed with concern for smaller things, too, like getting places on time and tying his shoes the right way.

One day at the dinner table, when Ian was eight years old, Timothy said, "Boys, we have something to tell you. Mum is sick. She will have to spend some time in the hospital so that she can get better."

"Why is she sick?" asked Daniel.

"She felt a lump in her chest and went to the doctor to get it checked. He said that it is a bad lump. Mum will need treatment for a while so that it goes away. We'll give her a lot of hugs and kisses to help her, okay?"

The boys nodded.

Judith had been with her children whenever they wanted her, but that was going to change. She wouldn't always be waiting for them when they came home from school. She put her hands to her breasts, trying to memorize their shape.

My endocrinologist followed a cautious approach to prescribing my testosterone. He decided to try a low dose initially. First, he ordered a blood test to make sure I was generally healthy and to determine where my female hormones were at.

In the lab, the technician asked me if I was afraid of needles.

"I'd better not be," I said. "I am going to start doing my own injections soon."

"Oh, really? What for?"

I'd sure stepped into that one. I couldn't contain my excitement about beginning testosterone, so I dug myself a deeper hole, and told her that I was transitioning.

"Why would you want to do that? You're a beautiful woman."

I gulped some air, and mumbled something about not feeling like one.

Soon, I got my first prescription, and a supportive nurse showed me how to draw my medication from its bottle and inject it into my thigh. During my initial three months on testosterone, I felt awful – exhausted and depressed. My body changed infuriatingly slowly.

Most people tried to remember to use my new name and male pronouns, but there were plenty of slip-ups. I typically felt shy about correcting people unless I knew them well. Ian, however, was terrific. If someone referred to me as "she," he would look all around the room saying, "She? Who? Where?" until everyone was laughing. This tactic brought conversation to a complete halt and gave people time to think about what they'd said. Most got it right after a few moments like that.

Despite being showered with congratulations and encouragement from friends and colleagues, I was a fragile, self-conscious kid that summer. My parents were trying but still struggling to come to terms with my decision. I forced myself to keep calling them, making contact again and again, all of us stuttering through uncomfortable conversations about their dog, their horse, and the weather. I think we all knew that eventually it *should* get easier.

My periods stopped, so the medication must have suppressed my natal hormones to some extent. However, the testosterone levels in my blood were not yet anywhere close to being in the normal male range. I continued to feel depleted.

Even though I had plenty of generous, loving friends, I was convinced I would never again be in a romantic relationship. *Who could be attracted to a guy with a vagina? How could anyone love me intimately* and *treat me like a man?*

I gloomily decided that if I was destined to be single and lonely forever, I had better at least adopt a dog with whom I could share my life (and my running). I moved to one of the only rental apartments in the city that allowed pets, in a decrepit area with a reputation for knifings. The day after getting my keys, I went to Winnipeg Animal Services and surveyed the dogs. A blue merle, Aussie-looking something, who I eventually learned was a Louisiana Catahoula mix, stared at me with one blue eye and one brown eye, sitting as prettily as she could while wagging her tail back and forth furiously and panting hard in the summer heat.

I asked to take her into the enclosed outdoor area where customers could endeavour to learn about and play with their potential pets prior to adoption. As soon as she touched the grass, the poor dog defecated and urinated, and then ran in circles, crazed, taking no notice of me whatsoever. Eventually she stopped running to pick up a hard plastic toy that she ripped into small shards.

I called Ian and said, grinning from ear to ear as I watched her, "This dog seems totally wild and destructive, but I don't think I can put her back in that cage. I think I'm getting this dog."

The long walk back to my apartment helped to calm my new companion. For the first few days, she shied away when I put my hand out too quickly to pet her, and she wouldn't eat. Not knowing that she was already fully house-trained, I tied her up in my kitchen as a precaution on her first night home, with a few towels put down on the floor for a makeshift bed. When I approached her, the dog rolled over, belly up, and growled softly at me. I jumped back, assuming she was threatening me. She growled again, louder and louder, until I talked to her. I wondered just what sort of animal I'd vowed to share my living space with. I cautiously tried to rub her belly and she turned her body into my hand in obvious pleasure. When I stopped stroking her, she growled again. I patted her once more and the growling stopped, at which point it dawned on me – what I thought was a threat was in fact a plea for *snuggles!* Soon afterwards, she was not only let loose, but was sleeping with me on my (single) bed.

Quinoa, as I called her, didn't know or care that I was going to change my name, or that I was taking hormones. She had no need for pronouns. She walked happily with me as I entered a frightening and potentially dangerous few months of my life, where I appeared androgynous. In public, strangers would sometimes address me as female and then act confused or annoyed when they heard me correct them with my deepening voice. Others switched pronouns mid-conversation without comment.

Quinoa turned out to be a cuddly, gentle suck of a dog determined to teach me about the importance of physical touch. Growing up uncomfortable with my own body, I had often avoided hugs and other contact. Now I lavished affection and caring on Quinoa and learned how to snuggle for the first time.

I went back to the endocrinologist after the initial three months and said that everything was great. I was afraid that if I told him I wasn't feeling well, he would want to halt my treatment. He ordered blood work and then increased my dosage to put me into a more typical testosterone range for an XY male. I started to recover my usual energy. I noticed my voice continuing to drop, and my face shape changing more. When I called home, my Dad repeatedly mistook me for my older brother, and was flabbergasted, not in a good way, each time I told him it was me.

One day, I noticed that dozens of distractions had disappeared. I now went into the bathroom without cringing and mentally altering the sign on the door. I interacted with people without silently correcting their use of pronouns for me. I stopped being stressed out at the thought of wearing formal clothes. People asked me to explain how I felt since transitioning.

I could only respond by saying, "I feel more like myself."

I became comfortable, focused, and happy. My life felt simpler.

I also noticed that women sometimes crossed the street if I walked behind them, something that had never happened before. I was saddened by this response to what was such a celebrated development for me, but I recognized what I saw. Once as a teenager, I was jogging my familiar circuit on a quiet forest path through a park, when I heard bicycle tires skidding on the gavel behind me, and a male voice called out, "Hey, beautiful." I ignored the man as he looped around me several more times and repeated the same words over. Thankfully, he did nothing more than terrify me.

Now, I was still short, white, and middle-class, but perceived as male. I started to be extra careful not to behave in ways that might be alarming to women. I could only imagine what difference it must make in this regard to be a bigger man of colour – to be feared and unable to do much about it.

As my friendship with Ian deepened, I started to feel so close to him I almost couldn't stand it. We worked in different departments at the office, and didn't see much of each other on the job. After work

I'd call him, or he'd call me, staying on the phone for hours. Or we'd meet for tea somewhere and talk until closing, and then take Quinoa for an extra long walk.

One day Ian and I were both sent to a conference out of town. He invited me to his room in our hotel and, as usual, we talked until it was late. When I got up to leave, Ian looked fiercely into my eyes and wrapped his arms around me, kissing me and pushing me down onto the bed. My heart pounded in my ears as I felt his body on top of mine, and, after a year of bounded companionship, I realized I had a lover.

"I really don't know what I'm doing," said Ian.

He was a gay man, and had never encountered my type of anatomy before.

"Me, neither."

We messed around like teenagers all night, touching.

"Does that feel good?" Ian asked many times.

I didn't bother to come out yet again, this time as gay. Ian and I lived our lives and let people figure it out – or not. My parents understood our relationship quickly, and showed that they liked Ian. They were thrilled to see how happy I was.

Some of our work colleagues became utterly mystified.

"So, are you straight now?" One of them asked Ian.

"Yeah, I thought you hated anything to do with the female body because you're gay," said another.

Ian's response was simple. "Trevor's a guy. I like guys."

Vancouver, 1975

Judith was given a radical mastectomy. Surgeons removed all of her breast tissue, including her nipples, and much of her chest muscle. A skin graft was taken from her thigh and used to cover her breast area. She had a painful, slow recovery, including a troublesome infection of her thigh wound, but she made it.

A few months after surgery, it suddenly dawned on her that the "normal" she was waiting for would not return. She was getting used to gingerly hugging Ian and Daniel when they left for school in the morning, trying not to let any part of them touch her front. All the things she used to do with ease – carrying the groceries, vacuuming the floors – were near-impossible chores now. Her blouses were newly shapeless, so she got into the habit of wearing a sweater or vest to obscure her sunken chest.

Top Surgery: Spring, 2009

I had my breasts removed because I hated them. At the time of the surgery, being able to feed a baby from my own body was the last thing on my mind. I was a transgender man in a gay relationship. It had taken me years to figure out who I was, and now that I knew, I couldn't get the surgery done fast enough.

I was more than embarrassed by my breasts. They horrified me. I slouched to hide them, and wore baggy shirts and sweaters over a compression shirt to disguise their shape. I overdressed in the summer time to avoid people seeing the lumps on my chest. I hadn't been swimming in years.

For a person with typical female anatomy, my breasts were quite small, but they were big enough to give me away. Strangers still sometimes identified me as a woman even after months of hormone therapy.

Gender-confirming surgeries are now covered in some Canadian provinces by public health insurance, but at the time mine wasn't. I did some reading and decided to consult a plastic surgeon in Vancouver who had experience doing male chest-contouring surgery. This procedure is different from a breast reduction, in which the breasts are made smaller but continue to have a feminine shape. With male chest-contouring, the goal is to create a male-appearing top. This means leaving some of the breast tissue to look like pectoral muscles and trying to carefully preserve the nipples. It was a work of art that would cost me four thousand dollars.

I hoped my breasts were small enough that the surgeon would be able to remove tissue via an incision going around each areola. For larger-chested trans guys, the nipples are removed entirely and kept on a moist saline sponge until later in the procedure when they are re-positioned and reattached.

The technique I wanted applied to my chest minimizes scarring. The nerves (and milk ducts, not that I cared) directly underneath the nipples and areolae need not be cut, so sensation in the chest can often be regained fairly soon after the surgery.

Ian and I had a close look at some surgical outcomes online. Many trans guys post photos of themselves to document their tran-sitions and compare notes with others. They also warn one another about poor surgeons who don't differentiate between mastectomies and male chest contouring, leaving their patients without nipples or with strangely shaped chests.

The surgeon I entrusted with sculpting my body was not just any regular lipo guy out to make a buck; Dr. Cameron Bowman was a rock star. For real. He played keyboard in a relatively well-known '80s Vancouver band called Barney Bentall and the Legendary Hearts. The reason I chose him to be my surgeon was that after his days as a musician, Bowman accepted a fellowship position in Belgium to study gender-confirming surgeries. He returned to Vancouver to be Western Canada's only fellowship-trained surgeon in this specialized area.

I told Dr. Bowman that maintaining nipple sensation was important to me and he agreed to do his best. We also both wanted me to be comfortable going barechested in public.

Ian and I flew to Vancouver and stayed with our friends, Amanda and Sid, for a time before and after the procedure. My own parents live only forty-five minutes away from the city but I didn't see them on this trip. I didn't tell them that I was in the province at all.

Ian suggested taking some photos of the breasts I was so eager to be rid of. I just wanted the surgery done, but I could see his point – to help mark a momentous decision and remember where I'd come from.

The day before the surgery, we went to the nudist Wreck Beach on the UBC campus, one of the most beautiful beaches in the world. I rarely went there as a student, and had never taken my clothes off. We found a quiet spot and undressed together. I've never looked at Ian's photos, nor at the technical ones the surgeon took.

That night, Ian and I went out for dinner at the Naam, Vancouver's oldest natural foods restaurant. I ate a vegetarian burger and whopping mountain of yam fries, and afterwards felt too nervous for any of it to settle in my stomach. I was going to be put under and cut open early the next morning. I suddenly became vibrantly aware of the risks of any surgical operation. I might react to the anesthesia, or suffer from a postoperative infection. The surgeon had told me that there was a minute risk of encountering trouble with the nerves in my shoulders or arms. I reminded myself of how ashamed I felt of my breasts and how badly I wanted to feel like a "normal" guy.

In the morning, Ian and I reported to the front desk at the clinic and I was instructed to put on a gown and swallow some pills with as little water as possible. After I met the anesthesiologist and greeted Dr. Bowman once more, we were finally ready. I counted as I was told, and the lights of the operating room faded away.

I woke up vomiting identifiable chunks of food from the Naam's kitchen. There was intense pain underneath and around my left nipple. On my right side I felt nothing. The warmth of Ian's touch on my head was deeply comforting. Soon, Dr. Bowman came by to check on me, and was pleased to note my pain. "Wow! Really? It hurts there? He's pointing at his nipple," he said to Ian. "It sounds like some of the nerves are still attached then. That's a great sign."

Amanda and Sid kept us company and made me smoothies in the days after the operation. Ian and I took slow, cautious walks around their neighbourhood to help my body clear the effects of the anesthetic more quickly. In the initial days, I could move my arms very little and required Ian's help for everything. He dressed me and gave me gentle sponge baths. We'd been instructed to leave my incisions alone as they were covered with special, breathable bandages. We watched all the available episodes of *In Treatment*, an HBO series about a psychiatrist, having given up on *Rome* for being far too gory for post-surgery.

We visited Ian's parents a few times on this trip. They lived frugally in the same house where Ian had grown up, in the now magnificently wealthy Dunbar neighbourhood of Vancouver. Judith went grocery shopping daily and carried her bags home by hand, in keeping with her doctor's orders from four decades ago that she should practice modest weight-bearing exercises to rebuild muscle in her chest. Judith and Timothy were gentle and gracious, treating me cautiously because of my surgery, but without asking a word about the procedure or the reasons for it.

After five days, we went back to the clinic for a checkup. An assistant surgeon removed the dressing on my left side to reveal a small pool of foul-smelling blood. "It looks open!" she said. I saw my wound moving up and down above my beating heart. I became nauseous. The room turned a speckled greyish-black and I felt Ian's arms supporting my body. I passed out for a brief moment and then came to.

The surgeon immediately began cleaning the incision and realized that everything was fine underneath the muck. Indeed, my chest was not open! We had misunderstood the care instructions and should have had the dressings changed much earlier.

The rest of my recuperation went quickly and I was thrilled with the result. I could wear fitted t-shirts without becoming a woman to the rest of the world.

In July, about two months after my surgery, Ian got hired for a brief gig in Toronto. We decided to make a family road trip out of it, dog included. At the first lake along the highway, I changed into shorts and splashed around with Quinoa, finally free to go swimming after years of abstinence. We continued our drive at a leisurely pace so that the dog and I could swim at every opportunity, both of us bursting forth with exuberance over and over again.

A few months later, I found myself in a cramped changing room with both male and female colleagues and, for the first time, I didn't need or want to hide myself. I saw one of the women there looking at me, and so I said, "What? This surgery cost me four grand. I better show off my chest, don't you think? Milk it for all it's worth?"

She smiled and pointed out that "milking it" was exactly what I couldn't do anymore. Her comment gave me little pause. I finally felt...*sexy*, a word I could never have imagined applied to myself before my surgery.

Ian and I started to explore more deeply. He'd touch me, and I would jump. *Is that my body, really? That? THERE?*

He kissed me, distracted me, coaxed me. I loved his kisses. His eyes told me that I was the hottest guy he'd ever seen. Suddenly, I realized that I was okay. I was great.

Just a year after my surgery, Ian and I talked for the first time about starting a family. The thought had not crossed my mind until I transitioned. Suddenly, I had new space in my soul to care for others.

I wasn't sure I liked kids. I hadn't spent much time with any, and I was a bit scared of the ones I knew. Kids say exactly what they are thinking, including things like, "Are you a boy or a girl?"

It seems, too, that many can tell in an instant if an adult is not feeling confident. Luckily for me, our baby would be born a baby and not a kid, and we would have time to get to know each other well before the need to negotiate over candy, bedtimes, or car keys.

I also took courage from the fact that Ian was, and is, amazing with kids. Friends of ours have been surprised more than once to hear their normally standoffish babies and toddlers crying for him, asking to be held, played with, and read to. Ian had assumed that as a gay man, he'd never have children of his own.

As surprised and unprepared as we both were (neither of us had ever changed a diaper before our own kid was born), we knew that we wanted to raise a baby together. We wanted a little person to love, cuddle, delight in, and guide as best we could.

At first we considered adoption, but rapidly concluded that no one would let us adopt a kid. There is a substantial age difference between us, we don't have piles of money, and, yes, there's the transgender issue. Canadian courts have ruled that being transgender or deciding to transition should not affect child custody arrangements, but many people are still suspicious of transgender parents (a quick perusal of the comments on any article about transgender parenting provides copious proof). We assumed that we would be stuck on an adoption waiting list for years and never get a call.

We next looked into the homegrown variety. I think Ian was afraid to ask me if I would carry a baby. I had just transitioned and was finally feeling (mostly) good about my body. I can't remember who brought it up first. We sort of chatted about it together over many months and confirmed that it was something we both were certain we wanted. Ian was extremely gentle about discussing babymaking, although I know now he was badly hoping that I'd be willing to try. The temporary nature of pregnancy gave me the assurance I needed to be able to go ahead. If I felt wretched, excruciating gender dysphoria as a pregnant person, at least it would be over eventually.

Neither of us have any serious genetic diseases in our families. I was at an ideal, low-risk childbearing age. We approached various doctors about the plan to have a child and none could foresee problems. I was advised to stop taking testosterone, wait a while for my system to sort itself out, and then try. Doctors said my voice would continue to be low and my facial hair would keep growing (an immense source of comfort for me, but which I now realize was also great personal luck – I've since met trans guys whose facial hair fell out and voices became higher in pitch when they went off testosterone), but, on the inside, my female hormones would start up again, reducing my muscle tone, redistributing my body fat, and preparing my womb for potential pregnancy.

A very traditional couple, we chose to marry and then give it a go. We were so conventional and *mainstream*, in fact, that our due date, April 17, 2011, was precisely forty weeks from the day of our wedding. We married at home in our back yard in the presence of friends and family who came from Winnipeg, Vancouver, Ontario, Nova Scotia, Montana, and Australia-via-Turkey to be with us.

When we were planning our pregnancy, we spent a lot of time with our friends Simone and Teddy, whom we knew from work. They had two kids, Tim and Samantha, aged four and one. We loved our friends' empathetic, thoughtful parenting style, and tried to soak up as much information and experience as we could. We often helped with the standard dinner-hour frenzy and then hung around for much-anticipated "adult time" after the kids were in bed, when we talked endlessly about birth, babies, and work.

Simone had planned to have Tim at home, under the care of a midwife, but ended up in the hospital after a long, exhausting labour. The birth of her daughter, at home, was a completely different experience. Simone told us she wished that she had read Ina May Gaskin's *Guide to Childbirth* before having Tim. The book is a cornerstone of the natural childbirth movement, Ina May being the world's most famous midwife. A strong advocate of natural childbirth, she is also the only midwife to have a medical technique – the Gaskin maneuver – named after her. The first half of the book is a compilation of personal birth stories, from labours that took mere hours to those that went on for many days. Simone didn't know until reading Gaskin's guidebook that a long labour could be normal and healthy. I bought the book and listened for more advice from Simone, meted out bit by bit over wine for her, and chamomile tea for me.

Reading Ina May was pure inspiration for me at the time, although the writing was very mother, mother, mother, mom, mom, mom, WOMAN!!! I expected all books about pregnancy to be that way, and hopefully assumed that if Ina May had known about people like me, she would have included more gender-neutral language.[34]

"As soon as you pee on the stick, you have to call the midwifery clinic, before telling Ian!" Simone had joked. Midwives were few and far between in Winnipeg and demand for them vastly outstripped supply.

I was pretty sure I wanted a natural, midwife-attended home birth. I couldn't imagine showing up at a hospital during labour and explaining over and over again to strange nurses and doctors as the shifts changed that, "Well, oh, just a minute, oooooowwwwweeeeeeee, well, I was born female, uh, hooooooooooh, haaaaaaaaaaaaah, and then I took male hormones, heeeeeeeeeeeeee, but we saw my endocrinologist who said..."

If we got into a midwifery clinic, we would be attended by the same team of three practitioners during pregnancy, labour, birth, and postpartum (six weeks). Hopefully we would never have to enter a hospital at all.

Ian and I were in a motel on the road when we got our positive pregnancy test. I was shaking, both from excitement at our news and at the thought of telling an unknown receptionist that I was a pregnant guy in need of midwifery services.

I called the clinic long distance, and told the woman on the phone that we had just taken our pregnancy test. We thought we were about three and a half weeks pregnant.

"Congratulations!" she said. "I will need to speak with your wife or girlfriend."

Here we go, I thought. "Well, I'm actually the one having the

---

[34] I met Ina May in 2014 when we spoke together on a panel at a birth conference. When I thanked her for her work and acknowledged how essential it was to my birth experience, she was polite. In 2015, I was shocked when Ina May signed a letter that argued against the need for gender-inclusive language and questioned whether trans people should be included in midwives' scope of practice. It can be viewed here: http://goo.gl/oqstzi.

baby. I'm transgender. That means I was born female..." It was the first of many times that I would give this explication. The woman took my information down without comment. She said we'd get a phone call in about three weeks if we were accepted. If not, we'd receive a letter in the mail.

When we arrived home from our adventures there was no phone message and nothing waiting for us in the mail. A month had passed. Maybe we were too unusual for the midwives, who typically only take the most average, low-risk cases. Complicated pregnancies are always left to the obstetricians. Although I should have been as low risk as anyone according to my GP and endocrinologist, we speculated that the midwives might have worried about the effect of my pre-pregnancy testosterone use on the fetus.

I was most concerned with how we were going to get the baby out, but Ian was starting to think of life with the actual baby. Which room would become the baby's room? What colour should it be? We decided on a bright, gender-neutral yellow and Ian sewed some cheerful curtains to match. There remained the question of a crib, a change table, a stroller, a car seat, receiving blankets, clothes, and probably a bunch of other stuff we'd never even heard of.

What would he or she eat?

Ian, being a true Winnipeger, is always on the lookout for the best deals. Living in this city is cheap, as it is located in the middle of nowhere and, depending on the season, it's alternately bone-achingly cold or swarming with mosquitoes bigger than your head. Housing prices are low, so are salaries, and finding items at a reduced price is the preferred sport and birthright of the Winnipeg local. Fifty-percent-off old cauliflower, two-for-one bottles of pop, and marked-down short-dated organic milk are all considered excellent buys. The savings are so great, really, that it is as if the store is paying us money to take these things off its shelves. If we don't get them, we are the losers. Never mind that the cauliflower was already going off, we shouldn't drink pop anyway, and nobody knows what to do with three jugs of milk in a family of two. We get cheap chocolates even cheaper the day after Easter, and cinnamon hearts for half-price post-Valentines' Day. We often pay for Groupon discounts, even though by now we've missed the expiration date for seeing the Da Vinci Exhibit, we forgot about the one for ceramics until after the discount period was over (we went anyway and paid full price), and we've realized that we have to get our house professionally cleaned four times in the first two weeks of January in order to redeem our Groupons at the sale price we bought them for (this sparkling start had better bring us good luck and health in the New Year).

When Ian learned early in our pregnancy, in the fall of 2010, that baby formula companies would send free samples, he became excited. He supplied them with our address and the anticipated due date of our baby, and then eagerly checked the mail. We happily received big tubs that were hardly sample size! Included was information on how to prepare the food and feed it to our baby, as well as how our baby would grow and develop. They even provided instructions on breast-feeding, noting that this is, in fact, the best way to feed a baby.

Ian once saw a bumper sticker that read, "My baby is exclusively breastfed. Not one drop of formula!"

That is how the breast milk versus formula debate gets inflamed and ugly, isn't it? "Breast is best," but if it isn't available, there are alternatives. That is the miracle of modern living.

We were sure that breastfeeding wouldn't be possible for us, so we were happy for the support of the friendly people from the formula companies, and especially for the free gifts.

We had a good start researching different types of formula, and now we needed a delivery system. We read about the Bisphenol A (BPA) controversy[35] and decided that there was no way our little baby was going to be ingesting weird chemicals. We found some used "Born-Free" bottles in great condition that were guaranteed BPA-free.

---

[35] BPA is often found in hard, clear plastics and is believed to be an endocrine disruptor that mimics estrogen.

We were getting ready.

After waiting and waiting to hear from the midwives, suddenly the calls flooded in. We were accepted by three out of the four midwifery clinics in Winnipeg, a situation practically unheard of. We made an appointment with the first one that had contacted us, and then informed the others that we had found care.

We learned that the midwives had not been intimidated in the slightest by our queer family – they had chosen to prioritize us. As part of their mission, they serve "marginalized communities." We were incredibly touched to be welcomed in this way, and a bit worried (*in what ways might we be marginalized by the health care system?*).

I was aware, however, that having a midwife was no guarantee of a stress-free home birth. Simone had warned me, "With Tim's birth, my labour was so long. Eventually, I was exhausted and scared, and feeling so vulnerable. I think the people around me had a hard time seeing me in such pain. They caught my fear and amplified it. The midwives started to talk to me about going to the hospital, which I hadn't wanted to do, but the mere mention of the word was enough. I agreed to go, and it was such a disaster. In hindsight, there was nothing actually wrong with my labour – it was just long. The baby's heart rate was good and my vitals were fine. For Samantha's birth, I told everyone that they should not speak the word 'hospital' within earshot of me unless the midwives thought my life or the baby's was at risk."

I couldn't imagine my determined and strong-willed friend caving the way she supposedly did. Behind her five foot five frame, friendly smile, and business-like hairdo and dress, there is fire, especially where her children are involved. Not exactly a pushover or a conformist, this is the same woman who still breastfeeds her five-year-old because she and he both want to (nursing toddlers and older children is standard outside of Western culture) and explained to her dentist that there is "not a chance" that she'll stop nursing her two-year-old anytime soon. "Sugary juice drinks and candy, not nursing, lead to dental caries," she said with confidence, having read enough academic articles on the subject to know more than the dentist.

At our initial meeting, our midwife, Mandy, mentioned something about how she liked to see adequate "progress" of about 1 cm dilation per hour, and in the back of my mind a red flag appeared. Didn't Ina May Gaskin say that dilation of the cervix is a wildly unpredictable process whereby the body leads and the health care professionals must patiently follow? I knew it was possible to dilate only two centimetres over the course of many hours and then another eight in 30 minutes, rendering average dilation per hour meaningless.

I couldn't contain my excitement over the pregnancy itself and having found a midwife to care for us. I let the mention of "progress per hour" slide. Mandy seemed friendly and otherwise flexible.

For the first 12 weeks or so, we kept our pregnancy private. We told my parents and Ian's, and a few close friends – the people who we knew would be ecstatic, and the only people we'd want to talk to if I miscarried.

I experienced a lot of nausea, known to me as "all-day sickness," which was frustrating as well as hard to disguise around others. Triggers included the smell of most cooked foods, cigarette smoke (even a hint of it from someone walking on the opposite sidewalk from me), and car exhaust. There were a few occasions when I stayed in the bathroom for much of the day. I craved dairy throughout the pregnancy. Ian made me sweet, icy, milk-based smoothies that I could usually keep down.

At the end of the first trimester I wasn't showing at all yet, but we decided to share our news with our work colleagues and casual acquaintances. The pregnancy was well established. Everyone was excited and congratulatory. A few people asked us how we knew the pregnancy would be safe, so we related our conversations with my endocrinologist and other doctors.

One co-worker, Dan, asked, "But what about the breastfeeding?"

Was not being able to breastfeed a reason not to have a baby? We reminded him that Ian had been adopted and fed on formula. Dan politely backed down, but then talked at length about how great a responsibility it is to have children, as if we hadn't thought of that.

The most common result, however, of telling people that I was pregnant, was that they started using female pronouns and calling me "mom." These were people who had met me when they thought I was a woman, and then watched me transition to male. For the past two years, they knew I was Trevor and had seen me using the men's bathroom and wearing men's clothes. I had a beard that I refused to ever shave and I spoke in a decent-sounding baritone. Suddenly, my transition was reversed in the eyes of our colleagues because we were starting a family.

When I corrected one woman, Jess, she told me, firmly, "If you're giving birth, then you're a mother."

I wondered about all the women who adopted babies but didn't give birth to them. Did Jess feel they were a different class of "mother"? Were the women who gave up their children for adoption the "real" mothers because they had given birth?

I had a hard time responding to statements like hers, not because I believed them, but because they revealed how poorly I was under-stood by people with whom I thought I had good relationships. Some felt they had a right to name my identity for me. I didn't know where to start. Besides, I was trying valiantly to keep my food down, an effort that went largely unnoticed but took up much of my concentration.

Another colleague asked us soon after we became pregnant, "Well, did you, umm, enjoy the process, you know, of making the baby? Cuz, I hope you did. I hope it's not horrible that I'm asking you."

Regardless of whether it was horrible, she blustered on. "I mean, it hasn't always been entirely pleasant for me. Sex, that is. Anyway, I'm just wondering, did you like it?"

I'm sure most people wonder this. How do the cisgender gay man and the trans guy make whoopee?

Trust plus Time.

Ian knows that I am a man, and I trust this. Despite my unique physical traits, he always treats me in a way that matches how I feel.

Opening up to let out a baby, however, especially while some medical professional is shoving her hands inside me, was not something I could see myself doing. I would have to focus on parts of me that I didn't feel belonged to me, and that I was constantly surprised I had.

Everything I read said that, where possible, minimal interference during labour, pushing, and birth makes the whole process safer. As a trans person, I wholeheartedly agreed. Birth has a natural rhythm. If you let your body do what it is supposed to, in most cases everything will be just fine. In the event that you are one of those unlucky birthers with some kind of complication, the midwife or doctor will step in and do whatever needs to be done. In Manitoba where midwifery is legal, we can have the best of both words: natural birth at home with top-of-the-line medical treatment as backup. For me the problem was that I defined "interference" extremely broadly. The term included, obviously, pelvic checks, but also feeling my body being watched closely and hearing distracting medical talk.

Trans guys are notorious for avoiding PAP smears. At clinics that serve the trans population, they put up posters reminding us "non-biological" men (as a friend of mine puts it, does this mean we're made of styrofoam or something?) that if we still have female organs, we can get cancer in them and they need to be checked regularly.

When anyone aside from Ian comes close to touching my down-there parts, they close up tight. My deepest fear during my pregnancy was that if I had a pelvic exam in labour, my muscles would contract and I would never open up again. That baby could stay stuck inside for weeks, maybe even years. I'd be forever wearing massive sweaters to hide my permanently pregnant body.

I started to fantasize daily about labouring and pushing the baby out so fast that our midwife wouldn't have time to get to our house.

This type of rapid birth is known as a "precipitous labour" and many people fear it because it can be an intense, out-of-control experience. Our midwife said most cases of precipitous labour result in perfectly healthy babies because all the circumstances have to be just right for a baby to come out so quickly. The baby would be well-positioned, with the hips opening at just the right angle and the cervix fully dilating and becoming completely effaced.

I dreamed of being on a walk at my favourite park just outside of the city, and suddenly, labour would start, out would come the baby, and I'd walk back to the car carrying my new infant with my faithful dog trotting at my side (probably after she'd enthusiastically polished off the placenta – let's be realistic). Despite my daydreams, I knew that I had to prepare for a certain amount of medical intervention.

I felt utterly stuck and fearful about the upcoming birth, so I went to see a good therapist that Ian had once worked with. She was sympathetic but had some trouble understanding my problem. She kept talking about how I had to "heal this old wound." I tried to imagine what this wound would be or how I might heal it, but the metaphor of injury and recovery simply couldn't describe my situation. I was a guy with typical female body parts, attempting to do what some might argue is a rather female task, and I felt terrified by the idea of doing it in front of others.

At the end of a visit with Simone, she loaned me a copy of the book, *Breastfeeding After Reduction Surgery: Defining Your Own Success* by Diana West. Simone was a volunteer leader with La Leche League, an international breastfeeding support organization.

She said, "I don't know if you want this. It might just be too painful and frustrating to read, or frankly irrelevant to you."

She knew that my surgery had been extensive. She said that if I could produce milk, it might only be drops.

Breastfeeding after surgery? Drops of breast milk? I had assumed that nothing would be possible and hadn't given it a second thought.

When I read the book, I realized that there was no way for me to know how much milk I could produce unless I tried. Even my surgeon couldn't tell me how many milk ducts he severed or how much glandular tissue was removed. In general, surprisingly little is known about breast anatomy. We do know, however, that pregnancy hormones drive the body into high gear, developing more breast tissue and sometimes healing milk duct injuries, a process called re-canalization.

I quickly discovered that books on breastfeeding tend to begin with a heavy-handed, guilt-inducing chapter about why nursing is much more normal, from the baby's perspective, than formula: feeding artificial milk increases chances of asthma, allergies, cancer, childhood diabetes, obesity, and dozens of other problems. Diana's book brought an essential nuance to this discussion by stating that breastfeeding does not need to be all or nothing. You can define your own success and feel good about doing what you can instead of being remorseful over not exclusively breastfeeding. Even drops of breast milk would be important for our baby's health. Tiny amounts are packed with infection-fighting antibodies, for instance.

Some of the differences between bottle and breast don't even come from the milk itself, but from the action of nursing. Suckling a breast (or chest) promotes normal jaw development while using a bottle does not.[36] Even if our baby had only formula, I could feed him at my chest using an at-breast supplementer, maybe keeping him from one day needing some of the dentist's more torturous devices.

A supplementer consists of a bottle of supplement with a long, thin tube going into it. You put the other end of the tube next to your nipple and then latch the baby onto the tube and your nipple at the same time. This way, the baby gets the milk that the parent can produce and the supplement through the tube, too. Using a supplementer avoids the "nipple confusion" that can come from bottle-feeding. Since sucking on a bottle is a different action from suckling at the chest, young babies who are given artificial nipples such as bottles and pacifiers may have difficulty breastfeeding. In addition, these infants may develop a preference for the faster flow of the bottle over the breast and begin refusing the chest altogether. Keeping the baby at the chest helps to stimulate the parent's own tissues to create more milk – breastfeeding depends on the feedback of a supply and demand system.

I also learned that breastfeeding is a simple, effective method of parenting, independent of its usefulness as a means of delivering food. Babies nurse to cope with stress or pain, and to fall asleep. I could see from Simone's parenting example that nursing is an ideal way to help a toddler handle big emotions like anger, frustration, and fear.

---

[36] Palmer, "The Influence of Breastfeeding on the Development of the Oral Cavity."

"Tell me your coming out story," I said to Ian.

"Which one?"

"Parents."

"Oh." He paused.

Pregnancy seemed like a good time to slow down and share, especially on days when I was feeling tired or sick. I couldn't believe I hadn't asked this question before. I wanted to know everything there was to know about my new hubby. I loved his every detail – physical, emotional, historical.

"I came home from my first day of university and told them. My mom cried. She was worried for me. She thought I would have a difficult life because of being gay. My dad said that for the first time he was glad I wasn't really his son."

"Oh, wow. But things got better?"

When I'd met Ian's parents, they were kind, welcoming, and generous with what they had, and they seemed supportive of our relationship.

"Yeah. Slowly. They are different people now."

Ian's mom and dad were both excited to finally welcome a grandchild. They never said a word about the unorthodox means by which this was coming about.

It was striking for both of us to read about breastfeeding, keeping in mind that Ian only had formula from day one. Most North Americans of his parents' generation did not nurse. An adoptive parent inducing lactation (breastfeeding without pregnancy, often using a combination of physical and hormonal preparation) was virtually unheard of. It was hard not to think of what Ian missed, although he received the standard infant nutrition of the time.

One article I came across left a stronger impression on us than the rest. It was written by Marsha Walker, RN, IBCLC (International Board-Certified Lactation Consultant), and had the ominous title, "Just One Bottle Won't Hurt – Or Will It?" Ian and I read it together and learned that one formula feeding would completely alter the gut flora of a baby for several weeks to come, even if every other feeding the baby had was human milk.

The infant digestive tract is not ready to handle anything other than milk from its own species for about six months after birth. By four to six months of age, the digestive system is finally more mature and is much closer to an adult one in terms of what it can do.

So what exactly can happen if a baby has something other than human milk before the digestive tract is mature? As Walker explains, babies exposed to cow's milk-based formula have an increased risk of developing allergies and even diabetes, especially if these problems run in their families. At birth, the mucosa of the GI tract are not fully closed, allowing whole proteins and pathogens to get through and into the blood stream where they may be perceived as foreign objects. The infant's body then produces antigens to the invaders and thus becomes sensitized. This can happen in just one feeding of formula to a normally breast-fed baby. No matter how hard they try, the formula companies cannot yet produce a food that doesn't completely alter the PH of the infant's gut, nor expose babies to an increased risk of allergies and disease.

Ian and I had believed that formula was fine – the standard – but breast milk was optimal since it lowered babies' risks of all kinds of diseases and problems. After reading more about the topic, we had a shift in perspective. As lactation consultant Diane Wiessinger argued in her essay, "Watch Your Language," we came to believe that human milk was appropriate and formula was, well, a special alternative that might cause health problems. Formula harms some babies. We no longer wanted to give it to ours. The goal became exclusive breast milk. I started hoping that if I did everything just right, I would somehow magically produce a full supply of milk.

I was kind of scared to be pregnant. Maybe somewhere in the back of my mind I was anxious because of having taken synthetic hormones before our baby was conceived. Were the doctors really right that nothing would be affected? I had a few nightmares about double-headed babies with three arms, but in the light of day, I worried most about diseases like allergies, asthma, and cancer, which seem to be running rampant in our times.

One of the first things I realized about nursing was how difficult it is to learn to do so in our culture. Stories abound of parents trying desperately to breastfeed and failing. Babies mysteriously refuse to latch, somehow not knowing what is good for them. Nipples become cracked and sore to the point where the pain simply cannot be tolerated. Breasts regularly seem to produce inadequate milk. So many of us intend to breastfeed because we've been told it is the "best" thing for our children, but it seemed much easier said than done.

I decided I had to learn as much as I possibly could. My challenges would be far greater than most. Even perfectly equipped cisgender women often find breastfeeding terribly difficult, so I had to be ultra-prepared.

The various breastfeeding guidebooks mentioned several factors that count toward success. First, it is helpful to have an undisturbed birth, even a home birth, where parent and baby are not separated and can have some privacy and quiet time together in the first few hours of life. Midwives who attend home births are specifically trained to empower their clients and avoid technological interventions where possible.[37] The less outside interference, the more likely it is that your baby will be able to figure out how to latch on. People who use

---

[37] Midwives Alliance of North America Board of Directors, "Core competencies."

midwives have lower rates of unplanned c-sections, episiotomies (the "down-there" cut that it hurts to think about), vacuum extractor deliveries (doesn't every gay househusband know that vacuums don't work well on anything larger than a pebble?), forceps (I'm sure you get the idea), and other interventions. Babies who come out on their own time, in their own way, and then get to be with their parents immediately afterwards tend to do better at breastfeeding. They are alert, calm, and focused.

Having already been accepted into a midwifery practice, our next step was to hire a doula. This is a person whose sole job during labour is to provide support – emotional, physical, spiritual, or informational, but not medical. He or she cannot practice medicine in any way, nor check the health of the birthing parent or baby. Having a doula is another factor known to increase the chances of a natural birth and successful nursing.

The word doula was coined in 1969 by anthropologist Dana Raphael and comes from a Greek term that means "woman who serves." A doula will do whatever needs doing, including getting you food, walking your dog, suggesting varying labour positions, or doing your laundry and cleaning up after the birth. A doula is frequently, but not always, a woman who has given birth herself.

When we interviewed doulas, I found all of them to be lovely, but there was only one who I could envision allowing to see my naked, birthing, male-identified self. She was a solidly-built lesbian called Emily who was completely at home with our gay-transgender partnership. Emily didn't have any kids of her own but was obviously passionate about supporting the natural birth process. She wasn't a doula aspiring to be a higher-earning midwife, but rather she was a doula for the sake of being a doula. In a few months' time, Emily planned to visit and study birth work at "The Farm," an intentional community in Tennessee that includes Ina May Gaskin's midwifery centre. Ours would be the next birth she attended after taking Ina May's course. We were convinced.

The books also say that you must have support from others in your community. You should attend La Leche League meetings and spend time with people who are nursing their own babies. Witnessing breastfeeding is critical. *Our Babies, Ourselves,* by Meredith Small, includes a story she learned from Diane Wiessinger about a zoo gorilla that was unable to breastfeed her first baby. She tried to do it, but placed the back of her baby's head against her nipple. Afraid that the little one would starve, the zookeepers took the baby from her and raised it as an orphan. During her next pregnancy, they arranged for humans to breastfeed their babies in front of the gorilla. She was successful in nurturing her second baby.[38]

Evidently nursing is a natural process but it is also learned through observation and sharing. I remember seeing a woman nursing her toddler on a train once when I was a teenager, and hearing others around us remark that she should be more discreet. I had seen Simone breastfeed her kids, and we had another friend who breastfed her baby (always carefully covered by a cape), so I had kind of witnessed nursing in action a few times. Attending an all-female La Leche League meeting would be another matter.

---

[38] Small, *Our Babies, Ourselves,* Page 178.

Into my second trimester my pregnancy started to show a bit. To people who didn't know, I looked like I had a small beer belly. Our colleagues started dropping off garbage bags and diaper boxes full of tiny, gender-neutral baby clothes, gadgets, and toys.

We didn't know the sex of our baby because we declined the standard 20-week ultrasound. Various natural-minded birth books argue that ultrasounds during normal, healthy pregnancies are unnecessary and may have some negative effects on the fetus. Even the FDA warns on its website, "Ultrasound energy delivered to the fetus cannot be regarded as completely innocuous. Laboratory studies have shown that diagnostic levels of ultrasound can produce physical effects in tissue, such as mechanical vibrations and rise in temperature."[39] The eventual effects of these tissue changes are unknown, although some researchers suspect neurodevelopmental differences as a possibility.[40]

We discussed our decision with our midwife, Mandy, for at least an hour.

"I don't want to tell you that you can't have a homebirth without an ultrasound," she said. "I don't think that's fair. I'll have to go over it with the rest of my practice group though, and see if the others agree to it."

I'd read the guidelines regarding homebirths in Manitoba, but I didn't recall any mention of ultrasounds. Mandy said she wanted an

---

[39] US Food and Drug Administration, "Fetal keepsake videos."

[40] Rodgers, "Questions About Prenatal Ultrasound and the Alarming Increase in Autism."

ultrasound primarily to show where the placenta was lying. Placenta previa, a condition where the placenta covers the cervix, could be life threatening if undiagnosed at the time of birth. However, Mandy did say that the position of the placenta could change dramatically between week 20 and the end of the pregnancy. Most people diagnosed early on with placenta previa no longer have it closer to their due date because as the uterus expands to accommodate the growing baby, the placenta has more room to move. I didn't want a test that could result in a false positive and a lot of unnecessary anxiety, followed by more tests.

"But the statistics show no improvement in birth outcomes with the use of routine ultrasound," I said.

"Yes, that's true. And there is nearly always heavy bleeding to indicate the possibility of placenta previa, so you get some warning. If you have above average bleeding, we would definitely do an ultrasound to check. But we medical providers really like to have the 20-week ultrasound so that we know ahead of time."

We talked in circles, going over the same points again. Mandy listened to us respectfully, but said she would book the ultrasound and that we could cancel it if we wanted, which was what we did.

At our next meeting, Mandy told us that the rest of her practice group still supported our plan to have a home birth. We took pains to reiterate that if anything seemed amiss at any point, we wouldn't hesitate to have an ultrasound to check things out. She seemed satisfied with that. I began to have the feeling that the generous appointment times afforded to midwifery clients could unintentionally increase parental stress if they involved drawn-out negotiations like we just experienced.

I barely exercised for much of the initial five months of pregnancy. I felt sick and exhausted, and used all my limited energy to work at my job – and to grow a baby, as Ian reminded me.

"Of course you're tired!" he would say. "You're making a new being inside yourself."

One morning in late November, Ian brought me breakfast in bed, as he often did since I always woke up overwhelmed by nausea and immediately requiring food.

"Thanks so mu---," I spat my cereal back into the bowl. "What is *in* here?"

Ian had a terribly guilty look on his face, reminiscent of Quinoa when she's been in the garbage eating rancid chicken fat.

"Well, you didn't notice it in the spaghetti last night, so I put a fish oil tablet in your breakfast, too."

"What do you mean? Fish oil? In cereal?"

"I opened the capsule and mixed it with the milk."

I'd been avoiding my daily fish oil and prenatal vitamin. I hate taking pills anyway, but during the pregnancy, swallowing them often brought on even more nausea.

I made Ian try my breakfast. He did, spat it out, and made a face. We both burst out laughing. The dog, however, lapped the cereal with vigour. Only later, following 36 hours of constant diarrhea, did we learn that dogs are generally lactose intolerant.

After that episode I agreed to take the fish oil pills voluntarily and endure whatever loathsome aftertaste they inspired. Friends told me that my nausea would fade soon.

It was hard to live with someone who was experiencing life as usual while I could barely keep up with basic responsibilities. Ian was very sympathetic and grateful to me for what I was doing, but I felt like a foreigner visiting an atmosphere that had twenty percent less oxygen than what I was used to. I dreaded the approach of the cooking, baking, gift-buying, and all-day gatherings that would come with the winter holiday season. In January, Ian and I usually went to visit our families in Vancouver, but this year I knew I would want to stay home. In addition to the exhaustion factor, I didn't want my parents to see my pregnant body and switch over to using female pronouns the way others around me had done. Ian got hired for some work in Ontario, and I looked forward to spending time on my own at home, moving at a slower pace.

Sometimes all the reading and learning I was doing seemed like an enormous, pointless investment of time and emotion. I could feel myself wanting more and more to be able to breastfeed as I learned about how important it was. I could also feel how much more difficult the loss was going to be if it wasn't possible.

Starting in the second trimester of the pregnancy, I occasionally tried to see if any colostrum might come from my nipples. Simone had shown me, and I'd read in my various books, how to express milk by hand.

Colostrum is a special type of milk that is produced during pregnancy and the first few days after birth before the regular milk starts to come in. There is usually very little of it, but it is rich in nutrients and antibodies that protect the newborn. It is known in the birth world as "liquid gold." Some people can express small amounts after about 25 weeks' gestation, or might even leak, while others don't get anything out until after birth.

One day in December, I was lazing about in bed dealing with a nasty headache on top of my usual nausea. I thought to try hand expressing again. I prepared myself for the usual disappointment and scoffed a bit at my witless tenacity. Nevertheless, I took my forefinger and thumb, as I'd been shown, on either side of what remained of my "breast," and pushed in towards my chest in the direction of my nipple. I saw that the nipple looked a bit shiny. Moist even. I touched it. Yes, it was wet. It didn't look anything like milk. There was so little fluid that it was hard to say if it had the usual golden color of colostrum or what. But it was wet.

I jumped up and down, my head pounding, and hugged the dog. Then I phoned Ian and told him. I phoned Simone and told her. I left a joyous message for Mandy letting her know, too. Then I phoned my friend Louise and everyone else I thought might care or even just listen. I called my mom and I talked about all sorts of things, but I didn't tell her my good news, even though I badly wanted to.

I spent the rest of the day proudly strutting around the house shirtless, frequently testing to see if I could still get something out. That evening I asked Simone to look and tell me that it was what I thought it was. She confirmed, "Trevor, that's colostrum!"

I began painstakingly collecting my precious liquid. Amusingly, I already had the right tool for the job: small syringes left over from when I used to inject testosterone. Over the course of a two-day period, I would collect as much as I could in a syringe, storing it in the fridge between tries. I labeled the syringe with the date, put it in a ziplock bag and stuck it in the freezer. By the end of the pregnancy I had about 40 or 50 syringes, each containing about 0.5 ml of colostrum – a total of maybe 20 or 25ml. A newborn will take about this much on her first day of life, and soon after increase her intake to several hundred ml per day. Each saved syringe represented about half an hour spent squeezing colostrum out drop by drop.

Now that I knew some of my milk ducts were still intact, I was giddily optimistic. Many people successfully breastfeed despite having c-sections, being separated from their babies after birth, and not nursing frequently. I secretly hoped that if I did everything perfectly to maximize my milk supply I would somehow make enough for our baby. I was determined to have a natural birth, and then to breastfeed continuously, day and night so that my body would get the message to make milk. I learned about foods and teas that support milk production, and yoga poses to promote good circulation in my chest tissue. I realized that I wanted to breastfeed more than anything, just a year and a half after the surgery that removed my breasts.

Many books advise drawing inspiration from one's sisters around the world and throughout history who have experienced birth. I didn't feel this sort of kinship. I was not a woman, and my vision of birth did not include connecting with others – not humans at least. I thought that in early labour I would love to have close friends around to lighten the mood. For the actual birth, I still felt that in my transgender body, I would need total privacy. I couldn't stand the idea of being watched by cisgender, female medical professionals who would be observing, studying, and evaluating my body. Even more so, I couldn't see myself enduring pelvic exams and monitoring without shutting down in every way. My therapist said that I should talk to my midwives about my issues, an obvious suggestion that was a complete revelation for me. Talk to them. Explain my problem. I would try that.

After speaking first with a few close friends, I learned that my predicament was not utterly unique to me. Nobody likes Paps or pelvics, some people despise them, and a few people, like myself, cannot tolerate them.

One friend I talked to said that some of what I was describing was familiar to her. She had suffered early childhood abuse of which she has no clear memory. She experiences vivid, horrifying flashbacks that occur in the presence of certain triggers, such as the scent of alcohol. Through therapy and discussions with a few family members who had limited knowledge of what had gone on, she'd realized that she was a survivor. Her greatest fear during her pregnancy was that some aspect of labour or birth would trigger a flashback for her, rendering her incapable of focusing on opening up. Essentially, she and I both worried about being overcome by fear, pain, and tightness – not simply because birthing can be physically painful and scary, but because labour and its accompanying medical interventions could force each of us to feel deeply connected to difficult core memories, thoughts, and images that we couldn't control.

She told me about a book that she found helpful – *When Survivors Give Birth* by Penny Simkin, a famous American doula. I recognized her name from major bestselling birth books like *Pregnancy, Childbirth and the Newborn* and *The Birth Partner*. This one, though, seemed to have had a small print run and then was forgotten. It was not at our public library, the university library, any local bookstore, or available anywhere online. Finally, Ian found a small website offering the book for sale, but its order form wasn't working. He called the number listed.

"Hello," an older, chirpy-sounding female voice answered.

"Hi," said Ian. "I'd like to order a book by Penny Simkin."

"This is Penny. Which book would you like?"

Ian explained our situation.

"Wow," said Penny, taking it all in. "I hadn't ever thought of that. I can see how this could be really tough for your partner. Do you have a good doula? What kind of birth are you planning? How has the pregnancy been so far?"

Ian was tickled to be chatting with the great Penny Simkin. They stayed on the phone for twenty minutes, sharing details and insights.

Penny said, "I'd love to know if my book is helpful. Would you please keep in touch and let me know how things go?"

"Yes, absolutely."

A few days later, a thin, highly informative, and sadly under-read volume arrived in the mail.

I was shocked to realize that according to the book's definition, I had experienced verbal sexual abuse by my violin teacher. She had yelled at me about my genitals and made me present myself in certain ways according to my supposed gender, *to look sexy*. Looking back, this label seems to fit my emotional memory of the situation, although I hadn't thought of it as abuse at the time. It made sense that if anyone is forced to conform to a gender role for the pleasure of others, it is a form of verbal sexual abuse, or gender identity abuse.

From Penny's book I learned that being in control of my health care during labour and birth and avoiding my triggers (especially pelvic exams), if possible, would help me cope. Small details like asking others in the room to be near my head rather than my nether region during an exam could improve my sense of privacy. It would be important to understand what the midwife was going to do, and why, and to have time to consent.

Most importantly, I recognized my feelings and my fears in the stories and descriptions I found in the book. I now had a context for my emotions. Although nothing in the book addressed transgender identities, it was close enough that I could use it to frame my problem somewhat and explain it to my midwives.

And explain it I did – again and again. I worked up the courage to talk to my primary midwife, Mandy, about it. This took over an hour, but she seemed to understand me eventually. I then explained the situation to our doula, Emily. Another hour, but she got it too. She assured me that in birth, although some decisions must be made quickly, it is rarely absolutely necessary to begin a procedure without giving the client a moment to gather himself.

Next, I had to talk it over with the second midwife, Kaly. She thought I meant that I wanted the perfect birth experience, regardless of whether or not my baby lived. (Note to midwives who may be reading this: clients generally do not want dead babies.) Two more hours of talking about my humiliating problem and how much I hated "that" region of my body, and finally she agreed. I didn't want excessive pelvic exams if none were medically indicated. If she observed some kind of problem, then obviously I would consent to anything at all including placing live-to-national-television cameras inside my down-there parts if it would help to get the baby out safely. Under normal circumstances, I thought I could best birth the baby if left undisturbed.

Early in the New Year, while Ian was in Ontario and I wanted to do nothing but read, sleep, and "bask" in the frigid Winnipeg sun, I discovered I couldn't zip my usual parka over my belly anymore so I went to Mountain Equipment Co-op to try to find one that would work.

"May I help you?" asked a store employee as I perused some marked-down XXL men's parkas.

I hesitated.

"I'm looking for a parka that will fit right to the end of pregnancy," I said, not specifying the owner of the gestating body in question.

"For your wife?"

"Ummmm...yeah. She likes walking outside but the standard maternity coats just don't do the job in this climate."

"Unfortunately we don't have a maternity parka. How tall is she?"

"About my height."

"That XXL will be way too big then."

"But do you think it will fit over the belly in late pregnancy?"

"Maybe, although every woman is different in how she carries a baby. It's a lot of money to spend on a coat that won't fit well and will only get a few months' use."

I bought it anyway and immediately took Quinoa out for a long walk. My reflection in the windows we passed showed an enormous grey parka, all bunched up in the arms, with only glasses, nose, mouth, calves, and boots visible. Perfect. On the parkway I unclipped the leash and sat on a bench to watch my dog digging in the snow in search of gophers.

When I got back home there was a message waiting for me. Simone and her family were going swimming at the Y that evening and wondered if I wanted to come along. I agreed – swimming sounded like a blissful idea for my sore back. I was six months pregnant. We could use the family changeroom together and Teddy, Simone's husband, promised to stay nearby in the pool in case anyone tried to give me trouble.

When we arrived, Simone went to work out in the weight room while the rest of us headed for the pool. I changed in a stall and then walked onto the deck with a towel wrapped around me. I quickly slipped into the water and stayed there. I felt my tired muscles releasing.

Thirty minutes later, Simone splashed in beside me.

"Trevor, I'm so shaken right now. I was on a machine and this big guy told me to get off because he wanted it. I said no, that I wasn't done yet. He straddled the machine between me and the handle bars and put his face right up to mine and told me to move."

"That's ridiculous. Are you okay?"

"I just can't stop shaking. This man threatened me physically with his huge body and tried to push me around."

"What did you do?"

"I talked to a staff member but he didn't say he'd do anything. He mumbled 'Oh yeah, that's RJ,' and said he was sorry that happened to me."

After we got out of the water we went to the front desk together. Simone had regained her composure.

"I am filing a complaint," she said. "A man harassed me in the weight room and then your staff member didn't take it seriously. I would like to speak with the director as soon as possible. I'm a regular member here."

On that day it was easier to be a pregnant man than a woman attending the Y in Winnipeg.

I didn't quite get what the big deal was about La Leche League. Simone talked about the meetings and work she did with reverence. LLL seemed like some secret society with its "leaders." Besides, any group with a name that had one letter repeated three times in a row just had to be fanatical or at least semi-religious. My family doctor, too, said LLL was a bit like a cult.

Why? I wondered. *All this over feeding babies?* I knew by this point that breastfeeding was not necessarily easy, and I'd read over and over again that it is important to see it happening in order to learn. I didn't get why a breastfeeding group should be any different than a bakery or a bicycle shop or a library. People come, they get what they need, and they go home, right? I didn't yet have a deep understanding of the cultural significance and history behind breastfeeding in North America. I had no idea that in another couple of years, I would feel more scrutinized for nursing my child much beyond the age of one than I did for nursing as a man.

Simone was undecided about asking the other leaders if I could attend the group. I was surprised. She explained that the meetings are intense.

"Women come in with their nipples cracked and bleeding. They sob uncontrollably while telling their stories. A La Leche League meeting is often the only place where they are comfortable to breastfeed without covering up. Sometimes even their husbands don't support them."

Simone worried that if I were present at a meeting, the women there would behave differently. They might hide their breasts, and they might hesitate to discuss their problems openly. She insisted that it wasn't my fault – it was just the way things were. She said she would help me any time I wanted and that she could try to gather together a small group of LLL leaders to meet with me.

I understood. The last thing I wanted to do was make anyone uncomfortable.

Ian disagreed.

"You need help as much as everyone else does," he said. "What about our baby? Our baby deserves to be breastfed."

Every pregnant person needs to see nursing in action, the guidebooks claimed. *Peer support is a major factor in breastfeeding success...* Except for me?

Ian and I were cautiously celebrating the development of our baby to a point where he or she would be viable outside my body. This new life was becoming real to us. We accumulated more and more baby clothes from generous friends and colleagues, and started thinking seriously about names.

At work one morning, a colleague took me aside and asked, "Are you going to keep the baby?"

"As opposed to...? What? This baby was very much planned and we are really excited."

The guy muttered something about how he "just didn't know." He certainly knew that we'd been married the previous summer.

At home, I told Ian what had happened. He was spitting mad.

"I wonder how many straight, married couples are ever asked whether they are going to keep their babies, or abort them, or give them up for adoption?"

Especially at 24 weeks' gestation.

A few months later, Simone suddenly announced that I was allowed to attend a La Leche League meeting. She'd asked her co-leaders for permission. Although some of them confided to Simone that they thought I was delusional for believing I could breastfeed, they agreed that I could come. I was surprised, elated, and petrified all at once.

Before my due date, there was only one meeting left scheduled at a time I could make. I arrived early so as not to be an unexplained guy walking in late after all the introductions were over. My voice trembled a little as I greeted Simone and her kids in the church basement where the meeting was to take place.

I waited in nervous silence for a few minutes. Parents trundled in slowly with kids in tow, quietly taking seats around the room in a rough circle.

Simone started the meeting off.

"LLL is a place for mothers to support one another and share information and ideas. Parents," she said with a smile in my direction, "are encouraged to take home what works for them and leave the rest behind."

She had warned me ahead of time that she might have trouble remembering to use language that included me. She was accustomed to doing the LLL welcome introduction talking about how "some *moms* may find XYZ while other *mothers* prefer ABC." The point of such wording was to avoid giving medical advice and keep with general suggestions that drew from personal experiences and intuition. Likely no one had considered breastfeeding dads in 1957 when LLL was founded.

"Yeah, I understand. That's okay. But give it a try, the mental gymnastics are fantastic for the brain," I'd told her.

When it was my turn to introduce myself at the meeting, I gave a carefully planned out "I'm a transgender person" spiel.

"My name is Trevor. My baby is due April 17th. I am able to be pregnant because I am transgender. That means I was born female, but I transitioned to male by taking hormones and having chest surgery. When we decided to start a family, I went off the hormones to become pregnant. I don't know how much I'll be able to breastfeed because of my surgery but I want to learn as much as I can and do my best."

When I dared to look up I saw heads nodding and welcoming smiles on most faces. I heard a couple of 'wow's and 'cool's, too. I was obviously pregnant at this point, so they knew I was the real thing. I wasn't sure how fully the group understood what I'd said. There were many nuances I didn't include for the sake of simplicity. I didn't mention that I was *assigned* female at birth because of my genitals, but never really felt female. The narrative that is currently best understood in our culture seems to be one of being born in one gender and then becoming the other at a later date, so that was what I provided. There was no time to explain that having top surgery was the most freeing decision I'd ever made for myself, and I would never regret it, yet I had a tremendous desire to breastfeed in some capacity. I had a sense, however, that the people in the room didn't expect to learn anything more than that I was trying to do what was best for my baby and me. They supported me.

After the introductions and an ice-breaker, some people brought up specific problems they wanted help with. Soon enough, tears were streaming down the faces of a few parents. I saw that folks really do wait all month for the one day when they can vent, rage, grieve, learn, and celebrate about breastfeeding unreservedly in front of one another.

One woman spoke about taking her nursing one-year-old to the doctor for a checkup. She was told that her baby was too skinny and that she should stop breastfeeding her immediately and feed her formula and fatty foods.

"He yelled at me in his office. I'm sure everyone could hear from the waiting room. He said I'm malnourishing my child!"

At home, the mom looked up her daughter's weight on the World Health Organization's (WHO) baby charts and found that she was in the normal range for her age. She realized her doctor had used much older charts that had been developed based on a sample of primarily white, formula-fed babies born between 1929 and 1975 in Ohio. It is now known that breastfed babies gain weight more slowly than formula-fed babies after their first few months of life. The more rapid, later growth of formula-fed babies may reflect obesity rather than health. The WHO charts were developed in 2006 and were based on breastfed babies' growth patterns[41].

At the meeting, we all quickly chimed in to reassure her. Yes, the WHO charts are the most accurate ones and are now considered the standard with which all babies' health, including formula-fed ones, should be measured. Yes, the WHO recommends breastfeeding for two years or beyond and the American Academy of Pediatrics for 12 months or as long as parent and baby desire. Yes, if her baby was happy and energetic, she was probably just fine.

Another parent explained how she had trouble making enough milk in the beginning. Her baby was premature, and she had to supplement heavily with formula. Over the next few weeks, she went to the hospital night and day for feedings every three hours. Now, months later, she was finally down to one formula feeding per day. A leader gently asked her why she thought her baby still needed the supplemental feeding. Did she seem hungry? Was she not gaining enough weight? The mom admitted that the baby was gaining well and seemed content, but she couldn't give up the extra feeding, even just to try for a few days. She wouldn't. Simone reassured her that she had done an amazing job, pumping and nursing so conscientiously when her baby was sick. The group murmured in agreement with Simone's praise.

Yet another parent burst into tears when she told of her struggles with depression. She had to take antidepressants in order to be a competent, healthy mom, but she had already tried each possible drug considered to be safely compatible with breastfeeding. She needed something different, a medication that might pass into her milk and harm her baby. She couldn't bear the thought of stopping nursing.

---

[41] Bonyata, "Average Growth Patterns of Breastfed Babies."

"Oh, that's very difficult, indeed. How old is your baby?" asked one of the leaders.

"She's...two. My doctor says I should just stop breastfeeding. But nursing means so much to me. It helps me so much to have this deep connection with my child."

"Wow, that is hard."

"My whole family is just telling me to wean. I don't think any of them understand what it means to me and my daughter."

"It is a completely personal decision that only you can make," said the leader. "No one should pressure you either way. If you decide to take the new medication, we can talk about gentle ways of weaning."

The parent was the expert on herself and her baby, and was treated as such.

Following the structured part of the meeting, several women came up to me to say that they were amazed by my courage and determination to breastfeed. I left knowing that the work done in that church basement was essential.

During the pregnancy, I thought a lot about what I would need to get through labour. I knew I had to learn how to open, but I also imagined that I would have to have great stamina. I didn't know how long my labour was going to take. For many people, such as Simone, having a first baby could mean several days of intense contractions.

Ian had the idea to mount inspirational photos on the walls of our so-called "birth room" (it would be the baby's bedroom, formerly the guest bedroom, formerly the office). We chose pictures that made me feel strong when I looked at them. The first was of me carrying a canoe above my head through the forest in Algonquin Park in Ontario. This was our last camping trip together before the arrival of our new family member. I was about six weeks pregnant at the time and just beginning to notice some awful morning sickness. I would carry the canoe over the rocky paths, saying aloud, even if I felt like I could barely manage another moment, "I'm strong!"

The other two photos that we put up were of me balancing in yoga poses. Just into my second trimester I started to experience nasty back and hip pain on one side. I assumed that in a pregnancy everything gets more and more uncomfortable as you go along, so I feared the worst. Ian mentioned my troubles to our yoga teacher, Mark. He explained that I didn't want to attend a class as a pregnant dude, and Mark generously offered to teach me all by myself once a week for the rest of the pregnancy. We could work from Geeta Iyengar's book, Iyengar Yoga for Motherhood (yes, indeed, this would mean more reading about spiritual, womanly aspects of pregnancy and birth while changing language and pronouns as I went along). I gratefully accepted.

With Mark's help I soon established a daily routine of poses that strengthened my back and geared my whole body towards birth. In one of my affirming photos, I am performing a headstand late in the pregnancy, around week 36. In the other, I'm enjoying half-moon pose, standing on one leg with the other stretched out behind me, and reaching for the sky with my upper arm. I could feel the strength of my body and the patience of my mind, a way of being that I hoped I could carry with me into labour.

Knowing that I likely would not make enough milk, Ian and I started to think about other options. Our baby would definitely get a nice amount of my own colostrum, from the freezer stash as well as (hopefully) freshly made right after the birth. This in itself was amazing, but we had to plan for ongoing needs.

Simone said that she would always be willing to nurse our baby, if we were comfortable with it. Some people are excellent at pumping, while others do not respond well to a plastic machine yanking at their boobs. Simone fell into the latter category, and said she couldn't pump for us at all. Ian and I planned to bring our newborn to her house once a day for nursing. Babies need to eat so frequently though that, while helpful, this wouldn't entirely solve our problem.

I mentioned to Teddy how grateful we were for his wife's offer to care for our baby in such a physical and generous way.

He grinned, "Well, you know she does have a bit of an ulterior motive. She loves to nurse babies. We can't afford to have another one, but maybe she can get her fix this way."

I didn't get this part of breastfeeding yet. For me, wanting to nurse was entirely about knowing how good it is for babies. I didn't anticipate it being enjoyable on my end. In fact, I worried that I would hate it because I have sensitive skin and sometimes find it almost painful to be touched. I didn't know how I was going to put up with a baby sucking on my nipples all the time, but I hoped I could find a way to do it for our kiddo's sake. I also worried that nursing would feel like a feminine task and bring back the intense anguish and gender dysphoria I felt before I had chest surgery.

We received an offer of donated milk early on that bothered me. This one came from a potential doula that we had interviewed before we found Emily. We'd explained to her our whole situation, including the breastfeeding, and she immediately, without hesitation, offered to nurse our child.

"You know," she said. "If you want his first taste of food to be breast milk, I'd nurse your baby."

I couldn't even imagine what a nursing relationship would feel like, good or bad, but I was sure that the very first time breastfeeding my baby – just after the birth – would be indescribably intimate. I had to be the one to do it or at least I needed the opportunity to try. I was repulsed by the idea of a paid doula getting to have that moment. Something about the way she put it made me feel she had a selfish motive – that she wanted to be the heroine who nursed the baby because I couldn't, rather than do everything possible to support me so that I could.

We had another friend, Lisa, who told us she'd had tons of milk with each of her kids. Her youngest was now 8 months old. She and I had long conversations about my potentially rather limited milk-making capacity. She said the most important thing was to nurse as much as possible in the very beginning. She felt this was how she ended up with a huge milk supply of her own. She reminded me that removing as much milk as possible, as frequently as one can, tells the body to make more milk.

Lisa never offered to pump for us and I didn't ask. Was it the unspoken question on her mind, too? Or did it never occur to her at all? Did she think I would consider it weird or gross to accept milk from somebody else? Several times I thought I should just ask and find out but it felt like I would be demanding too much even by mentioning it.

When another friend told me about a Facebook site called Human Milk 4 Human Babies, where strangers get together to share milk, I thought it was preposterous and dangerous. Who would want to accept bodily fluids from someone they didn't know, and feed them to their baby? In the middle of our second trimester, Health Canada issued a warning against this kind of milk sharing.[42] Mandy spoke to us about it, schooling us in the risks associated with milk sharing. Ian and I quickly agreed that we would have nothing to do with informal sharing. We would look for milk from people we knew very well, and we were a little anxious even about that. If we didn't have enough, we would use formula.

---

[42] Health Canada, "Health Canada raises concerns about the use of unprocessed human milk."

Near the end of our pregnancy I finally started to feel well. My nausea was gone and the back pain was manageable thanks to daily yoga. I exercised, rested, and ate good food. I found it harder to organize my thoughts and keep up with rapid conversations, which left me flustered at work more than once. Some of my fearful thoughts about the birth itself began to fade.

The midwives seemed to become increasingly stressed out as our due date approached. One had to go off call because of an injury, and another was ill for a few weeks. At week 36, an overworked Mandy told me she wasn't sure if we could still have a home birth.

"The other team members are not comfortable with your birth plan. They would attend you in hospital, but not at home."

"Do you know what they are not comfortable with?" I asked. "Is it the ultrasound? If they need it, we'll do an ultrasound in order to have a home birth."

"I don't think it's anything specific like that," she said. "I can talk to them about it again and see. Maybe you can meet with them before the birth."

The backup midwives said they were too busy to meet with us. Mandy was exhausted. We were sent for an ultrasound anyway because my belly appeared to be measuring slightly small for week 36, but the results were normal. The placenta was fine.

At week 37, Mandy phoned to say that we could have a home birth if I went into labour when she was on call. The backups had agreed to attend us at home as second midwives but not as the primary midwife responsible for care. Mandy gave us her on-call dates. I wrote them into the calendar and rubbed my belly for good luck.

Winnipeg being what it is (tiny), I heard the next day through the cousin of the ex of a friend that there had been a managers' meeting at work to discuss whether or not I should be paid "maternity" leave. Some argued that since I identify as male, I didn't qualify for the additional money. Thankfully, they decided without any input from me that carrying and birthing a baby is what qualifies, regardless of gender. I would be given the appropriate compensation.

Winnipeg has a major doctor shortage so I originally found mine, Dr. Enn, through the city's helpline. I didn't choose him based on recommendations or anything I knew about him, but because he was one of the few MDs taking patients at the time. When I first met him I hadn't yet transitioned but was already planning to, and I didn't know how he would feel about trans people.

I introduced myself, and then said, "I really want to transition to male. I've wanted to for a long time. I've been seeing a clinical psychologist about it and she thinks it's a good idea for me."

"Okay. That's fine," he said in a monotone, without looking up from my newly created chart. He told me he'd had other trans patients in the past, and that was the end of the conversation.

My doctor tends to seem like he's dozing during appointments. He leans back in his chair, his shoulders hunched over and eyes almost closed. Only on one occasion, when I had a potentially serious problem, did he perk up, open his eyes slightly more, and offer proactive, sage advice. Then he slid back down in his chair and yawned.

One day very late in our pregnancy, we went to him to ask if it would be possible for Ian to breastfeed as well. We were still trying to figure out how to feed our baby the best food possible.

He thought for a moment about Ian's question. "Well, your testosterone would get in the way. Yes, domperidone can induce lactation in biological males in rare cases. You would have a major increase in breast tissue though. It would be permanent. But the testosterone would really prevent you from making much milk," he theorized in the absence of much research at all.

Domperidone is a drug mostly prescribed to combat gastro-intestinal problems, such as nausea in cancer patients. As a quirky side effect that is not yet fully understood, it also seems to increase milk production in lactating parents. [43] Even more interesting, some cisgender, male patients taking domperidone for its more conventional purpose start producing small amounts of milk.[44]

If I was brave enough to be a breastfeeding man, why shouldn't Ian try it too, he'd reasoned? Each drop was precious, after all. But, he had no interest in adjusting his testosterone levels or increasing his chest tissue.

"I was hoping I'd be good for something at least," said Ian.

We could say, however, that we did consider every conceivable way to feed our baby.

---

[43] Newman, "Domperidone, getting started."

[44] Hospital for Sick Children, "Breastfeeding without pregnancy."

Ian and I knew one couple that forged a milk-sharing path ahead of us: Nila and Lucy are a highly intelligent, moving and shaking pair that we found through a mutual friend. Nila trained as a doula, and both are incredibly knowledgeable about natural birth. When we first met them, they were working on getting the birth registration form changed in Manitoba. It currently has a place for "mother" and "father or other parent." Lucy had given birth, so she took the mother category, but Nila was not content to be classified as an "other" and, by implication, less primary parent.

It had vaguely occurred to me that I would have to suffer yet another indignity in my gender-variant life as a result of this pregnancy. It already says F for female on my driver's license and passport. On my birth certificate, the word FEMALE looms as large as my new name. I supposed I could also be a bearded, male-identified "mother" on paper.

I try to be lighthearted about the ridiculous incongruity between my appearance and my legal documents, but I sometimes worry about my safety if I have to show my ID to somebody unsympathetic. When Ian and I traveled to Nepal for our honeymoon we took with us a fake letter of explanation just in case there was trouble, hoping that any sheet of paper with "Government of Canada" and the maple leaf on it would be shown some respect. Luckily we never had to use it.

Nila and Lucy invited us to participate in their campaign to change the birth registration form, and we hesitantly agreed. We attended a meeting with the director of Winnipeg's Rainbow Resource

Centre to discuss our issues.

Lucy sat down with her baby and got out the contraption I'd been reading about: the at-breast supplementer. I'd tried to imagine how I would use it from the descriptions I'd come across, but found it difficult to visualize. I watched as Lucy latched the baby on to her breast first, and then poked the tube of the supplementer into the side of the baby's mouth. She placed the bottle on a table beside her. I saw the milk shoot quickly up the tube as the baby suckled. Suddenly, I knew I could do this, too. It wasn't going to be so bad.

I don't remember much about that meeting other than seeing the supplementer, but near the end, Ian paused, looked around the room, and said, "This is where activism happens!" Neither of us had ever planned to be involved in politics.

More meetings took place and we were promised that the people at Vital Statistics were trying their best to accommodate us. In the meantime, Ian and I decided we would send our baby's birth registration form in with a small essay explaining how we'd had him and that we were both his genetic fathers.

For the most part, we weren't thinking about our rights on paper. We wanted to know how to protect our baby's flesh and blood through human milk and were eager to hear the stories of anyone in a situation similar to ours.

Nila had an older child, Rachel, from a previous relationship, so she and her partner had decided that Lucy would carry and give birth to their next child. When she was twenty, Lucy had had a breast reduction surgery. She was glad she had it, but she knew when she conceived that her milk production might be affected.

At the time that Nila birthed Rachel, she'd had plenty of milk. She hoped she could re-lactate relatively easily by pumping and taking domperidone (although she didn't use birth control pills to simulate the hormonal effects of pregnancy the way some parents have done when inducing lactation). That way she could have a nursing relationship with their baby and provide some additional milk. She gained about 80 pounds from taking the medication, but she was unable to produce more than a few drops of milk. After the birth, Lucy found that her milk supply couldn't keep up with the new baby's needs. With four breasts ready and available, the two parents didn't have enough for their baby.

Through a friend, they found an ideal donor, a doctor's wife who had already been saving up a stash for another baby. This woman gave them a six-week supply, and started saving all over again for the original recipient baby who wasn't yet due.

We had another friend, Elaine, who was nursing her nine-month-old. She'd offered to pump for us as we got close to the third trimester of the pregnancy. This seemed like plenty of time to get a small stash going in the freezer. We bought Elaine milk storage bags that fit her breast pump and she commenced operations.

After filling four precious bags for us, Elaine came down with shingles and had to stop pumping. A few months later, her symptoms were finally gone and we hoped she'd be able to try again. However, her boy had dropped lower on the weight charts at his most recent pediatric visit. Elaine needed to get all the milk into him that she could.

I welcome this sensation. *I am opening. I am opening, and I welcome this sensation.*

Every year in Winnipeg there are two awe-inspiring natural events. In late fall or early winter, the Assiniboine and Red rivers freeze over, and in late spring, they break up. Their meeting place, the Forks, in what is now the downtown, has been a spiritually and culturally significant place for aboriginal peoples for thousands of years.

I like to walk by the rivers every day to see what they are up to, especially when temperatures are changing fast. This year, I wondered whether my waters or the rivers' would start to flow first.

Simone had wisely advised, "Waiting for labour to start is the worst. If you get a social invite, go for it. Keeping yourself busy makes the time go much faster."

Ian and I did pretty well for ourselves on this score. We went to restaurants where I could barely squeeze myself between the bench and the table. I often had a strong urge to move my body, and one night we danced to live Latin American music at a bar, with no particular reaction from the other patrons.

About a week before our due date, Ian and I went to dinner at the home of a couple, Jill and Derek, who we knew from work. It was mid-April, but we were served an astonishing Thanksgiving-type feast, complete with turkey, stuffing, wild rice, cranberry sauce, gravy, salad and dessert. After dinner we drank cup after cup of mint tea, chatting until late. Nobody wanted to call an end to the evening.

Around midnight I excused myself to use the washroom and saw that I had lost a part of my mucus plug. I told Ian it was time to head home. I went into labour on a very full stomach. After we had sent a message to Simone and other close family and friends, I convinced Ian that he should go to bed on his own to get some rest, although cramps kept me awake.

At 2am, I attacked the piles of dishes that decorated our kitchen, and tried to get a feel for how to cope with contractions. At the start of one, I'd lean against the counter and breathe deeply, allowing myself to experience the sensation fully. I chose to vocalize a low, yoga-inspired "Om" during the most intense moments. Within a few hours, the contractions became milder and I went to bed to rest, awake, until morning.

After breakfast, Ian and I went to see how the Forks were doing that day.

With contractions ten minutes apart, we sat on the steps at the edge of the water, watching chunks of ice float past.

"What breed is your dog?"

Oh, no, somebody is trying to talk to us.

"Cat... a... houla," I spat out. "She likes... birds."

The woman wanted to know how old our dog was, her name, and where this unusual breed originated. I looked straight ahead, breathed deeply, and took my inspiration from the ice that moved relentlessly no matter what was in its path. Ian handled the rest of the conversation.

We walked a little way down the river. During contractions I befriended whichever tree was closest, leaning into it with all my weight. Passersby politely averted their eyes just as they would for a reeling drunk or a woman singing loudly to herself.

We put our glamorous canine in our car and wandered into the market to get lunch. We sat down at a sushi restaurant. A few people shot side-glances at us from behind their newspapers, but no more than usual. Our server quickly took our order and disappeared. I managed to eat some miso soup and rolls between moments of increasing intensity.

When we went home, I found it hard to be there. I needed movement. We went out for a long, incredibly slow walk at dusk. We would go a few paces, and then stop for me to lean into Ian during a contraction. Then we'd walk a few more paces, and stop for another contraction. Cyclists whizzed past us from time to time.

That evening, the contractions became serious. Ian started to fill the birth tub with warm water, and I called our doula. This was the beginning of active labour. By early morning, things were going fast. I was sick to my stomach, a common sign of transition (yes, that's what it's called), which leads to pushing.

We phoned the midwives. As soon as Mandy arrived, she got out her portable ultrasound unit, called a Doppler. The sound of the baby's heartbeat was loud. I knew right away that the beat was about 120 per minute – for many years, that had been my warm-up speed for the famous Schradieck violin exercises that I'd practiced daily. It was a normal heartbeat for a full term baby.

Mandy measured my pulse as well. Some time prior to the pregnancy, I had figured out for myself that I needed to concentrate on relaxing the core of my body and breathing deeply in order to have a normal pulse measurement. Otherwise, without fail, my GP would tell me that it was a little high and I should come back in a month to be checked again just to be sure. Throughout the pregnancy, this measurement was done at every appointment, so I was practiced. Mandy said my pulse was fine. She took my temperature under my arm and was satisfied with that, too.

With the rising sun and the intrusion of medical gear, labour immediately slowed down to infrequent, mild cramps. I spent the day getting in and out of the birth tub, but nothing (measurable) happened. Mandy checked with the Doppler every 15 minutes.

A second midwife, Lily, arrived in the afternoon. She was one of the ones who had said she would not attend us at home unless Mandy was the primary. When Mandy told her how long labour had been going on, Lily replied with annoyance, "We really should have seen a baby by now."

Mandy suggested trying to relax and have a little bit of wine to get my labour to pick up. "And, you know, I'll give you a bit of time with Ian. Being sexy can be very helpful, too."

We obediently went into our bedroom. We nervously sipped some wine, wondering if this birth would end at the hospital in front of a pile of doctors and nurses. We took off our clothes and touched each other with deliberate hands. We were awkwardly beginning to connect and do what we needed to do to birth our baby.

Annoyed Midwife burst in. "I just need to have a little listen with the Doppler," she announced. Ian reefed on the blanket to cover himself.

Yes, this was sexy. We listened to the bock-bock of the hand-held Doppler. Again, the baby's heartbeat was excellent.

Ian and I went outside for a walk. We didn't get past our own front steps when we both started to cry. We held each other, and apologized to each other, for what exactly we weren't sure. I called Simone.

"I am failing to progress," I said, using the common medical phrase for not dilating as fast as health professionals would prefer.

"Wow, still in labour?" she asked. "You must be feeling so tired by now."

"No! I feel fine!" I realized my tone was angry and defiant. I was healthy. My vital signs and the baby's were good.

I asked her how long her labour took with Tim, even though I remembered the answer. I needed to hear it again.

"Fifty-four hours. Look, if you're feeling fine, then just keep going. You can do it. It's normal to have a long labour. Many people do."

We went back into our house and wondered what to do next. Our doula and her student cooked us a beautiful meal, encouraging us to rest and simply enjoy the down time we happened to be getting.

We went out for a slow walk around the block with the restriction that the midwives wanted us back within 15 minutes for the next Doppler measurement. We played hooky and took an extra five.

By early evening, Mandy said she needed to do a pelvic exam to see how dilated I was so that she could work out her call schedule. She needed to know if she should stay with us or leave, or ask for a replacement to come. I forgot what I had read in Ina May's book – that dilation is not a good indication of whether birth is imminent. A person might take days to dilate from 0 to 3 cm and then get to 10 in an hour or two. Experiencing distress can cause dilation to reverse temporarily.

I allowed the check. It was painful, and the contractions were excruciating while lying on my back. I realized that as Ian was holding me through it, he was crying for me. He knew how humiliated and violated I felt. I told him that I was okay. The midwife found that I was 7 cm along, so she needed to stay.

In the end, we had our original two midwives, plus two complete stranger midwives and a student tagging along. The extras were required because my labour was taking so long that the first two midwives needed to be relieved. But they didn't go.

Annoyed Midwife did manage to make at least one dreadfully embarrassing contribution to the process at hand. She tried to teach me how to do a sort of feminine, sexy labour dance during a contraction where you bend your knees and wiggle your butt from side to side. I gamely tried this a few times, but it didn't feel like a level playing field: the distinctly *not* pregnant, fully clothed, female-identified midwife versus me, a mostly naked, laboring man.

Mandy believed the baby was stuck in an awkward position. She said that before the local hospital fixed its old clunky elevator, sometimes the jolt as the elevator started to drop would help move a baby. Pregnant people going down to the basement to have c-sections due to stalled labour quickly had natural births, apparently on account of this bumpy ride. So, I decided to try doing a headstand to jiggle my baby around. As soon as one contraction was over, I kicked myself up into position against a wall. Our hope was that once I was upside down, the baby could dislodge from its poor position in my pelvis and then try again to move down. I stayed up until I felt the next contraction coming. I don't know if the headstand helped our baby to come out, but it sure made me feel amazingly powerful. Even Skeptical Midwife said excitedly, "Most people can't do that at any point in their life, let alone during labour!"

Later in the evening, Mandy got a couple of Doppler measurements in a row that were a bit fast. She thought that perhaps I'd been in the warm birth tub for too long and that this was causing stress on the baby. Mandy started an IV and gave me some fluids, unknowingly hanging the bag from the Medicine Buddha Thangka painting that Ian and I had brought home from Nepal. I thought of the artist and his family who we had met, and knew that they would find this use of his work most appropriate.

Mandy said she wanted to break my waters "to speed things along" (read: to bring on excruciating pain). I had trouble understanding her reasoning, and Ian had finally succumbed to a nap after spending 48 hours awake. I was scared that breaking the waters would be extremely painful for me and that it might send labour into high gear before we were ready for it. I wanted to be sure that the baby's heart rate had come back down to a healthy speed before trying anything that could cause more distress. Mandy insisted that we had to do it and that there would be no risk to the baby. She woke up Ian and asked him to move so that we could use the bed.

I later had a chance at a public lecture to ask the famous French obstetrician Michel Odent about this procedure. He explained that nowadays we know irrefutably in scientific terms that breaking the waters doesn't help labour go faster and can sometimes cause dangerous problems. However, it is often a temptation too great to resist. He said in his beautiful accent, "It is like zee midwife iss a child wit a balloon. She looks inside and sees dis perrrrfect, smooth, round bag of waters and she must go wit her needle 'pop'!" [45]

Mandy popped, and then she panicked. "I have a fetal heart rate of 80! I need another pair of hands in here!"

Another midwife rushed into our bedroom. Meanwhile, Ian put his hand on my wrist to check my pulse. What he felt matched the sound coming from the Doppler unit. My midwife had picked up my heart rate instead of the baby's. Since an adult heart rate is much slower than a baby's, she thought that she had nicked an umbilical vein while breaking the waters or that the baby had dropped down firmly onto the umbilical cord, restricting blood flow.

Ian repeated several times. "No, that's Trevor's pulse. You're hearing Trevor's heart rate. Eighty is Trevor!"

Mandy realized her mistake and calmed down. I didn't. I was overwhelmed by terror and impossibly painful contractions. I had thought our baby was about to die.

But a mantra came from my doula. "I am opening," she said. I repeated after her.

"And I welcome this sensation."

Sometimes I could barely get through the words, but I kept on saying them. Every time I said "opening" I imagined myself opening just a little more. Every time I said "welcome" I focused on and accepted the pain a little more instead of trying to get away from it.

Eventually, despite a roomful of fearful onlookers, Jacob was born. Ian caught him as he came out. Someone said, "Put him on Trevor's chest!" with great urgency in her voice.

As if Ian didn't know that I needed to hold the baby. He put the baby on me and then hovered between us and the midwives, holding our space. One of them handed him a gungy old gym towel that was close by on a shelf.

"Not that," Ian told her. "The soft receiving blankets. Give me a receiving blanket."

"But those ones are so nice."

---

[45] Odent, public lecture.

"*Yes.* I know, I made them. Give me one, please."

We dried our newborn gingerly. Jenny, one of the more confident, fresher-faced midwives listened to our baby's breathing and heart and said everything was okay, but that she was waiting for the lungs to inflate more fully. We waited and spoke to our child softly.

"Is it a boy or a girl?" asked one of the midwives who was hovering at one end of the cramped room.

Ian looked up, incredulous.

"I need something to mark down on my form!"

"He's a...oh, did I spill the beans? Oops..." said Mandy.

Ian and I hadn't looked yet. I didn't care, and never cared during the pregnancy, what our baby's sex was.

Jacob, as we called him, was out and completely healthy. We waited for his cord to stop pulsating and then Ian cut it. I am trans and I opened.

Part Two: The Milk

The moment I'd been anticipating and reading about for months on end had finally arrived! It was time to feed this baby. I'd learned that a healthy, full-term infant can figure out, pretty much on her own, how to latch on and suckle within as little as twenty minutes after birth. Through all my diligent studying, I thought I discovered that the key to breastfeeding is simple noninterference. The birth parent should not be separated from the baby after birth. No one should poke, prod or otherwise disturb the baby. The atmosphere should be calm. If the birth parent lies back on some pillows and places the baby on his or her chest, the baby will often find and latch onto the nipple without any special help. During the pregnancy, I dreamed of this scenario every day. In labour, I told myself that I was going drug-free through all those hours so that my baby would be ready to nurse from birth. According to La Leche League leaders I knew, an epidural taken by the birth parent can negatively affect the baby's coordination and alertness for as long as several days after the end of labour.

When Jacob was born and Ian brought him to my chest for the first time, I felt such incredible awe. He was fragile, tiny, perfect and as slippery as a sardine. I could barely figure out how to hold him. I clutched his moist little body and supported his head and neck. I moved slowly, deliberately, cautiously. He mouthed weakly at my chest, and I felt helpless and immobilized like a nervous young music student who had suddenly been handed a Stradiviarius and told, "Go ahead and play but be certain you don't damage it. You know this is worth millions of dollars, right?" I didn't know how to help him. Jacob and I tried for a few minutes to no avail and then he fell asleep, exhausted.

All I could think about was trying to latch this baby on. I could feel the clock ticking. Articles and books on breastfeeding emphasize the importance of latching the baby within the first hour after birth. The suckling action of the baby's mouth helps to stimulate prolactin receptor sites in the mammary tissue that determine how much milk the parent will make for months to come.[46] The tissue continues to change for about six weeks after birth, but that first hour is the most precious. I had read in Ina May Gaskin's *Guide to Breastfeeding* that it is best to latch a baby on in a variety of positions immediately after birth so as to activate as many different receptor sites as possible.[47] Now, in this vital moment, I couldn't latch my baby on at all.

"Maybe he should try sitting on the toilet." *What?* In my newborn-induced stupor, I gradually became aware that the midwives had been whispering to each other in the hall for some time. I saw Mandy check her watch, looking anxious. Then I remembered that I hadn't yet birthed the placenta. Protocol dictates a hospital transfer if the placenta isn't out within half an hour of the birth, and we were past that deadline.

I was given an injection of synthetic oxytocin, a powerful drug that causes the uterus to contract. No placenta. I tried sitting on the toilet as instructed. No placenta. I couldn't pee so the midwives put in a catheter since sometimes a full bladder can get in the way of the placenta coming out. Still nothing. "It's been an hour. This is my limit. We *have* to go to the hospital," said Mandy.

She had already given us more time than she was supposed to and I assumed we had no choice. My mind started to race. How would we get to the hospital? Did we have to go in an ambulance or could we drive? Could Jacob and Ian come with me? Did this mean we had to strap our newborn into a car seat when all we wanted was to hold him close? I pictured our tiny baby in a hospital full of germs and wondered if it would be safer for him to stay home. But then, how

---

[46] Marasco and West, "How to get your milk supply off to a good start."

[47] Gaskin, *Guide to Breastfeeding.*

would I ever latch him on?

Midwife Jenny went into the other room where Emma, another fresh midwife, was cleaning up from the birth. "You're good at getting placentas out," Jenny said. "Get in there."

Emma felt my abdomen. "I'm sure it's fully detached from the uterus. It's just stuck around a corner or something." She grabbed the cord with both hands and pulled firmly, and the placenta flew out of me. I could have kissed her. Finally I was going to get to focus on my little baby and nurse him. I turned to Ian who was sitting beside me with Jacob on his chest and I held my arms open to my son.

"Okay, so let's check to see if there's any tearing. Spread your legs open."

Tearing? I couldn't have cared less about sewing up some minor imperfection in my down-there-bits. I had to hold and feed my son.

"Oh yes, there's a small tear. It would be easiest if Ian keeps holding him for a bit I think."

The midwives applied some local anaesthetic and stitched me up. It was a painful process, made much worse by listening to Jacob cry beside me while I ached to hold him. I felt stricken at having that part of me examined and touched after the monumental work of labour and birth. It seemed like I had maintained the emotional stamina for labour, no matter how long it was, and I'd prepared for and made it through birthing, but after all that, I had nothing left. As deep as I looked within for another morsel of patience, of being able to hang on and cope, I was done. I felt traumatized and invaded.

At long last, I got to put Jacob to my chest but, again, I didn't know what to do. Jenny asked if she could help me to latch him on. I felt I could trust her because she had breastfed two of her own babies (my primary and secondary midwives and doula were all childless). In the meantime, Ian phoned Simone and asked her to come as soon as she could.

Jenny put a stack of pillows at my side and placed Jacob on top of them so that his mouth was at about the height of my nipple. She encouraged me to slouch forward a little, which made my chest tissue less taut than it was when I leaned back. Then she held his body with her fingers tips supporting his neck and she moved his head towards me. At the same time, she squeezed the tissue on either side of my nipple to make a fleshy sandwich for his teeny mouth. She moved my nipple along his upper lip and he opened his mouth wide, searching. At this precise moment Jenny swiftly shoved Jacob into my chest and he immediately started to suckle. It was an hour and a half after the birth. We had missed the critical first hour but at least he was finally eating.

"Hear that?! He's swallowing!" Jenny announced. "Oh, that was a big swallow right there. And *there*. Again. *There*. Hear it?"

Jacob was making an unmistakable gulping sound with every few sucks. I was overjoyed and more than a bit surprised. It was intense and somewhat unpleasant to feel him pulling so strongly on my skin. "It hurts a little. Is that normal?"

"Well, you've never had a baby sucking on your nipple before. You'll get used to it."

Jenny repeatedly latched Jacob onto either side of my chest. "He has to do this enough that he'll remember how. I think he's swallowing more colostrum than most babies usually get at the beginning. The hand expressing that you did during the pregnancy must have really helped."

Jacob was getting *more* colostrum than most babies? This was incredible. Maybe I would have enough milk for him after all. There was just one thing that worried me very much. It was great that Jenny was here to latch Jacob on for me, but how was I going to do this on my own? I grabbed my tissue with my hand and squeezed on it like Jenny had and in doing so my arm obscured my view of Jacob's mouth. I couldn't see enough to know when I should move him onto my nipple. Ian tried to position Jacob while I made the "breast sandwich" but we fumbled repeatedly. We were stuck.

Simone walked in and saw me trying to latch Jacob on and

thought to herself, *This is impossible. He just doesn't have any breast tissue for a baby to latch on to. I don't think this can be done. He is going to be devastated when it doesn't work out.* But she didn't say that at the time.

She took Ian out of the room and tried to prepare him for my inevitable failure. She said, "Trevor wants to breastfeed so badly but it's really not possible. You will have to be ready to support him through a lot of grief. You will have to be very strong."

Still, Simone was willing to try. She and Ian came back in together, and she said, "That looks very awkward for you, Trevor. What if you try grabbing your breast from below so that you can still see what's going on?"

I paused briefly over the word "breast." I was indeed trying to breastfeed, but I don't have (or want) breasts. I have nipples with a teeny-weeny bit of mammary tissue around them and luckily a few intact milk ducts. Maybe I was intending to chestfeed; or nurse, the term with which I eventually became most comfortable.

I tried what Simone suggested and it worked. Jacob latched and suckled. But it hurt me just a little more.

"It is fine from Jacob's perspective. This latch might make you sore though. Ideally you should get more tissue into his mouth to make it more comfortable for you."

I knew that if my milk came in more fully, my tissue might change and perhaps become slightly more voluminous. This normally happens on day three or four after birth, so I hoped I simply needed to get through the next few days with some minor pain.

I tried to let go of the sandwich and Jacob immediately slipped off. I re-latched him. Simone assured me that he would get stronger and might be able to hold on without help when he grew bigger. In the meantime I needed to constantly grip my meager tissue to help him hang on, and endure the accompanying soreness.

After getting things sorted out with the placenta and the stitches, and beginning feeding, Ian and I both called our parents. Everyone was incredibly excited and happy to hear the news. We asked my mom to get on a plane as soon as she could to come visit. Ian snapped a few photos of our newborn and sent off an update to our work colleagues and friends.

We learned from a friend about how our new addition was also announced at work during a meeting. The manager said, "Trevor and Ian have a healthy baby. It's a boy."

"For now!" called out a woman, giving rise to derisive laughter.

Even years later, I think of her making that joke when she thought I'd never know, and how the rest of the group laughed thinking I'd never hear. Do they expect that my kid will be trans because I am? Do they assume that if he was, it would be devastating? Do they observe my child's gender expression with a critical gaze, trying to judge whether he is growing up to be "normal?"

Despite the physical challenges, the first two days of feeding my baby were absolute bliss. Ian and I held him constantly and I fed him as I had intended, which was all the time. If he opened his eyes, I fed him. If he wriggled in his sleep, I put him to my chest. Jacob was eager and determined to eat and he seemed strong and healthy. The day after his birth he'd lost about five percent of his birth weight, but this is considered normal. I kept nursing.

By his third day of life, the loss was at seven percent and his pees and poos were not copious. The midwife visited and suggested supplementing. Soon after she left, Jacob gave us some decent output and I was thrilled as I'd never been before with excrement. I talked the situation over with Simone and we agreed that I could wait one more day before supplementing with my saved colostrum. In Manitoba, the guidelines say that eight percent is the maximum acceptable newborn weight loss, but in other provinces and countries a weight loss of up to twelve percent may be considered normal. Jacob was definitely not dehydrated, and we hoped that the situation might turn around soon on its own.

That night was the worst of my life. I would feed Jacob in bed, and then gently try to put him down. He'd wake up and cry and so I'd feed him again. Then I'd try to put him down once more and lie down beside him, but he'd immediately wake and cry. When he nursed, I could no longer hear the frequent gulping sounds that had been so exciting to everyone on Jacob's first day of life. We swaddled him, which calmed him for a moment until he managed to wriggle one arm out, and then the other arm, followed by his legs. Ian suggested supplementing in the middle of the night, but I didn't want to try it at such a time without any help. I had heard that nighttime is always the hardest – the time when sleep-deprived parents crack open cans of formula thinking the baby is hungry when really he's crying for some other inexplicable reason. We held off, and Ian ended up spending the rest of the night holding and rocking Jacob.

The next morning Jacob had a small pee. I showed the diaper to Simone, who came by to check on us on her way to work. She said it was too dark and that we should start supplementing. After our terrible, sleepless night, Ian and I agreed. Mandy came over shortly after and weighed him. He had now lost twelve percent of his birth weight.

We got the colostrum syringes out of the freezer. Jacob was fussing, and Mandy said to him, "Oh, you poor little guy. I know, you're soooooo hungry. Don't worry, we'll get some food into your belly. You poor thing. Such a hungry little baby. It's okay little Jacob, food is on the way."

I felt a lump in my throat. Tears welled in my eyes. Had I been starving our newborn? Had he cried last night because we were torturing him with hunger? I sobbed for the next four hours as we tried to get the hang of feeding him the supplement, all the while with Mandy talking in her sympathetic baby voice. I was desperately thirsty but didn't think to pause to get water or ask for any.

Everyone was aware of the value and irreplaceability of my saved colostrum, and we were all on edge. The volume in each container was so little that the milk thawed quickly in Ian's hands. The first syringe of carefully collected "liquid gold" dribbled past Jacob's mouth and down my stomach. I had trouble seeing through my tears. We were trying to use the at-chest supplementer for the first time and it was awkward and painstaking. We used a homemade version that consisted of an irritatingly short, narrow feeding tube (provided by Mandy) going into the syringe of colostrum. I had to place the end of the tube just beside my nipple and then latch the baby onto my nipple and the tube at the same time. I felt I needed at least two pairs of hands to accomplish this. Mandy and Ian helped to position the tube while I made the breast tissue sandwich for Jacob and guided his head. Ian held the syringe close to my chest since the tube wasn't long enough for us to place it somewhere more comfortable. Learning to use this system involved much trial and error.

Eventually, I called Simone, still in tears, and begged her to come over again. When she arrived she saw that the first task at hand was to calm me down. "Jacob is fine. Yes, he is ready for your milk to come in, but he is fine. He is not dehydrated. It is time to supplement now, but losing 12% of birth weight is not unheard of. Managing the supplementer is awful. I had to do it with Tim in the beginning, so I know. It's super hard. But we'll do it."

The best part about Simone coming over was that Mandy then felt comfortable enough with the situation to leave. Simone's presence was confident and assertive. She knew what she was doing, and she addressed me gently and sensitively.

Before she went, Mandy explained, "Don't worry about warming the milk for Jacob. Keep it cool while using it, and then you can put it in the fridge after. If you warm it up, you have to throw out any that he didn't finish in that feeding. They give cold milk to babies in the NICU all the time, to help them stay alert enough to continue eating. Otherwise, they can fall asleep before they are full."

As soon as Mandy left, I was able to relax a little and things went better. We stopped spilling so much colostrum and Jacob was calmer, too.

The supplementer allows me to feed Jacob whatever my own body can make at the same time as the supplement, which is amazing. At least he can be fed completely at my chest. Despite this, supplementing changed our feeding relationship entirely. Jacob and I now had a cold, plastic tube placed between us. Sometimes Jacob sucked so hard that the tube made dark angry marks on my areola. I checked inside his mouth to make sure it wasn't giving him sores. This was now the best possible way to feed our baby, but I had to spend time grieving the loss of the natural, beautiful nursing that we were able to do during his first few days.

The most painful part of it all was to think that this was of my own doing. Just a few years ago, I had breasts that likely could have nourished him perfectly and I chose to get rid of them. I remember reading before my procedure that anyone who goes through such a surgery must grieve for what they leave behind. At the time this surgery was imperative – I needed it in order to be mentally healthy. I did not experience any sense of loss whatsoever. Now my whole body ached to feed my baby and I can only describe what I felt about my failure to do so as a deep mourning.

That night, after our first day of supplementing, I dreamed that Ian and I were sitting next to each other on an airplane that was diving. We knew that the plane was going to crash and that we were both going to be killed. I was trying to tell Ian I loved him. I mouthed the words; I felt like I shouted them, but they couldn't be heard. When I woke up, the feeling of desperation stayed with me. Breastfeeding said, "I love you" to my baby, and that night I knew I couldn't do it anymore, or at least not in the usual way that is so simple and profound.

The day that we started supplementing, we knew we were in trouble for human milk. We had those few small bags from Elaine plus the syringes I'd collected during the pregnancy. We estimated that this would last Jacob until the next morning.

Simone nursed Jacob when she came over to help teach me to use the supplementer. For her, this was pure pleasure. "All the joy of nursing a sweet little newborn, and none of the sleepless nights!" she said. It was difficult to watch someone else nursing my baby. Simone's breasts had plenty of flesh for him to latch onto, and lots of milk for him to gulp. She had so much milk, even, that it surprised Jacob. When her milk let down for him, he raised his eyebrows and swallowed as fast as he could. He pulled off and coughed and spluttered some, then was eager for more. This was what he'd been waiting for. I worried that after nursing from Simone, he wouldn't want my chest anymore. Yet I encouraged her to nurse him as much as she liked because I'd rather that he got her milk than formula.

Ian rented a hospital grade breast pump so that I could try, whenever I wasn't nursing Jacob, to stimulate my remaining mammary tissue to tell my body to make more milk. Breastfeeding being a supply and demand system, I made it my goal to increase demand as much as possible with the hope of inducing a correlating supply.

We called our friends, Nila and Lucy, to tell them the news. Without hesitation, they offered us donor milk from their own small stash and some milk-making medication and herbs. Lucy came over and immediately started preparing a galactagogue tea. This is the strangest breastfeeding word I've encountered so far. I learned from Fiona Giles' book, *Fresh Milk: The Secret Life of Breasts,* that galactagogue and galaxy share the same origin in Roman mythology. Apparently Zeus tried to hook up his mortal baby for a drink from the goddess, Juno, while she was asleep so that the child would become immortal through her milk. Juno woke in surprise and took the babe off her breast, spraying milk all over outer space and creating the Milky Way. So now we have galactagogues, which are defined as substances that help to increase milk production when they are ingested. [48]

Some birth enthusiasts are witches – the real kind, not those insulting Halloween personas. Over steaming cauldrons they combine herbal brews for all sorts of things including strengthening the uterus, mitigating the effects of postpartum depression, soothing the poor sexy bits, and, of course, making more milk. Lucy put together a concoction of fennel, anise, nettle, and alfalfa. She listed off the ingredients and then she paused. "Do you want to take goat's rue?"

I knew why she was asking. Goat's rue is a galactagogue because it is purported to "build and restore breast tissue," according to the claim on a bottle I saw. Lucy was asking me if I wanted my chest to potentially get bigger.

"Yes, absolutely, yes, I want it. I'll do anything that will give me a better chance of feeding this baby."

I could barely believe the words I heard coming out of my mouth. After everything – my transition, the hormones, the four thousand dollar surgery – I didn't hesitate to hope for more mammary tissue.

I started drinking Lucy's tea and I took pills of fenugreek and blessed thistle. Lucy also gave me some of her own domperidone pills to use on the weekend until I could get a doctor's prescription. I tried using the pump Ian brought home but I couldn't get out a single drop

---

[48] Giles, *Fresh Milk*, 1-2.

with it. I found this rather discouraging, although the books claim that just using the pump to stimulate the mammary tissue is helpful. I reminded myself that some people cannot pump much milk even when they actually have plenty.

Ian drove Lucy back home late that evening, leaving me alone with the baby and my thoughts. I had been sure that if I didn't have enough milk, we'd supplement with whatever human milk we could and then feed our baby formula. Despite having read about the risks of formula, I had imagined that I would feel fine knowing that we'd done whatever we could to give him human milk. Instead, I felt absolutely desperate to find a donor somehow. As I looked at my sensitive, perfect, soft-skinned baby, my whole body hurt at the idea of feeding him formula on his fifth day of life. Ian came home and eyed his trove of free sample formula, but I had an overwhelming instinct that the packaged, processed food would not be healthy for Jacob at this point.

We were grateful for the two bags of frozen milk Nila and Lucy gave us. I asked Nila, "But what about your baby? Do you have enough milk for her?"

She said, "No, we don't, but that's okay," and chuckled. "It's different now. Amy's six months old. She gets some formula sometimes and it's a drag, but it's not the same as when they're only a few days old."

Her own baby was going to have formula in place of the human milk she gave us. We could hardly imagine a time when we'd feel as relaxed about this as she did, but we accepted the gift without any more questions.

We didn't know what to do with it, though. We'd promised ourselves before he was born that we wouldn't risk exposing our baby to possible disease through donated milk. We'd never even met Nila's donor. Her name was Sherry and she was Mormon. She was a founding member of the Human Milk 4 Human Babies web site. This was all we knew of her.

I called Elaine to thank her for the milk she'd given us before she got shingles. I tried to pick a moment to call when I felt fairly cheerful and brave about things but as soon as I started to talk I burst into tears. "Without you, Jacob would have had formula already yesterday," I sobbed. Elaine said she might be able to come by after work to see us. We were truly scrounging, trying to get from one feeding to the next.

I started to look up official milk banks online. We decided during the pregnancy that we wouldn't go this route because milk from a bank is very expensive. Now, I felt like several grand would be a worthwhile investment to protect Jacob's digestive tract for his first weeks. I found a few banks that said they would sell milk to healthy, full term babies only if they had extra. Most banks said they would give milk exclusively to very sick babies with prescriptions for it. I called several locations but all were closed for the weekend.

Ian went online, too. He looked at the Human Milk 4 Human Babies Facebook group. I was surprised to see him posting but I didn't say anything. We saw that Nila and Lucy had already written about us on the site the day Jacob was born, mentioning that we might be in need of milk.

Soon enough the phone rang; someone had seen our post. Perhaps this wasn't going to be as hard as we first thought. I chatted for a while, trying to get a feel for this well-meaning stranger. I imagined I was doing something in between conducting a job interview and deciding on a potential date. The woman, Kathleen, seemed to be trying hard to make a good impression. Too hard. She ate only organic foods, never had a drop of alcohol, wasn't on any prescription drugs, and had only ever had one partner. I kept listening. She mentioned that she hadn't nursed a baby in a year but was still lactating and wanted to build up her supply. This made no sense to me. Why would you want to build up your supply if you didn't have a baby to nurse?

We had talked for quite a while when Kathleen finally mentioned, casually, that she smoked cigarettes and occasionally enjoyed weed. She said she was telling me this just to be honest and straightforward with me. "I'd even be willing to cut it down to three cigarettes a day for your baby. And I'd give up the pot entirely for you guys."

I used the handy excuse that I'd need to talk these things over with my partner. I hung up and threw the phone across the bed. I was learning that health and lifestyle choices mean different things to different people. I hadn't even thought to ask about smoking, yet it should have been one of my first questions.

According to some health care providers, marijuana use while breastfeeding is a big no-no because it may affect brain development in infants when they are exposed through milk. The research done so far has been minimal, but it has shown that THC, the principle psychoactive compound in marijuana, gets transferred into breast milk and that it seems to delay motor development in the first year[49]. Smoking cigarettes while breastfeeding is discouraged due to the health hazards of the smoke, but also because nicotine is transferred into breast milk and may upset a baby's stomach[50]. Despite this, many experts advise parents who cannot quit smoking to breastfeed anyway because it is better to breastfeed while smoking than to formula feed while smoking. Breastfeeding seems to protect the infant's lungs from some of the dangers of the smoke[51]. Ian called Kathleen back and thanked her for the generous offer but declined.

Elaine came by in the afternoon to see what she could do. For the first time since the birth, I made my way downstairs. We hung around together in the living room, me nursing Jacob and Elaine hooking herself up to the pump we'd rented. She got out a few ounces, enough for one or maybe two feedings. Then she headed home to look after her own family.

Ian read about a beautifully simple solution to part of our milk sharing problem. Pasteurization. It is done with cow's milk all the time, so why couldn't we pasteurize human milk to kill any dangerous pathogens it contained? Google revealed that some HIV-positive women in impoverished countries pasteurize their own freshly expressed milk before feeding it safely to their babies. Researchers have developed an easy method that can be used anywhere with few

---

[49] Djulus, "Marijuana use and breastfeeding."

[50] Bonyata, "Breastfeeding and cigarette smoking."

[51] Bonyata, "Breastfeeding and cigarette smoking."

supplies. You place 50ml of milk in a glass container, and put it in a pan with 450ml of water. Bring the water to a rolling boil and then remove and cool the milk. Bye-bye, HIV, and other scary things.[52] We now knew what to do with Sherry's milk until we had a chance to meet her and learn more about her.

In the meantime, my own chest tissue was changing. Fast. My skin started to feel tight. Then hot, and even hotter. The midwife, Jenny, who had helped latch Jacob the first time had offered to come back if we needed her. We called, and she came over that day, a Sunday evening. She spent about two hours with us, first listening to me crying about how guilty I felt that I couldn't feed Jacob.

"What you are doing for him, feeding him at the breast, providing him with such closeness, is amazing for him. Everyone feels like this around four or five days after the birth. If it wasn't about the breast milk, it would be about something else. You are doing everything right for him."

Having assuaged some of the hormonally-intensified guilt, we managed to get down to business. Whatever milk I did have was trying to come in, and my chest was engorged. I had a variety of little and big, hard lumps all over my chest and in my armpits. They hurt to the touch. It was suddenly much harder to make a nice "breast" tissue sandwich for Jacob and latch him on because the tissue was so full and tight. Jenny showed me how to massage the tissues towards the nipples, encouraging the milk to flow out[53]. We weren't sure if all the milk being produced had a way to get out or what would happen to me if it didn't. If I had milk backing up behind severed milk ducts, how would my body cope? Together we reread sections of Diana West's book, *Defining Your Own Success: Breastfeeding After Reduction Surgery*. It seemed that if the milk couldn't get out through the

---

[52] Yang, "HIV in breast milk killed by flash-heating."

[53] Diana West later explained to me that since some of the fluid in my chest was lymph, it might be most helpful to massage in the direction that the lymph should drain – toward the armpits.

nipple, it would hurt for a while and then my body would slowly re-absorb the milk and stop producing it in those places. Jenny suggested using caution with the domperidone and the herbs so that I wouldn't cause myself even more pain by making more milk that couldn't get out. She hoped, though, that some of the hard spots would drain to the nipples.

We tried using the pump to see if it could help work out some of the engorgement. I still didn't produce a single drop of milk but it seemed like the swelling did go down a bit. Afterwards it was easier for Jacob to nurse.

Jenny gave me a few parting tips. I should take a hot shower before nursing sessions to help the fluid flow better. If things got really bad and painful, I was to apply cold, raw grated potato to the lumps, which I did later that night with good results.

Next, Simone came over and, seeing the pump, asked if she could try it, too. She said she wasn't a good pumper but that she'd see what she could do with a high quality pump. Ian sterilized the equipment for her and she started up, just as Elaine had done a few hours earlier. Simone got out about three ounces, enough for another two or three feedings, and also nursed Jacob after I had fed him as much as I could. We now probably had enough milk to get through that night.

Simone looked at me with her soft, kind eyes and said gently, "You know, Trevor, formula is a miracle. It's a lifesaver. I know that around here it is the 'F' word, and it is for me, too. But this is exactly the kind of situation where a baby can benefit tremendously from formula."

I nodded and tried to produce a smile. I knew that what she was saying was true. I fought back my tears as she continued.

"You have done everything you can to make as much milk as possible. His latch is awesome and he is very persistent. I get upset when people don't try because they don't know how important it is. Or worse, when they are discouraged from breastfeeding altogether."

She was right. Formula kills babies in poverty-stricken countries where parents mix it with dirty water.[54] Breastfeeding would be the ideal means of feeding their babies safely in a precarious environment, but many have been convinced by the formula companies that the manufactured product is better, more modern. To me, it is the greatest crime of healthcare practices in the developing world.

We have clean water in our cozy home in Winnipeg, Canada. Jacob was not going to die if he ate some formula, and if there wasn't enough donor milk, we ought to be grateful that researchers have developed a substitute. In addition, today's formula is far more advanced and nutritionally complete than it was even a few decades ago, when Ian was formula-fed. I began to come to terms with the inevitable, but I hoped that perhaps we could just make it through his first week with only human milk.

Simone took the pump home with her to try over the next few days. She thought that if she used it regularly her supply should respond. Simone, the woman who had said she hated pumping and that she would never pump for us, was taking back home a fancy, hospital-grade electric pump. We were certainly beginning to have the sense that we were supported by a generous village.

I was glad she took it, but at the same time I felt sorry to be giving Simone the pump. It was the only one we had, and we'd initially got it so that I could try to stimulate my supply whenever Jacob wasn't nursing. Giving it to Simone was giving up in a way, and admitting that I had very little milk. I couldn't feed my own baby and we'd have to find milk or formula elsewhere.

The same evening, we got in touch with a few milky moms that our doula, Emily, had scared up. Alexa was mother to a toddler and a seven-month-old baby. She immediately expressed some milk for us after talking to Emily. She called her back though, saying that her milk didn't look fatty enough for a newborn. Ian and I felt that any human milk would be better for Jacob than formula so we asked if we

---

[54] Williams, "Baby health crisis in Indonesia as formula companies push products."

could collect it anyway.

She agreed. Emily told us ahead of time that Alexa attended a Mennonite church with her husband, who was ethnically Mennonite. Emily assured us that the couple was also very open-minded. The previous year, Ian and I had volunteered alongside some Mennonites, sandbagging against spring flooding when the furious Red River threatened a number of homes. We didn't mention anything about our queer relationship, in fact, maybe we behaved a bit less freely than usual, refraining from holding hands or sitting too close when we broke for lunch. Now we were about to receive bags of milk from a Mennonite family – an intimate exchange. Alexa was interested to know about the baby and family she was helping, so Ian explained our situation. She didn't seem troubled knowing that we were a gay, transgender couple. There was a baby in need and she was going to do what she could to help, no different than a church-basement-lady baking cookies for a good cause. She promised to ask other ladies at her church if they might also be able to contribute milk.

Emily also put us in touch with Laura, a woman with three kids, the youngest of whom was only two months old. She said she'd never had any trouble producing milk and that she'd take this as a challenge. Right away, she offered to pump milk for us for at least one month and see what we felt like doing after that.

Ian went out that evening to pick up the milk from our newfound donors. He collected a whopping sixteen ounces, an amount of milk that would probably see Jacob through two whole days if we used the supplementer with the utmost caution and didn't spill anything. He made arrangements to visit both donors again in two days' time, or earlier. Ian breathed a sigh of relief, and then realized he was completely exhausted both from daily life with a newborn and from the stress of trying to gather the perfect baby food. It suddenly occurred to him while he was driving home that he hadn't eaten all day. He stopped at the nearest McDonalds' drive-thru, the cooler of precious human milk sitting on the seat beside him.

It was Mandy on the phone again, on day five after Jacob's birth.

"Did you guys look online for breast milk?" she asked.

I was nervous. Health Canada warned against milk sharing, and the midwives were definitely not allowed to condone it. Ian and I had reminded each other that milk sharing, to our knowledge, was not actually illegal. Still, we wanted, and had wanted all along, to stay on the good side of the midwives and then finish up with them after Jacob reached six weeks of age, the time when infants in midwifery care normally move to pediatricians.

I blushed and stammered. I didn't know what to say. I said no. Ian came home soon after the conversation and I told him what happened. He pointed out that the midwives might be keeping track of us on the Facebook milk sharing site. They could easily have seen our post.

We knew of another queer couple whose midwives had chosen to call Child and Family Services before their baby was even born. We were well aware of being a highly unusual couple who may be subject to prejudice. It was the flip side of being identified as part of a marginalized population and therefore prioritized for receiving midwifery care. We could also see that midwives had power in the medical system. With one phone call, they could make a family's life hell for the foreseeable future.

When Mandy came over later that day, she asked again if we'd looked for milk online. This time I said, well, yes, but that we hadn't accepted anything. Mandy said that Kaly, the other midwife, had a friend who told her about our post. How many gay couples in Winnipeg with a five-day-old baby would be searching the internet for milk? *Oops.*

We had a discussion with Mandy about interviewing donors and pasteurizing milk. I was nervous and probably red in the face the whole time, but Mandy didn't seem any different than usual. She said that pasteurizing the milk we got would allay her fears about the safe handling and storage of milk. If the donor uses dirty pumping equipment or leaves the milk out too long, you could get bacteria that need to be killed by heat, she warned.

We nodded vigorously in agreement, or as much so as one can on day six with a newborn. We certainly didn't mind being cautious and pasteurizing the milk, but bacteria introduced by laissez-faire handling was not foremost on our minds.

Breast milk has extraordinary properties that include being able to attack bacteria. For this reason, breast milk keeps far longer in the fridge than formula does, and you can even leave it out for several hours at room temperature after pumping it if you then use it right away[55].

The current expert advice is that sterilization of bottles before every feeding is not required, even when giving formula. Now they say to wash bottles with soap and water the same as one would for regular dishes and cutlery. As long as the baby is healthy and full-term, occasional exposure to normal household germs is fine, and even beneficial. Ian and I were still far more concerned about the possibility of unknown medications, drugs, alcohol, caffeine, nicotine, and STDs in donor milk than we were about some common bacteria.

Mandy wasn't so worried about these issues. She said that milk banks interview their donors, and she didn't see how us conducting the interviews would be much different. For each batch of milk, a bank combines donations from at least three different women. This is

---

[55] Mohrbacher, "Why do milk storage guidelines differ?"

supposed to help dilute any unwanted drugs or toxins that escape their screening process. We were certain that we'd need far more than three donors to feed Jacob, so relying on dilution would be even more effective in our case.

We showed Mandy that we'd done thorough reading and she seemed to think that she'd warned us thoroughly enough about casual milk donation to move on. She gave me a doctor's prescription for domperidone, did a quick baby check, and left. I returned to feeling more exhausted than anxious and once again paid attention to the baby, who, I suddenly remembered, was the whole point of all the torment in the first place. I even tried to take time to enjoy him in his newness.

For Jacob's first trip outside, our destination was my beloved bakery, Le Croissant, a Winnipeg institution that is only half a block away from our house. It's the good stuff, meaning almost entirely white bread, made by French people. The bakery is only open in the mornings. If you go towards closing there is generally nothing left. I've shopped there two or three times a week since I moved into this neighborhood almost three years ago: I'm an addict. The chocolate almond croissants, creamy Saint-André cheese, perfectly crusty baguettes, fluffy egg bread, and cave-aged Gruyere call to me from down the road – literally. The bakery staff keep our phone number on file and let us know when our favourites are fresh out of the oven.

My Mom was visiting from Vancouver, and she, Jacob, Ian, and I all went together on a crisp, sunny morning. We walked gingerly down the sidewalk. I carried Jacob first on my shaky postpartum legs. Then Ian took his turn showing our baby the outdoors. As I opened the door to the bakery, we were greeted with the warm sweet scent of fresh bread. It felt luxurious to leave our house and baby-feeding woes for a few minutes.

The bakery owner, Fabienne, and her assistant Nel, gushed over the newborn. "Ooooh, so cute!"

They asked what his name was, how old he was, how much he weighed. They wanted to know how long my Mom was staying, and where she was from. What did she think of her grandchild?

We were all skirting the question that was on their minds. Where did this baby come from? *Where was the mother?* We didn't offer any explanation. We bought our croissants and went home, pleased to have shown off Jacob.

The next time I trundled off to the bakery it was just me and Jacob who went. Nel was the only one behind the counter and the shop was quiet.

Nel said, "So, how's Mommy doing?"

"Who?"

She laughed nervously and then pursued again, "Well, did you guys adopt or what?"

"Oh, you just thought I was getting really fat over the winter, did you?"

That made her really nervous. I laughed and let her off the hook. I told her I was transgender and Ian was my partner. I had our baby myself.

Oh, now she got it. "Good for you. Congratulations. I think that's great," she said.

She'd been bursting with curiosity for days. I smiled and walked home. Maybe I would tell her about how I was nursing the next time around.

Jenny, the sweet midwife who was so helpful, said that there are freezer stashes all over Winnipeg. There are people who have been storing breast milk for all kinds of reasons, and have ended up with more of it than they could ever need. In fact, during any given week, a parent nearby is probably pouring milk down the drain. Probably as well, their eyes are welling up with tears because it took a lot of effort to pump and collect that milk, and they know how precious it is. Maybe they thought they'd go back to work and so they tried fiercely to produce extra milk ahead of time and then realized they didn't need quite that much. Now it's been sitting in the freezer for too long. Maybe this parent pumped milk for the babysitter to use, but then the baby refused to take a bottle. Or maybe their baby died and they had to pump for a while in order to be comfortable. Now they are finally throwing away their last physical connection between their own body and their baby's. There is always a story behind a bag of pumped milk.

Whatever the reason, there are these freezer stores, waiting like hidden treasure in ordinary Winnipeg houses. We knew that they existed, but we had no idea how to find them if they weren't listed on Human Milk 4 Human Babies. A few people are aware of the Facebook sites that allow people in need to find those with excess. Most have never heard of such a thing. So we looked far and wide, and we were happy to pay for shipping milk from anywhere, or drive for hours to go collecting. Ian didn't only join the Manitoba chapter of Human Milk 4 Human Babies – he now belonged to the Ontario, Saskatchewan, and North Dakota community pages as well.

In Jacob's first week, there was a posting on the North Dakota site about a sizable amount of pumped milk from a healthy woman. We jumped on it, and Sherry offered to help arrange transportation since her mother was going to be driving from North Dakota into Winnipeg later in the week. This supply could really put us in good stead for a while, and we even had someone ready to deliver it for us. We responded to the offer only to find out that we were too late. Someone else in need had already laid claim. We began checking Facebook compulsively for new posts and private messages.

It was in this critical week that I was finally prompted to take back some of my hateful words about social networking sites. At one time, I *may* have been heard to say, "Facebook is a waste of time. Everything about it is superficial. Why should I join when one of its first sign-up questions is about my gender?"

I had refused to join Facebook for years. Privacy was of the utmost importance for me as a closeted trans person, and Facebook seemed determined to do away with it entirely. I had different layers of friends who knew varying details about me, and even called me by separate names, but their social circles overlapped. I couldn't manage a networking site when I had multiple personas. Everyone else loved Facebook and I had to hate it.

Now Facebook was feeding my baby. I nursed the baby, changed the baby, and checked messages. Ian, a longtime Facebook devotee, had a grin as wide as a crocodile's when I finally pronounced my adoration for the biggest, most wonderful time suck in history.

If you've ever cared for a dog or a baby, you've spent time worrying about feces. The vet wants to know if you remembered to collect a sample. How has the stool changed? What is it normally? What colour? Consistency? Time of day? Straining at all?

"Okay, well since you didn't take a sample, I'll have to get one now so we can run some tests. Just relax, Rover. Why don't you give Rover a big hug around the neck to keep him from turning around and biting me? That's perfect."

It's the same thing with babies (hopefully minus the biting part). The simplest rule of breastfeeding is that if an adequate amount of food is going in, there will be ample wet and dirty diapers. The first poop that comes out after birth is called meconium, a dark substance stickier than molasses. After the initial few days, the stool should gradually change to looking mustardy in colour. It still sticks to everything, although less so than before, and you can stretch it out like a wad of bubble gum (I've done this, but not on purpose). Eventually baby poop can become quite loose because human milk is a natural laxative that helps to clean out the baby's insides and get things going after all those months of in utero digestion.

Since we knew Jacob wasn't regaining his birth weight quickly enough, we had to carefully watch his poops and pees. After we starting supplementing, the pees came in fast and wet. We didn't see any poop at all for a few days in a row. Several breastfeeding books enthuse about an "okay" diaper, meaning that the number two in the diaper is about the size of an okay sign you can make with your thumb and forefinger. At most we were getting smears.

We were scheduled to have a break from the midwives for a few days, but Mandy was concerned to hear from me over the phone that there hadn't been any poop. I was worried, too. I wanted that poop. I wanted to see it, smell it, touch it. I was ready to throw a party for Jacob's first "okay" diaper. We waited. We looked at Jacob and he looked back at us, utterly content, but poo-free.

Mandy sent Kaly over to weigh the baby just to check that everything was still all right. As she arrived, she said, "Yeah, this scale I've got... There's something wrong with it. So the weight will probably be wrong, but don't worry about that. Last week Mandy and I discovered that our two scales were totally out from each other. Anyway, I'll weigh him, but it'll probably be really out. But don't worry, *okay?*"

Ah, these were the comforting words of a medical professional who relies almost entirely on a baby's weight gain as the basis for determining health. The number she got was 2740 grams, apparently down from two days before. She repeated that we ought not to worry about this at all.

Kaly asked if I burped Jacob regularly. I said no, I hadn't thought to. She showed me the current approved burping technique, which is to sit the baby on your knee, supporting his head, and *rub* his back, rather than pat or whack as some of our own parents might have done. She did manage to get a burp out of him, and said in a sweet, babyish voice, "There, that's better Jacob, isn't it? Now you'll have lots more room for breast milk with that air out of your tummy."

I felt the lump from a few days ago coming back up into my throat. Kaly left, saying she'd be back tomorrow to re-weigh, and I burst into tears. There was no way not to spend the rest of the day and all night worrying that Jacob wasn't getting enough food or that something else was wrong. I knew the scale was probably calibrated incorrectly but its authoritative number stuck in my head.

We were told to supplement Jacob as if I was making nothing for him at all. Mandy said that a baby born at his weight should be eating about 240ml (8 ounces) of milk per day. She instructed us to make sure we supplemented him at least this much during a 24-hour period.

We chose to feed Jacob on demand, as much as he wanted, whenever he wanted it. Having done this, I can't imagine how anyone can feed a baby on a schedule. Sometimes Jacob would cry as if the world was about to end when all he wanted was 5ml. Other times he'd have 80ml at once. He seemed to know exactly how much he needed and we were happy to oblige.

Keeping track of intake and output was fiendishly difficult, especially overnight. We kept a spreadsheet on the computer that included amount of supplement taken, pees celebrated (squirt, kitchen faucet, or major flooding so get another diaper and a new pair of pants) and poops let loose (smear, okay diaper, or poonami, if we'd ever be so lucky to get one).

At this stage, Jacob tended to be on or off, either peacefully asleep or awake and screaming for food. We'd all be cuddled up in our family bed, Jacob snuggled against my side with my arm wrapped around him. Usually, Ian was snoring. And then it would be like a fire alarm went off under the covers. "Wah-ah, wah-ah," Jacob cried his distinct newborn cry, his voice frighteningly high in pitch and intensity. I'd sit up with a start and hurry to get out the supplementer. Since the tubes we had available to us for the first few weeks were very short, I couldn't put the bottle of supplement down beside me: Ian had to hold it up close to my chest.

"Ian!" I'd nudge him awake. He would sit up next to me during the forty-five minute feeding, frequently dropping back to sleep and loosing his grip on the bottle. If we remembered to look at the level on the bottle at the beginning and end of a nighttime feeding we were very lucky. Immediately noting it on the laptop was rare.

I'm not sure we ever got an accurate tally of how much Jacob ate in one day. I always estimated numbers on the high side so that we could tell the midwives we were feeding him tons, hoping this would somehow keep them happier, even though I knew the numbers they cared about most came from the scale.

Kaly came back again the day after she'd used her cockeyed scale. This time she'd recalibrated it and Jacob's weight was met with approval although there had still been no poop. Right after she weighed him, he wanted to feed. Ian and I fumbled with the supplementer in front of Kaly, desperately trying to demonstrate competency with the evil device. After he was done, she asked to weigh him again. I rolled my eyes – this was getting to be a little much. The baby was eating well and was happy and hydrated.

Looking at the level on the bottle, Ian thought he'd had about 30 ml. Kaly did the second weigh, and said, "Well, Trevor, he took in 40 ml just now. That means you made 10ml."

I jumped up and hugged her, I was so incredibly happy to hear that I had made a quarter of what Jacob just ate. This was considerably more than the nothing I felt like I was providing.

Using the supplementer for virtually every feeding with Jacob made it seem like he was having only supplement. I could see and believe the level going down in the bottle, but couldn't observe that anything was coming out of my own body. We had heard him swallow colostrum for the first few days of his life, yet this now felt like a facade or at best a faint memory. On the other hand, there were times when Ian and I were trying to get him latched on with the tube and I thought it worked because I heard him gulping. Then Ian would say, "No, we've got to try again. Nothing's going up through the tube."

Moments like this when I knew that the contents of his hungry swallows could only be coming from me were triumphant, but I still felt deceived by my body. It was hard to believe that anything was happening in there to make milk. When I used a pump, nothing came out at all, and when I hand expressed, I got only drops.

I clung to Kaly's 10 ml measurement. The scale may very well have been wrong, or Ian may have misread or misremembered the level in the bottle. I didn't dare ever again to do a weight before and after a feeding. When asked, I just tell people, "I make about a quarter of what Jacob needs." I don't want to find out otherwise.

Later that day Ian's colleague from work, Grace, came over to visit. I asked her to wash her hands before coming into our room. I explained that this was just something we paranoid, overprotective new parents were asking everyone to do because of our week-old little baby.

She replied, "Germs are good for them. It's possible to be too cautious, you know." She washed her hands anyway, but after that I didn't let her hold him. She stood there, awkwardly, as Jacob stayed cocooned in my arms.

Of course, it was while Grace was over, hovering by the door to our bedroom, that we finally got the explosion we'd been waiting for. Jacob was wrapped in a receiving blanket, diaperless. Four days' worth of poop went all over Jacob, my legs, the receiving blanket, and our bed. I shrieked in surprise. "Oh, my! Oh, wow! Umm. What do we do?! Wipes? Ummm. He's still going. There's more! Ian? *Ian!*"

Grace watched in amusement. She had looked after her own nieces and nephews often enough to be quick and efficient at changing diapers. Here I was not letting her hold Jacob, and acting like doo-doo was a national emergency.

In fact, it was cause for major festivities. Jacob had produced his long awaited bowel movement after, rather than before, being weighed by the midwife. As it turned out, he was a baby who liked to poop no more frequently than every five days for the first five months of his life. Sometimes he held off as long as ten days. Contrary to what's in all the books, the midwives said that this is within the range of what is normal for a breastfed baby.

Our visitor wished us well and politely made a hasty retreat when Jacob fell asleep. Ian and I knew we should waste no time in sliding down into bed beside him to get some rest for ourselves. He'd probably be up again in an hour. I obediently closed my eyes and started to drift off.

"Remember when he was the size of a lentil?" asked Ian.

I opened my eyes, and smiled sleepily, trying to appreciate in spite of the exhaustion that Ian was having a "moment." At six weeks pregnant, the word "lentil" had overwhelmed me with nausea rather than affection. I was relieved the week that Babycenter.ca told us Jacob was the size of a blueberry, which was to me a relatively benign morsel.

Jacob had been either nursing or cuddled up with one of us since his birth. We were sure we recognized the little being who had developed inside me for all that time. We had both felt his kicking and squirming in utero, and he continued these familiar antics after we welcomed him Earthside.

"What day are we at now, Trevor?"

"Ten."

"Whoa." Ian rubbed his eyes. "I was ten days old when I was held by my parents for the first time."

The next day when Kaly came over again we tried hard to keep the appointment brief. Everyone, including my Mom who was still staying with us, was aware of the need to please her. A midwife had come to our house on ten out of Jacob's first twelve days. "Visits" were at least half an hour but sometimes several hours long. We were done with feeling monitored and interrogated. We were starting to get over the brand new parent, terrified-of-everything phase (*Dear G-d, his nose is broken! We've been too rough with him! Oh, that's just a booger.*) We were almost ready to start trusting ourselves. We could see that Jacob was content and thriving.

Besides, on this day we had another reason to see Kaly off faster. There was an attachment-minded families playgroup starting in a few minutes, and we wanted to go hunting for milk donors. "Attachment-minded" parents tend to sleep with their babies, keep infants close by at all times, and practice gentle forms of discipline with their older children, but best of all, they are nearly always die-hard breastfeeders. Sherry, the Mormon who supplied some of Jacob's first supplements, was a member of the group. We were approaching Easter weekend and most of our milk donors were going out of town for the holiday. We were coming up to our first of what would be many milky crunch periods and we knew it. Every drop was going to count.

In front of Kaly, I tried to be as relaxed and happy-looking as possible. Yes, it *was* a beautiful day. Sure, my stitches were feeling fine – wonderful, in fact. Nope, no need to check my stomach muscles. I could do situps right now but I won't because I want to take it easy.

No reason to strain myself. Oh, yes, Jacob's been eating perfectly. Uh oh, how to answer the sleeping question, I wondered. Was he sleeping happily through the night being a perfect baby? Wouldn't this suggest we weren't feeding him enough? No, I decided, he wasn't sleeping right through, but of course we didn't mind. Diapers? Oh, jeeeez, they've just been huge. Impossible, really, leaking out of everywhere. I mean, but not excessively or anything though. All normal. I thought maybe I should throw in something that demonstrated pure delight in our baby, not just the usual health check stuff.

"Kaly, you have to see this, it's so incredibly cute."

I leaned over and kissed Jacob on the nose. On cue, he lifted his head slightly and looked up, eyebrows raised.

"Isn't that the sweetest thing? He does that every time." I put on the doting parent voice pretty heavy.

"Oh, yeah that's super cute," she said. "Now...that may be a breastfeeding thing. When something touches baby's nose, mouth, or cheek, the instinctive reaction is to open the mouth and look in the direction of the nipple."

My attempt at casual, easy-going, now-get-out-of-here-because-obviously-everything's-fine conversation had backfired. Kaly went on, discussing theoretical aspects of breastfeeding. And how exactly was it that the baby knew what to do?

Ian interrupted to mention that we were going on our first real outing with Jacob. We told Kaly we were going to the parenting group.

"Oh, great! One of my good friends is in that group. They're a wonderful bunch."

Perfect, we thought. She'll have her own personal spy amongst our new friends.

Kaly left us and we were able to get going. It was our first time in the car since Jacob's birth, and by the time we made it to the playgroup, I was so exhausted that I didn't get further than Sherry and a few friends who were standing right by the entrance of the building. We chatted with them for a while and then I needed to sit down. The room was a bouncing, child-minding mess of parents and milk ducts. Far too tired to network as we'd hoped, we soon retreated back home.

My mom only stayed for one week, but it was better than nothing. She cooked for us every evening and took the dog out. She held Jacob while he slept and couldn't take her eyes off him. I wanted her there badly, but I wanted her to stay away, too.

A few years earlier, when I told my parents that I planned to transition, my Mom was worried. When she realized I was actually going to do it, I think she was sad and confused for a long time. I explained to her about the hormones I'd take and the surgery I'd have, and she asked, "But how could you mutilate your body like that?"

It wasn't mutilation at the time; it was immense relief. I felt firmly male, and I needed my physical self to resemble my inner being more closely. When I started taking the hormones and my voice began to deepen, I relaxed a little. I didn't mind hearing my own voice any more. I recognized myself when I spoke. My face shape started to change as my jawline became more pronounced, and I relaxed a little more. Peach fuzz thickened and darkened into a nearly respectable forest on my chin, above my lips, and along my cheeks. When I looked in the mirror, I started to feel like I knew the person looking back at me. He seemed happy and comfortable.

I never told my parents exactly when I was having chest surgery. I was nervous about being under anesthesia and cut open, and I didn't want to have to worry about somebody else's feelings at the same time. I couldn't get my Mom's word "mutilate" out of my head. I chose to spare her and myself and just go off and have the surgery without talking about it. She knew it was part of my long-term plans. I never told my parents about how scary it was when I puked as I came around after surgery or how it took a month to recover enough that I could play violin again. I didn't get to tell them how much relief I felt afterwards, either.

Now that Jacob was born and I was struggling to make milk for him, I didn't think I had a right to grieve my loss in front of my Mom. I was sure she'd tell me the surgery was a stupid thing to have done in the first place. I couldn't explain how it had made my joy and my pregnancy possible, and was also a source of deep sadness. I tried my best to be stoic during her visit.

On the morning of her flight back to Vancouver, we did some shopping and went for a walk at a provincial park outside of the city limits. Jacob got hungry in the car. We pulled over and I struggled to feed him on the side of a busy road. I couldn't hear whether or not he was swallowing, and wasn't sure if the tube was in the right place in his mouth. We tried to drive again, but a minute later he cried and we stopped to feed him once more. Mom was patient through it all and never once said anything about the inconvenience of having to bring a cooler of milk everywhere. She didn't remind me how fussy it was to have to nurse him with a feeding tube. She just quietly helped out with what she could and, on more than one occasion, sang high praise for human milk.

By the time we brought her to the airport I felt depleted in every way. As soon as she was out of sight, I felt the tears welling up in my eyes. I cried all the way home. We had got over the initial stressful days of trying to get breastfeeding working and finding a starter supply of donor milk. Mom had gone back home and now I had the space to mourn my decision to remove the breasts I had hated so much and that would have made the perfect food for my baby whenever he need- ed it. Ian listened to me weep several times a day for the next while.

Around this same time, Ian matter-of-factly began tearing down the inspirational photos we'd put up in the birth room. It was time to transform the space into the baby's room now that he had arrived. In response, I bawled with the self-possession of an infant enduring a heel prick test. I wasn't ready to see my photos come down. I still needed help remembering that I was strong. I had loved the end of the pregnancy, when I could feel Jacob perfectly protected inside me, and I missed it. I still sometimes touched my belly in memory of our symbiosis. Now he was outside and vulnerable, and we depended upon others' generosity and abundance to feed him. We kept those photos on the wall a while longer.

Ian later told me that at the time of my surgery, he wondered if we might have kids some day, and if I'd want to be able to feed them from my body. He knew that there was no way for him to suggest this to me at the time. He could see how desperately I wanted to have a body I was comfortable with. All he'd said was that he loved every part of me, and that it would be okay with him if I didn't want to go through with the surgery. I'd explained to him that maybe he didn't need me to have the surgery in order to love me, but that I needed it in order to love him. And, I don't think I'd make a different choice even if I could do it all again. I can't be Jacob's mother. I gave birth to him, but I am his breastfeeding dad.

In 1995, Ian's friend Lex called to say she'd seen on the news that the British Columbia adoption records were going to be opened. Just outside a small town in rural Nova Scotia, a friend of Melissa's came to tell her the same. Melissa and Ian both soon received letters in the mail stating that they had each agreed to disclose their identities to one another.

Ian planned a trip to visit a complete stranger, his birth mother. He flew to Halifax and took a bus as far as it went – to the town of Bridgewater. There, he met Melissa and her husband, not his father, and their two nearly-adult children.

The family drove him the hour to their 100-acre homestead. Their driveway was lined with mature pine trees, and their house surrounded by maples planted in honor of the births of their children. Inside, there was a beautiful, antique, fully-functioning stove and old wooden floors.

Ian and Melissa and her family spent days sharing food and stories. He quickly felt enveloped by warmth and generosity on the farm.

Upon the end of his visit, the family dropped Ian off at the bus stop in Bridgewater. They hugged him tightly, waved their goodbyes, and drove away. Tears streamed down Ian's face as he stood at the side of the highway.

For the first ten days of Jacob's life, it was entirely up to Ian to go out and pick up milk when it was available. In Jacob's first week I didn't even make it out the back gate let alone go off on a trip to meet and try to befriend some strangers doing us a huge favour. Ian drove all over the city in those early days picking up a bag of milk here or there from whoever offered. He was continually in a sleep-deprived fog from sitting up with Jacob and me to help during every feeding.

Before setting off on a milk run, he'd wait until Jacob had downed a good feed. As soon as Jacob took his last gulp, Ian knew he was on the clock because I'd need help with feeding again next time the baby was hungry. He did all this because of what we knew about the risks of formula-feeding, but also I'm sure because of the look he saw in my eyes when it seemed like there wouldn't be enough donor milk for Jacob. Ian knew how deep my pain went and so off he drove at a time when most parents would be trying to catch up on much-needed sleep or enjoying bonding time with their infant.

On day eleven after the birth, Ian and I both felt it would be good for Jacob and me to visit the milk donors in town. I wanted to meet in real life the people who were helping us in such a personal, intimate way. We also needed to show our immense appreciation and hopefully be friendly and interesting so that it wouldn't be too much of a chore for our donors to have to see us frequently for collections. This was also our last milk pickup before the Easter long weekend during which our donors would be away. We hoped that we would come home with a plentiful supply.

It was astonishing to me that some of our earliest, most generous milk donors were deeply religious, *and that they knew we were gay*. As a kid, I attended a public high school with a large proportion of fundamental Christian students as well as a devout Muslim family. I became best friends with the most reverent girl among the Muslim students. We got along very well in many ways. We were both smart and each of us disliked most sports. One day, she mentioned that she believed being gay was more reprehensible than murdering someone. I stayed silent. For years she remained my closest friend, at the same time as I was starting to work out my sexuality. A Christian girl at school used to approach me at recess and lunch breaks to whisper in my ear that gay people would "burn in hell forever and ever." I grew up with the impression that this is what people of faith believed.

First, we went to see Alexa, who attended a Mennonite church in Winnipeg. She hand expressed her milk. Pumping elicited traumatic memories from when her baby was a newborn struggling to gain weight. She wouldn't use one again, she said, but she had plenty of milk. She knew exactly where and how to squeeze her breasts to get an efficient spray going.

Alexa greeted us with canning jars of milk, explaining that she had a lot of extra jars at this time of year. She and her family lived in a small apartment but had found several people in Winnipeg who owned land and gardens they didn't use. One was an old woman whose unfenced yard attracted deer and sprouted vigorous weeds, but Alexa found that she could at least successfully grow potatoes and onions there. Working in the different gardens all summer long, the family grew enough produce to last them through a good portion of our interminable winter – a tremendous feat.

Ian was tickled to be getting milk from an experienced canner, who had food handling credentials any midwive ought to trust. We imagined milk from Alexa was also probably low in toxins since she grew and ate her own organic food.

One irony of acquiring donated breast milk is that many of our donors' own children have had formula. These determined parents had troubles early on but persevered and then came to produce copious supplies. Because of the work it took them to accomplish exclusive breastfeeding, they recognize how valuable their milk is and they seem eager to pass along the wealth.

Alexa told us her first baby was born near-term (not quite full term) and underweight. Alexa's labour had been induced early due to pre-eclampsia. Her milk was slow to come in, and for five days she pumped every three hours in a desperate attempt to plump up her baby. After a few days of much-needed formula, Alexa's milk arrived in full force. We said we were sorry to hear about the formula.

Alexa said, "Oh, that's okay," with the look of somebody who had spent time coming to terms with events that hadn't exactly matched her well-laid plans. We hung around for what we hoped was an appropriate but not overbearing amount of time talking about birth, babies, and milk. Before we left, Alexa casually whipped out her breasts and squirted some more food into the canning jars. "Just a little top-up," she said and smiled.

As gay men, we were sure spending a lot of time appreciating breasts – for their life-giving function.

Soon after that weekend, Alexa set her church in motion collecting milk. She told our story to her friend Leila, who swiftly pumped four very full bags of milk for Jacob. Alexa and Leila then cornered a pregnant first-time mom-to-be on a Sunday in church and told her what they were doing for us. When she later gave birth, she, too, gifted several bags to us. Finally, Alexa called yet another lactating Mennonite who wanted to help but didn't get anything out when she pumped. On the other hand, some of our secular work colleagues seemed to think that sharing breast milk was unappetizing, and wondered aloud why we didn't just give him formula "like normal people would do."

Next on our errands, we went to see Laura. Ian led me around to the back of her house, where we came in through the dimly lit kitchen. The counters and sink were piled high with dirty dishes. Toys, tools, and gadgets decorated the floor. Laura was sitting on a worn-out couch looking completely serene as she breastfed her two-month-old baby. I felt comfortable at once, since I had finally discovered a home as messy as our own filthy dust patch carpeted with dog hair.

Laura spoke with a sweet, gentle tone and was clearly happy to see our little guy. Jacob instantly started up crying and needed a diaper change. To calm him down, I automatically began to unbutton my shirt. Then I realized this would be the first time I'd nursed Jacob outside of the privacy of our own home or car. It certainly wouldn't be the last. Laura handed us four of our own "Born-free" bottles full of her milk and we were on our way.

It wasn't the most flattering question to ask of someone who had recently given birth, but it was understandable. "Trevor, are you pregnant again?" Simone's boy, Tim, asked me when Jacob was a few weeks old. "Your tummy looks really big!"

I sighed and explained to Tim that no, I wasn't pregnant again – it takes a while to lose the extra fat and fluid you gain during pregnancy. And, I should have added, a postpartum body is probably never going to be exactly as it was prior to growing new life.

The four-year-old was working to get me all figured out. During the pregnancy, he had wanted to know how I, a man, could be having a baby. We adults explained to him that I used to be a girl, and then I changed because I wanted to. I took a special kind of medicine to change. Since I had been a girl before, I had the parts necessary to have a baby. It was simple language, but it would do for now.

That night before going to bed, Tim was worried: "Mommy, do I have to change, like Trevor?"

"No, no Tim. You don't have to change. Well, you'll only change if you want to change." Simone was committed to answering him truthfully.

"I don't want to change."

"Okay, Tim," said Simone. "You don't have to change."

"Okay. Goodnight, Mommy." He was satisfied.

The next night, Tim said to Simone, sounding plaintive, "Mommy, I don't want you to change!"

"Don't worry, Tim, Mommy's not going to change!"

Simone and I laughed about this together later. Then we realized that we had neglected to mention to Tim that "changing genders" is a relatively rare occurrence. It wasn't something everybody did at a certain age. He would not, one day, eat a bologna sandwich for lunch, go to the dentist in the afternoon, and change his gender some time before dinner. All of Tim's friends and family wouldn't suddenly be unrecognizable to him from one day to the next.

I guess we also didn't make it clear to him that I wasn't quite what you would call a "girly girl" before my transition. I hadn't magically switched from being a girl to being a boy; I had always felt like a boy, and when I transitioned I was able to share that information with others. Most people who knew me saw it coming a long way off, and were happy for me when I finally made my great pronouncement at the age of twenty-three. Tim didn't meet me until after my transition, so it was hard for him to picture what I must have been like in my previous incarnation.

After Jacob was born, Tim was curious to see how I was feeding him. The first time he watched me using the at-chest supplementer, he laughed and exclaimed, "That's ridiculous!"

Simone went straight to educating, using her best La Leche League leader tone of voice.

She said, "When someone doesn't have enough of their own milk, they can put milk into a bottle like Trevor has there. See the tube going up from the bottle? Baby Jacob opens his mouth wide and latches onto the tube and Trevor's nipple at the same time so he gets Trevor's milk and the donated milk, too."

Tim came closer to better inspect what exactly I was doing.

"You're giving Jacob Daddy nanas!" he exclaimed.

"Nanas" was his word for nursing, which he still avidly pursued, especially at bedtime or if he hurt himself, like the previous day when he had walked smack into a telephone pole. He and his younger sister Samantha had a whole breastfeeding vocabulary and grammar worked out. Samantha called nursing "mamas." If she wanted to nurse more or lots, she'd demand "millia mamas." If one breast seemed to be running low and she wanted the other one, she'd say, "mama dat."

Jacob, at three weeks of age, always wanted "millia mamas." He demonstrated his enthusiasm by mouthing at my chest, persistently bobbing his head around to find my nipple. According to Tim, Jacob was a "nana pig." We reminded Tim that when he was a baby, he, too, had been a "nana pig." Tim laughed at this. Soon he walked around proudly nursing his sister's doll, showing us that he could grow up to be a breastfeeding man just like I had.

Like a kid learning to apply a math concept to apples just as well as to snowmobiles, Tim tested his understanding of transgender identities using different scenarios. "Did you notice, Trevor, that Papa Smurf doesn't have a wife, but he does have Baby Smurf? He must be transgender like you!"

Now it all made sense.

One day when Tim was at his drop-in daycare, he said to Sue, one of the adults watching him, "I know a man who gives his baby nanas."

Sue knew what "nanas" meant, and she laughed at Tim. "That's nonsense! You're very funny Tim, but it's impossible for a man to give a baby nanas."

The next time I saw Tim he asked me what I was doing with Jacob. Surprised at his question, I said I was nursing him. "How are you doing that?" he asked, laughing. "That's impossible!"

In addition to nursing Jacob whenever we visited her, Simone always pumped for us in the mornings. This was the time of day when she had the most milk. She knew that today, Easter Sunday, our meager stores had nearly run dry so she hoped she'd get plenty out. We had secured some milk via Facebook from another donor in Saskatoon but were still working on the details of how to ship the available milk to Winnipeg. In the meantime, we weren't sure if we would make it through the weekend.

After getting woken up early by her kids, Simone tried to savour what she could of her morning off at home. Tim asked for "nanas" and she agreed but specified that it had to happen lying down on her bed. She would nurse him and rest a little and then get up to do her ritual pumping for us. She cuddled and breastfed him, and glanced at the clock. Still early. She fell asleep for an hour and woke up to her four-year-old saying in his chirpiest voice, "Mommy, you're all dried up!"

Jacob was thirteen days old and we didn't know where to find our next fix.

The phone rang at 10:00 p.m. on that blurry, sleep-deprived Sunday evening. A man said he was here with the "sweet stuff." We had thought that this batch in from Saskatoon was going to arrive the following night, which would probably have been too late for us to stay off of formula entirely. By this point we were counting every drop.

We gladly accepted our mistake and Ian immediately went out in the dark and rain with a bottle of wine in hand. He found the address deep in the suburbs. The open garage door revealed two luxury SUVs with a cooler of breast milk sitting in between them: the holy grail. The man answered the door.

"Yes, that's it there. Please, take it."

Ian offered up the bottle of wine. The man, who had brought the cooler with him on his drive into Winnipeg from Saskatoon, said it was absolutely unnecessary.

"That's true. Please accept it. We are so grateful for this."

Susan, the donor, had posted that she had a four-month supply to give away. She was a math teacher, non-smoker, and non-drinker. Perfect. I felt I could understand someone who was a math teacher. Our next-door neighbor was a schoolteacher. One of our best friends was an education assistant. I always liked my math teachers when I was a kid (I think I had a crush on at least one of them). I felt confident about milk from a math teacher. Setting my nerdy fantasies aside, I also knew that Susan was a complete stranger to us and that we'd be pasteurizing her milk for sure.

Susan's baby was born without a suck reflex. The baby was

incapable of breastfeeding or bottle-feeding and was fed in the NICU with a tube down his throat. Susan pumped and saved her milk laboriously, hoping that her baby would one day drink it. Her fragile infant required thickened milk, otherwise he threw everything back up due to an immature stomach valve. Breast milk, the perfect food for almost all babies, is obstinate to remain in its natural state; it resists thickening. Susan's baby was never able to drink her milk.

We'd wondered whether this unlikely-sounding tale could be the real thing. Simone said she'd never heard of it and that personally, she'd be suspicious. A quick Google search confirmed the medical facts. In rare cases, babies absolutely cannot drink human milk. Lack of a suck reflex and the inability to keep milk down are both legitimate conditions. We were, rather embarrassingly, delighted at the possibility: another baby's terrible health struggles were our good fortune. This was not just average human milk, either – we had hit upon "liquid gold," the colostrum and early milk that breast milk junkies crave most.

We couldn't contain ourselves at the thought of a four-month supply of milk for Jacob. We'd talked about buying another freezer to store it all. We'd put the neighbours on alert about needing some interim freezer space until we could get everything sorted out. We were thrilled we wouldn't have to worry about milk in Jacob's early months.

When we opened up the cooler that Ian brought back from his trip to suburbia, we saw that this milk would probably last Jacob only about two weeks. It offered immense relief in our current state of crisis but was not the months' worth of milk that a constantly suckling baby would demand and stimulate. We then realized what Susan meant by a "four-month supply." This was the milk that she had pumped over the course of four months, not the amount of milk a baby would drink in four months. Susan's baby didn't breastfeed at all, and so her body didn't receive the message that suckling sends to make more, *make more*. Breast pumps are great, but they will never be as effective as healthy babies are at drawing out milk and showing the body that there is demand.

Nevertheless, it looked like Jacob would probably have nothing but human milk for his entire first month of life. My mind immediately started jumping ahead – I couldn't help wondering if perhaps we could get enough milk to go two months, or more. Any day closer to the time, around four to six months, when his digestive tract would be prepared for solid foods would be a better date to start with formula. For the next two weeks, while Jacob drank Susan's milk, we would continue collecting from our donors in town and searching for additional ones online.

Grateful for what we'd received, we asked Susan what we could do for her. She replied that we ought to donate to a charity of our choice. We sent a hundred bucks to Greenpeace.

If you have a new baby, expect to be at least one hour late for appointments. Better yet, try not to make appointments at all. This was what we learned in the first few weeks of Jacob's life.

Our midwife tried to make it sound like some remarkable milestone: Jacob's first checkup at the clinic. Prior to this, since we had a home birth, all the visits were done in our own home, at our own pace. For most of these checkups I stayed in bed with the baby and Ian was often in his bathrobe, no matter what the time of day.

I started getting ready to leave an hour before our clinic appointment. Surely this was plenty of time. I packed our "go-bag" with extra clothes, wipes, diapers, and receiving blankets. Ian put plenty of milk in a cooler. I fed the baby. I was about to put him in his car seat when he had a huge, explosive poop. Since Jacob still only pooped about every five days this was a real event. *No! Not just before they are going to weigh you!*

We spent a while cleaning him up and getting him into a new diaper, something which he immediately characterized as a serious injustice. I tried to breastfeed him quickly without any supplement to see if I could calm him down enough to put him in his seat. He got more and more worked up, and Ian asked above his cries, "Do you want to give him some actual milk?"

I was stunned. *Actual* milk? At first I thought he meant cow's milk.

I was about to exclaim, "Why on earth would we give him that?" We had plenty of human milk available. Cow's milk could bring on allergies and other problems. Formula would be a better choice! I thought after endless reading and discussion that Ian and I were on the same page with baby nutrition. Then I got it. He meant donor breast milk.

Ian brought the supplement over and I latched Jacob on with the tube. He started to eat and calm down.

"Did you say actual milk?" I said quietly to Ian.

He looked at me with sad eyes. "Yes. I'm so sorry. I meant donor milk. I need a better term for it. I didn't mean that what you make for him isn't actual milk. I'm so sorry."

I burst into tears. Sometimes I, too, think of the donor milk this way. Supplement is what Jacob gets in volume. I make a few squirts per feeding. The bags of milk in our freezers are Jacob's "real" food. My friend Lucy said that breastfeeding after reduction surgery is brutal, and I now know this was what she meant.

We called the midwife and said we were going to be rather delayed. We blamed everything on the explosive poop, and what a wonderful excuse it was.

At around two weeks of age, Jacob suddenly decided to almost double his intake of milk. He had hit the first of a series of major growth spurts that his milk-hoarding parents would come to fear. As he guzzled, we watched the bags of milk from Saskatoon rapidly dwindle in our freezer. By the following week, it was clear that we would have to come up with a new source imminently or we wouldn't make it through that first month exclusively on human milk after all. Once again, I found myself staring down the formula samples that were collecting dust in our cupboards.

In response to this latest crisis, we went breast pump happy. We were desperate for every swallow Jacob could have, so we were pleased to rent out pumps to anyone who'd use them.

We continued renting one for Simone because, as she'd explained, she got virtually nothing out with the basic hand pump she owned. Laura wondered if she, too, would do even better with a high quality pump. I finally had more energy and wanted to try again to pump in-between feedings. So, Ian went to the pharmacy across from the hospital and got in line to acquire two different rental pumps, one for Laura and one for me.

In keeping with his frequently outlandish style of humour, he imagined telling the clerk he was getting them for a quadruple-breasted "Orion slave girl" (of Star Trek infamy). He pictured the pump tubes going in every direction. This, in all likelihood, is not your average gay man's utmost fantasy. Ian thought, *But wouldn't we be swimming in milk then?*

What Ian conjured up as a Trekkie concoction was actually not far from the truth in certain contexts. In the US, prior to emancipation, enslaved Africans were forced to nurse white babies, often to the detriment of their own children. Historically, black parents' breasts have been sexualized and exploited, bought and sold. More recently, the for-profit American companies Medolac and Pro-lacta have collected breast milk to create sterilized or fortified human milk products that they then sell to hospital NICUs for as much as $180 per ounce.[56] The Black Mothers Breastfeeding Association called out Medolac in January of 2015 for specifically targeting low-income black women in Detroit as a source of valuable ingredients.[57] The group pointed out that since Medolac planned to pay the women $1 per ounce for their milk, there could be a strong incentive for them to feed government-subsidized formula to their own vulnerable infants. The company executive claimed they were "only trying to help mothers stay at home longer with their babies" *by paying them a pittance.*

The Human Milk 4 Human Babies group prohibits donors from selling their milk for money, although recipients are encouraged to help offset the costs associated with donating. As Ian and I were finding out, in addition to time, energy, and access to health care, donors often needed considerable equipment to establish, maintain, and share their oversupply.

There was something so impersonal about the breast pumps, Ian thought as he waited. He chatted with the woman behind him who was looking inquisitively at the two pumps in his arms. She said she was pumping milk for her baby, but that hers couldn't drink it yet.

Ian said quickly, "Oh, is that because your baby was born premature without a sucking reflex and the milk needs to be thickened so she can keep it down?"

---

[56] Pollack, "Breast milk becomes a commodity."

[57] Black Mothers' Breastfeeding Association, "Open letter to Medolac Laboratories from Detroit mothers."

Ian was probably better informed about lactation than many health care professionals. The woman confirmed his guess, albeit surprised that some stranger knew all about her child's condition. She added that she was thinking of donating her milk to a sick baby in the NICU. Ian knew that this wouldn't be allowed in the hospital since there is no formal milk bank in Winnipeg. In fact, as one nurse told a friend of ours, in the local hospitals, peer-to-peer milk sharing "isn't a grey area, it's a black area" and the practice would not be permitted, let alone facilitated. This woman would need to meet some parents in the NICU by chance and offer up her milk to them. Likely, a nurse would overhear and tell the recipients that they weren't allowed to use someone else's milk.

"Well," said Ian. "We don't have enough milk for our baby. Isn't that funny that your baby can't have breast milk? Because ours can *only* eat breast milk – he has allergies. It's so hard to find enough. I'm renting these pumps for donors to use."

The woman said, "Oh, is your baby at the hospital, too?"

Ian couldn't believe the words that had come out of his mouth. Of course, Jacob didn't have any allergies at all, although we wanted it to stay that way by keeping him on human milk. Ian realized he'd crossed over to the dark side, and tried to backtrack fast. "Ummm...no. I mean, he's healthy. He's perfectly healthy. He's at home with us."

Ian said, "Donating to a NICU baby would be the very best. If it doesn't work out for you though, maybe I can give you my phone number." He jotted it down on a scrap of paper to hand to her, ever hopeful.

Additional milk for Jacob never did materialize from the woman at the pharmacy. Maybe she found someone at the hospital to give her goods to, under the table. The high end breast pumps helped to maximize what Laura and Simone produced, but we still couldn't keep up with Jacob's growth spurt – he was eating considerably more than we were collecting on a daily basis.

And then, out of the blue, again Facebook delivered us yet another generous donor. Sheila lived in Thunder Bay, but nobody there had replied to her online offer of milk. Eventually she looked on the Manitoba site and contacted us. She'd pumped extra milk for her baby to have while she worked one day a week. Her partner had never convinced the babe to take a bottle so the milk sat there in the freezer. She was willing to ship us her stash of three hundred ounces and even offered to try to pump more for us after that.

The only question was how to get frozen milk from Thunder Bay to Winnipeg, a thirteen-hour drive. This was even further than Saskatoon, and we didn't have the convenience of a hand delivery from a friend. We learned quickly by reading online that milk can be shipped easily if it is well packed. It must travel in a sturdy, insulated cooler and there should be no space left unfilled on the inside, since pockets of air can warm quickly. Gaps around the milk should be stuffed with material like blankets or newspapers. The cooler's seams should be covered with tape to prevent air exchange with the outside. As long as there are at least 300 ounces or so of frozen milk, there's no need for dry ice.

After a few days of interrogating bus company employees to determine their apparently unpublished delivery schedule, Sheila was able to ship us the milk. Ian drove to the bus depot at the airport to pick up our sacred goods right when they arrived at 7:00 a.m. We didn't want the milk to sit around any longer than it already had.

Ian said to the front desk staff person, "Yes, I'm waiting for the Saskatoon bus."

"Oh, I'm sorry, that one doesn't get in for another two hours."

Ian squinted through his fuzzy eyes after a night of "sleep" with our three-week-old son. He turned around to go home, not knowing what he could possibly do with himself at the station for all that time. He would have to come back later. Then, suddenly jolted awake, he remembered. *This was the bus from Thunder Bay. We already got the stash from Saskatoon.*

He retrieved the package and drove away. Back at home, I paced with the baby, waiting anxiously to hear the door squeak open. When he arrived, he tore the tape from the big red cooler and lifted its lid to reveal a ten-day stockpile of baby food, still frozen solid. We were now certain that, barring a major power outage or freezer failure, Jacob's first month of life would be formula-free.

It was awkward to call people about milk. In the early days we phoned Alexa and Laura every other day to ask if they had anything more for Jacob. Most of the time they'd been able to pump or express something and Ian would drive off to pick it up even if it was only a few ounces' worth.

After we received our Saskatoon and Thunder Bay troves we settled down and acted somewhat less like a pair of stalkers. Once, we forced ourselves not to dial Laura's number for three days in a row. Surely she needed some peace and quiet to enjoy her own family.

"Hi, it's Laura calling," I heard her soft voice when I answered. "I haven't heard from you guys in a while. Is everything okay?"

This was true milky dedication. Laura was worried that something might be wrong with Jacob since we hadn't called. Deeply touched, we assured her that everything was well and that was, indeed, why she hadn't heard from us. Nevertheless, we gratefully rushed out and collected the milk she had waiting for our boy.

By the time I made it to an LLL meeting after Jacob was born, we pretty much had nursing worked out. To establish his latch in the first place required intensive one-on-one help, and holding out for a monthly meeting was not going to cut it. But now, with a five-week old baby, I was going to the group because I loved nursing. I loved talking about nursing, learning about nursing, and seeing other people and babies nursing.

LLL meetings would naturally be a perfect place to look for milk donors, but for reasons to do with liability and insurance, leaders could not discuss milk sharing between individuals. I didn't want to put Simone or the other leaders in a difficult position. One woman in the past had actively combed local meetings for milk donors, making everyone involved uncomfortable. Simone and I agreed that if it came up in conversation with someone after a meeting, she would decide not to listen and I could happily ferret out a new donor. Otherwise, I would keep my mouth shut on the donation front.

People slowly wandered into the meeting until there was a room full of about twenty people. When it was my turn to introduce myself, I gave my usual transgender spiel, and then added, "So I make a little bit of the milk that Jacob needs. He gets a lot through the supplementer, but I'm doing the best I can."

I was nursing Jacob while I spoke. I looked up from his little mouth clamped tight around my areola to see everyone smiling at us. A few people who I'd met at my first meeting back when I was pregnant were truly beaming. One of the leaders remarked at how amazing it was that I could use the challenging supplementer with such ease. I nursed Jacob through the whole meeting to keep him quiet and happy.

Simone asked if anyone had come that day with a particular question, and so we started in with our various nursing stories and problems. One woman was worried that her baby cried a lot in the evenings. "When he still cries even after I nurse him, I feel worried that there is something wrong with my milk. Maybe I don't make enough milk for him. I think I want to give him some formula."

I could speak to this point like no one else.

I said, "I can see the amount of food that my baby eats. I watch the volume of supplement go down in the bottle – I know he's had tons, and sometimes he still cries. Sometimes he's just fussy even if he's had plenty."

The La Leche League leaders loved this. "Yes," said Ana. "If your baby is gaining well and you are offering the breast whenever he wants, there is probably nothing wrong with your milk supply. Babies cry a lot for all sorts of reasons."

Here I was, the trans guy, offering concrete breastfeeding advice – and the LLL leaders were grateful for it.

Then, however, came the complaints about too much milk.

One woman was particularly vocal about her problem. "When will my supply adjust? I mean, it's been months now, and I still wake up to soaked bed sheets in the middle of the night."

Everyone groaned in sympathy.

Another chimed in, "Well, we're at month four and it is finally starting to get a little better. And by that I mean that I can wear the same nightgown two days in a row without reeking of sour milk." The others laughed.

They had no idea. Or maybe they did, but their problems were still problems. It was wonderful to have excess – still, what were they to do with it all? If these women's babies skipped one feeding in the night, their mattresses would be soaked with milk. If their babies slept through the night (for once!), the mothers had to get up and hand express in order to feel more comfortable. Listening to these stories made me realize what breastfeeding might have been like for Jacob and me if I'd never had my surgery. I, too, might well have had copious milk for my baby. I was healthy, I'd had a natural birth, and Jacob latched on strongly. Almost anyone in this situation would make plenty of milk. Now, I listened to these parents wanting to know what to do about leaking milk soiling their clothes, and I couldn't even let them know that we needed donor milk for our baby. I guess they assumed we were formula feeding, and probably they never even thought of sharing their milk.

There were a few new moms at the meeting who needed help latching their babies. Simone talked to each of them one at a time after the meeting was over. She is used to helping women latch their babies, and she is good at it. But this time she suddenly felt like she had her hands tied. After having nursed Jacob so much for me, it seemed most natural to simply demonstrate the correct latch instead of having to explain it in words. She badly wanted to pick up the newborn in front of her and physically show her parent what to do. What could be easier than an experienced breastfeeder latching on a new and confused baby? Simone knew she absolutely could not do this at a La Leche League meeting. She slowly found her words and facilitated the breastfeeding duos.

A woman called Carolyn approached me and introduced herself. "It's so amazing to see what you're doing for your baby," she said.

"Oh, thanks. And you know it's all breast milk that he's had so far." *I couldn't help it.*

"Really? How are you doing that?"

Yes, this was exactly the conversation I wanted to have. I explained to her about how we got donations from friends and people we met on the Human Milk 4 Human Babies site. Within a few minutes, she mentioned that she had some bags of milk in her freezer that had been there forever. Would we like them, if they were still good? She added that she could try and pump a little extra for us once in a while, too, if we needed.

For at least the first six weeks of Jacob's life, our days consisted of feeding the baby, changing the baby, checking Facebook, and running milk-related errands. Occasionally, we also slept.

One sunny day we began our routine of attempting to leave the house. We fed Jacob, changed him, and fed him again until he seemed willing to put up with some time sitting in the car. Our first stop was Hollow Reed Holistics, a wonderful, tiny shop that seems to regularly host much of Winnipeg's modest counterculture and alternative healing community. I opened the wooden door and immediately was bathed in the comforting, sweet scent of herbs. To increase my milk production, I was taking goat's rue, alfalfa, nettle, shatavari, and domperidone, as well as regularly eating oatmeal, soups, and coconut and almond milks. This time we were stocking up on fenugreek and blessed thistle, mainstays of my regimen. "Canada's leading breast-feeding expert," Dr. Jack Newman, claims that one must take enough fenugreek to smell like Indian food in order to have a beneficial effect on milk production.[58] I happily complied.

Next, we went to Alexa's place to pick up some milk. When we arrived, she and her family were out on the sidewalk enjoying the sun. She asked her husband Dave to run in and get the milk for us. While he went off to retrieve the good stuff, Jacob started to get fussy. He was obviously hungry. Alexa suggested we go across the street to her friendly neighbour's lawn. The grass looked inviting. We sat down and

---

[58] Newman and Pitman, *Guide to Breastfeeding*, p 74.

I unbuttoned my shirt.

We were on Furby Street, in a notoriously bad area close to downtown Winnipeg. Ian and I have both lived near there at different times in our lives. This was the same area where I'd found one of the only rentals that would allow a dog.

Now, I was a breastfeeding transgender man with my young baby and my gay husband. Things were very different. Jacob needed to eat. I positioned myself to face away from the street. I could see that Ian was glancing around, checking for onlookers. Jacob ate on and off a little, but it was hard to concentrate on him. A big, rough-looking guy and a woman walked up the sidewalk together in our direction. Ian moved to cover Jacob and me. As they came closer we could see that the woman was pregnant and the guy looked kindly and cheerful.

We were playing a dangerous game. There was no way to know who might come around the corner, what they might notice, what they might think, and, most importantly, how they might react. As gay and trans people well know, some individuals react to what they don't understand with anger, even violence. There are numerous stories of trans people being found out by accident and then murdered on the spot. This is why every November 20th, the transgender community around the world marks a Transgender Day of Remembrance for those we have lost through hate and prejudice the previous year. The vast majority of these murder victims are trans women of colour, though recent research has begun to shed light on the significant other forms of violence faced by trans men, including hate violence, sexual assault, and stalking.[59] I often move through the world with a lot of privilege as a white male who looks like any other. But my straight- and cis-passing privilege vanishes instantly when I nurse my baby. The act of nursing screams my queerness, whether I feel like coming out or not.

When I was thirteen years old, a young, gay man called Matthew

---

[59] Cook-Daniels, "Op-ed: Trans men experience far more violence than most people assume."

Shepard was brutally murdered in Laramie, Wyoming. Two guys at a bar tricked him into thinking they were gay, got him to follow them to their truck, and then took him out to a desolate road. They pistol-whipped and tortured him and tied him to a fence. When he was found eighteen hours later, his face was covered in blood except for where the tears had streamed down his cheeks. I had slowly gone over the newspaper article about his death during breakfast at my family's kitchen table. I read part of it aloud to my dad who was perusing the business news. Dad agreed that it was a terrible thing, and he advised me to stay away from gay people. I knew what he meant: gay people didn't deserve this kind of treatment, but it happened anyway. The best strategy for individual safety was to avoid being seen with them. I wondered how I could stay away from myself.

Ian, too, is wary. On a visit to Calgary years ago, as he approached the only gay bar, a man started chatting to him in an excited way. He said, "I've never been to a gay bar before. Are you heading there?"

Something about him seemed off to Ian, who didn't answer.

"Can I go with you?" The man seemed agitated. "I'm just really nervous to be going for the first time. I need somebody to go with."

Ian suddenly noticed other men closing in on them from both sides of the street. He bolted as fast as he could and barely made it into the bar, where the bouncer called the police. If he had slowed down to talk to the man or been too distracted by his questions, he would have been too late.

When we are together, Ian and I often hold hands, but we instinctively let go of each other when we both see someone heading towards us who we're not sure about. Our apprehension is something that we share and that brings us closer together, like other couples might enjoy a common interest in boating or fine art. After a few minutes of feeding Jacob on the grass in plain view on Furby Street, we thanked Alexa and Dave for the milk and said we had to go. We went to our sweltering vehicle in the sun at midday and I finished feeding Jacob sitting in the back seat, half in the car, half out. Ian crouched next to us, shielding us from sight.

Next on our list was picking up milk from Laura. She lived only a few minutes away from Alexa, but her house was unfortunately close to an Indian fast food joint. Ian and I were both famished. Having fed Jacob the best-known human food on the planet, we bought ourselves a dozen greasy samosas. Of course, it's impossible to turn down the free soft drink that comes along with the meal, so we enjoyed a high-sugar liquid to wash down the oil. We had our breast milk and that was all that mattered.

Both of Simone's kids were fascinated by her donations for Jacob. Whenever we arrived at their house, Tim would run to the fridge and get out the bags she had pumped. "Here's the milk for baby Jacob! Mommy made it for him because you don't make enough, Trevor."

We'd tell him thanks, but we should probably keep the milk in the fridge until we were ready to leave. He eventually caught on to this and starting bringing us the milk at the end of our visits.

Samantha and Tim became Simone's personal cheerleaders when she pumped. "Oh, I see a drop is coming out. Hmmm...That side isn't doing as well as the other side, Mommy. Oh, now it is speeding up. Way to go, Mommy!"

One day, Samantha was sitting on the floor, watching Simone pump. She reached up and grabbed the cords that ran from the machine to the suction cups on Simone's breasts and heaved on them to pull herself up to stand. The cups popped noisily as they were ripped from Simone's skin, and Samantha went crashing to the ground, landing in a puddle of milk and banging her head. Simone yelped in pain but then quickly had to nurse Samantha from her stinging breasts to calm her down. Everyone cried over the spilt milk.

After several weeks, nighttime feedings were becoming more manageable but still required special preparation. I would strap on my headlamp and flick the switch. Like a miner heading for a shift deep down under the earth's surface, I had food and drink to last about ten hours, all efficiently packed and readily accessible.

I was just trying to feed the baby.

We keep donor milk in a cooler with us in the bedroom so I don't have to get up and go downstairs to the kitchen to retrieve it for each nursing session. Our baby sleeps with us because the books say this is best for breastfeeding, not to mention that we love it this way ourselves. I feel him starting to stir, and I groggily get myself up in bed, with a heap of pillows around and behind me to prop us up. We keep a dim nightlight turned on, but positioning the feeding tube requires extraordinary measures. Using the headlamp, especially in the early months, was the only way to make it happen without blasting light at my sleeping husband.

One of the great benefits of breastfeeding is supposed to be its convenience. Yes, you have to feed more often. Babies can digest human milk more easily than formula, so their stomachs become empty faster and they need to eat frequently. It's true, too, that babies seem to love to nurse in the night.

On the other hand, people who breastfeed often say they prefer it because the milk is always there and ready to go. If you get delayed with your baby for hours at an airport, or wherever, it doesn't matter.

As long as you have access to water, your body will produce what your baby needs. And, a big-ticket benefit of breastfeeding for some folks is the ability to sleep at the same time as nourishing the baby. Many parents report that they simply sleep on their sides and don't even wake up for nursing once their baby is proficient at latching.

We gave ourselves the worst of both worlds. Feeding Jacob at night involves waking up fully and sitting up to position him. I don't have enough chest tissue to latch him on comfortably while lying on my side. Even the shortest outing necessitates packing a cooler of milk because Jacob needs to nurse so frequently. Once, I went out on a walk with the baby and had the misapprehension that because I would only be gone a short while, I didn't need to take along all the equipment. Half an hour later, Ian heard my hurried footsteps coming back down the path through the woods from a long way off: *Wah, ah, ah, ah! Wah, ah, ah, ah! Wah, ah, ah, ah!* Jacob's cries sounded in rhythm to my strides as I bumped along as quickly as I dared with my little baby.

Ian was usually selective about telling friends and colleagues that we were collecting donor milk for Jacob. We knew that not everyone would approve, and we had already faced enough judgment and suspicion over our queer identities. He posted on the Human Milk 4 Human Babies site to say that we still needed more milk but, to his dismay, his plea came up at the top of all his friends' news feeds. He quickly deleted the post and then learned how to comment without sharing to his own page, but not before some unintended "friends" saw what we were up to.

To our great fortune, one of them was a special young woman named Tara who Ian knew professionally. She told us she was throwing out cups of excess milk every week and that she'd love to donate. She also wanted to arrange some play dates. We thanked the all-knowing, all-powerful Facebook and Ian's slip-up, and accepted her goodwill.

We hit it off with Tara immediately. She carries her baby much of the time, picks him up when he cries, and is deeply committed to breastfeeding. She is a beautiful, mature young woman with a generous smile and short, dark hair that frames her face. She speaks to her charge in affectionate French.

Three years before, Tara survived advanced lymphoma by means of a stem cell transplant. Her doctors harvested her own stem cells and then wiped her clean of all her bone marrow before completing the transplant. It was a risky, last-ditch attempt to save her life, and it worked. After the procedure, she felt like a newborn. Her immune system was destroyed, she could hardly digest food, and she needed to sleep twenty hours a day, but with time, she recovered fully. As part of her treatment, Tara had surgery on her neck and shoulder that left a prominent scar and caused permanent weakness in her right arm.

Tara's doctors told her that women are typically infertile after receiving stem cell transplants. However, her cycle returned and she soon experienced a healthy pregnancy and carried her baby to term.

Tara was absolutely determined to breastfeed her baby, Hunter, despite her own health challenges. Breastfeeding can be hard on anyone's arms, but Tara truly had her work cut out for her. When Hunter was small she managed to hold him for hours every day while feeding. After a few months he became too wriggly for her to hold successsfully during nursing sessions, so she changed to feeding him lying down.

We had one obvious question about accepting donor milk from Tara. Would her history of cancer or any of her treatments affect the safety of her milk? It was uncomfortable to ask. She had made the decision to breastfeed her own baby and must have concluded that it was safe to do so. Asking her about it felt like asking her if she was harming her own child. Ian tried to phrase it politely somehow, but it came out sounding weird and made little sense.

"You know," he said. "Your milk, of course, is fine for your own baby. It might not be okay as donor milk though."

Tara didn't take offense to our fumbling. She said she was glad that we were careful about using donor milk. She had never wondered about the safety of her milk and none of her doctors had ever mentioned it to her. Suddenly, she started to question whether her medical history could indeed have an effect on her milk.

Tara contacted her doctors, who responded confidently that everything should be fine. She also asked Dr. Jack Newman, the breastfeeding expert, if he agreed. He emailed her back: "I do not see how it would be possible that any drugs would remain in your system after so long a period of time. Are there drugs that remain so tightly bound to your tissues that they would be still there almost three years later? I don't think so. Even if there were, if they were that tightly bound to your tissues, I could not see how they could get into the milk."

We proceeded with our milk collection and quickly formed a good friendship with Tara and Hunter. We were now one step closer to having a large enough pool of local parents providing ongoing donations to support Jacob's all-consuming habit.

One night when we were downtown together with Tara, enjoying a street festival, I wondered out loud if I'd be comfortable nursing Jacob there in public. A true ally, she immediately offered to nurse him for me, saying cheerily, "My boobs are your boobs!"

Sometimes, if I feel safe, I am almost cavalier about my unusual family situation. I can find myself correcting a nosy stranger on the street, "Oh, no, my partner is a *man*, my husband. I don't have a *wife*. I'm actually transgender. I birthed my baby myself, and I can even breastfeed him some. Great, isn't it?"

If I have plenty of time and energy, I'm quite willing to explain what we've done. I hope there can be some greater benefit beyond my personal circumstance to helping others learn. Most people respond well, with mild curiosity or amusement. Sometimes though, it just isn't the right moment to get into explanations about how transgender folks give birth. One evening, Jacob had just fallen asleep in a coffee shop and we needed to get going, when somebody asked us if we used a surrogate. Neither Ian nor I like to lie about anything. I said, "Isn't it wonderful that people can do that nowadays? Well, we have to go!"

On another occasion we were eating at our favourite restaurant in Winnipeg, a small, family-run Ethiopian joint downtown. We had our wedding dinner there, and we love the friendly staff. However, communication is a considerable challenge due to the language barrier. I thought I'd booked the dinner only to find out a week before our wedding that the restaurant had no record of the upcoming event. Luckily, they hadn't booked anything else either, so I simply booked again, this time in person. The actual day went well except for that there had been a misunderstanding over the number of guests, and there weren't enough chairs for everyone. Then, the restaurant owner who is also the chef forgot to include the samosas on our bill and we didn't notice, either. Weeks later, she grumpily mentioned it to us while her son pleaded with her to forget about it. We told them we'd be happy to pay for what we'd had, and all was well.

Ian and I both felt that there was no way we could successfully explain the origin of our child, even though I'm sure the well-meaning chef would have been delighted to hear all about it, if only we could get the message across. When we appeared at the restaurant with Jacob for the first time, she cooed over him for a good five minutes.

Then, she asked, "So, you get him in Canada? Or, international?"

Ian responded quickly, saying, "Yes, he is a local Winnipeg boy!"

The restaurant Momma approved heartily. "Very good, very good," she said. "Have a good night! See you again soon!"

When Jacob was about a month old, our friend Elaine produced a few additional precious bags of milk and asked her husband, Allen, to drop them off at our home. He arrived and we chatted politely with him as we always do with milk donors and their families. We admired his rambunctious, kicking eleven-month-old baby who was with him that evening while Elaine worked.

Eventually, Allen said he had to leave because his son was getting hungry and should be put to bed soon. They were going to stop and get some food for him on the way home. Ian, trying to be conversational and friendly, asked him what he was going to feed his baby.

Allen responded that he'd pick up some soymilk to mix with the formula he already had at home. Other typical foods for Nick were Cheerios, peeled grapes, and, for extra protein, hamburger helper, pureed in their new blender.

Ian was flabbergasted. "Oh, yeah, great. Well...Thanks so much. See you later!"

Allen was delivering breast milk to our doorstep and then going home and feeding his own baby formula. To boot, he was feeding the formula incorrectly, mixing it with soymilk instead of water. Powdered formula is so concentrated that combining it with anything other than water can put too much stress on young kidneys that must do the hard work of digesting the rich food.

We asked Elaine why Allen would ever feed formula when her milk was available in the freezer.

"I know!" she cried. "It's so frustrating, but I've given up. You might as well have my pumped milk for Jacob."

She explained that when Nick was younger, Allen found mixing formula easier and quicker than thawing her milk. Who wants to spend time thawing when you are alone with a hungry, crying baby? Now, Allen was mixing formula with soymilk to try to get Nick "back on track" with his weight gain. Their pediatrician was using the old, standard growth charts that were based on the weight gain of Caucasian formula-fed babies.

Luckily, the health care providers that Ian and I encountered mostly supported breastfeeding and the use of human milk. At six weeks of age, our midwifery care came to an end and we began regular visits with a nurse-practitioner, Helen, in a pediatric office. Helen's own mother had been a La Leche League leader, utterly committed to the cause even at the height of formula's golden age, back before the start of public health campaigns aimed to support breastfeeding. At one point during Helen's infancy, her mother required surgery and couldn't breastfeed for a brief period of time. She arranged for a friend to wet-nurse her daughter. Now, as a pediatric nurse, Helen was well aware of the difference between the formula-fed baby growth charts and the breastfed WHO ones. She seemed pleased and impressed at our own milk sharing exploits, although I don't think in her position as an employee of Manitoba Health she would be allowed to say so too blatantly. She discussed milk safety and pasteurization with us and seemed satisfied.

Then came the usual questions. Is he smiling yet? Has he rolled over? Is he sleeping for longer and longer stretches? Does he turn his head in response to sounds? And, *how many feedings a day does he have?*

Maybe she didn't understand our style of nursing quite so well after all. Was I supposed to count the five sucks he took before he got distracted by something as a "feeding"? What about when he ate for five minutes, took a ten-minute break, and then ate for another ten minutes? Was that two feedings or one? During his waking hours, Jacob rarely went longer than half an hour without nursing from the time he was born until he was about seven months old. Helen reluctantly agreed to write down "feeding on demand" in her chart since I refused to provide a number.

My family doctor, too, was breastfeeding-supportive in his own oddball kind of way. Before Jacob was born, he had told me that I should have no problems making enough milk for him.

"Breast size doesn't matter at all," he said. "Since you're producing colostrum already, you'll be fine. Just nurse very frequently and you will make enough. It's a supply-and-demand system. The more you breastfeed, the more milk your body will produce. It also helps to sleep with your baby so that you are close all the time."

What a refreshing perspective! Many of our friends complained about how their doctors would chide them for co-sleeping or feeding the baby "too much" at night, and then would turn around and recommended formula feeding because they felt the rate of weight gain was not sufficient. I knew my doctor was probably wrong about my ability to make milk after surgery, but I appreciated his faith in me, anyway. I didn't try to correct him.

"Now," he'd said, "they'll probably send a public health nurse around to yell at you if he loses some weight in the first week but don't worry about that. Twelve percent loss is normal for a breastfed baby."

When I told my doctor, a month or so after Jacob's birth, that I needed to supplement, he tsk-tsked me.

"What?! It's simple supply-and-demand, Trevor. I guess it works perfectly in India, doesn't it, where they carry their babies around everywhere? Oh, well, I suppose not everybody can do that in North America."

In fact, I *did* have the privilege of being able to spend 24 hours a day with my baby. I didn't have to worry about going back to work since I received a lump sum "maternity" benefit, parental employment insurance, *and* had a partner who had a stable job. We didn't use a stroller, a baby swing, a crib, or a playpen. I carried or wore Jacob everywhere to keep him close to me, and I truly did nurse him at every opportunity. I still did not make enough milk for him. Breast size may not matter, but having developed and intact mammary glands and milk ducts sure does.

Allen and Elaine's pediatrician, on the other hand, had no patience for breastfeeding. He also refused to take into account that baby Nick is part Asian and may naturally fall on the low end of the American *formula-fed* baby growth charts. The pediatrician looked at the numbers and declared that the child absolutely must be made to gain weight. No one looked at the bright, sparkling, ball of energy except to tell him to stop tugging on the curtains in the office because they might break.

Ian and I were happy to accept the occasional bag of pumped milk that Allen refused to feed to his own toddler. Every time I had contact with Allen, I was doubly grateful that Ian was so supportive of my efforts to nurse. It would have been impossible to keep Jacob away from formula if we weren't both passionate about feeding babies the way nature intended – using several freezers and a lot of plastic milk storage bags.

The most awkward moments in breast milk collection happen when Ian is picking up milk from a woman who isn't home. Her partner or older kid directs Ian to the freezer and all involved try to act cool and casual.

On one such occasion, Alexa's husband answered the door and quickly produced some canning jars. He mentioned that he was surprised we'd go to such lengths to keep Jacob on breast milk, criss-crossing the city as we do to procure it. Ian explained that it is a commitment we've made and it is just what we are doing.

"Trevor is making as much milk as he can. I can't contribute much of anything to the project."

"Haha, yeah, me neither. Well, I can squirt something out but it's a tiny amount."

"Yeah," said Ian. "Me, too. And it's only really needed earlier in the process."

They laughed sheepishly at their sophomoric joke as Ian got out his cooler for storing the bodily fluids of the other man's wife.

"Well, thanks a lot," said Ian.

"Any time. See you again soon."

At home, we listened to a frantic voicemail message. "I hope you haven't given Jacob anything from the jars with the really small amounts." It was Alexa's voice. "Those are yogurt cultures! Dave gave you the wrong jars by accident."

Luckily, we hadn't used them yet. Since no amount could be too small to save, no one had suspected that a few tablespoons of white stuff in a canning jar would be anything other than human milk.

A whole family needs to love and support breastfeeding for it to happen. It may look from the outside like an intimate connection between parent and baby that nobody could come between. In reality, breastfeeding requires acceptance and appreciation from the nursing pair's community. For every nursing couple, there are moments where the baby is screaming, the parent is crying in exhaustion, and neither of you can figure out what to do. If your partner right then chooses to say, "How about some formula?" you'll either kill them or give in and feed formula from a bottle.

Hubbies of milk donors get this. They've been there in the middle of the night through it all and they've chosen to say things like, "Honey, you're doing a great job. You're amazing. Why don't I run a bath for you and you can try breastfeeding in there? See if it works?"

And they definitely get that a few millilitres of extra milk are way too precious to throw out.

One day, when we were again getting low on donor milk and wondering when we'd have to start Jacob on formula, I noticed a new offer of milk posted on the Human Milk 4 Human Babies web site. *Just in time. I think I want to marry Facebook.* Then I saw that the offer was specifically addressed to Nila and Lucy's baby, Amy. However, it seemed that our friends had not responded. Did they not need the milk after all? It took all the decency I could muster not to contact the donor and try to get this milk for Jacob. Instead, I considerately telephoned Nila and told her about the post just in case she had missed it. She was grateful for the call and jumped on the offer.

Not long after this, when Jacob was just over one month old, Ian saw that there was yet another new donor: "Hi! I am a healthy lactating mom with lots of extra milk to spare." Ian sent her three messages within ten hours, feeling and acting like an obsessive admirer. No response.

We started to worry. Maybe we shouldn't have mentioned that we're a gay couple. If we didn't, though, what would we say to her when we met her? We weren't interested in lying or having dealings with homophobes. They could keep their sweet breast milk.

Finally, after we had decided that this Sandi woman must have been a social conservative who wanted nothing to do with us, she responded that we were welcome to a large deep freezer full of milk. She wanted to buy bread in bulk from Costco, she explained, but she just didn't have room for it because of all that breast milk. Was there any way we could come over sooner rather than later so she could go shopping?

You bet we could. Sandi lived out by the perimeter of the city. We got directions, grabbed a twenty-can cooler and were out the door. After a tough, noisy car ride with Jacob, we greeted Sandi with our warmest smiles. She opened the door wearing a sleek yoga outfit, and showed us into her spacious, immaculately-kept home. Her two-and-a-half-year-old dashed about with his light saber while her baby rocked in a motorized bassinet.

It was the true start of summer, and today was Jacob's first experience with real, uncomfortable heat. He was red in the face and endlessly fussy. I bounced him up and down, changed his diaper, and walked him around in Sandi's house. I badly wanted us to make a good impression on this extraordinary milk pumper. If we could secure her good graces we'd be set for a long time with food for Jacob. I assured Sandi that he was normally a lovely, happy baby (and we were usually quite capable of calming him down) but that we'd had a hard time in the car.

Sandi showed us into her garage where she kept her deep freezer. She opened the lid to reveal shopping bags piled upon shopping bags, each full of six-ounce breast milk storage bags. Our eyes widened. She picked up one of the grocery bags and dug around in it with her hand, the milky icicles clanging sonorously. We filled up our little cooler but didn't even make a dent in her stash.

"Would you guys mind coming back tomorrow to get more, now that you've seen what I've got?" she asked.

We had no trouble agreeing to return.

Sandi was producing enough milk to feed more than twins. She was pumping it for her second baby boy, born a few months before Jacob, six weeks premature. Her tiny baby, Dylan, had stayed in the hospital for five weeks, being fed with a gavage tube down his nose and throat until he began to be able to coordinate his own suck, swallow, and breathe pattern. He was only three pounds at birth, when most babies born at 34 weeks weigh around five pounds.

Sandi pumped her milk for him from the beginning, every five hours, and he never needed formula. As Dylan's lungs matured, hospital staff and lactation consultants encouraged Sandi to breastfeed him, but it never quite worked out. He seemed to feed much more efficiently using a bottle, and Sandi continued pumping. She produced so much more milk than he was able to take that she felt comfortable experimenting with pumping less frequently to see if she could regulate her supply downwards.

At about one month postpartum, Sandi developed a raging fever over the course of just a few hours. Barely able to stand up, she felt her chest and eventually located a small red spot where there was a blocked milk duct. She had mastitis, a condition where milk gets backed up in the breast and causes swelling and infection. Sandi's doctor explained that sometimes this can happen when the milk ducts aren't fully emptied by the end of a feeding or pumping session. She felt miserable and exhausted, and took antibiotics for one week until the infection cleared. Determined not to repeat the distressing episode, Sandi began to pump more frequently again, like she had just after her son's birth – at least every five hours (including during the night), and drawing out as much milk as she could each time.

She fed Dylan all he wanted from his bottle, but often found that there was plenty left over. She put the extra milk in the freezer just in case she might need it later on. She planned to keep up her rigorous pumping routine until her baby learned to breastfeed or turned one year old.

Of course, frequent pumping and fully draining the breasts at each session are both practices that help to prevent mastitis, but they might also tell the body to make more milk. *Gee, this baby is sure suckling a lot. I guess he needs more. Let's get going!* Sandi's body went into high gear. Her appetite skyrocketed and her waistline became narrower than ever before. Shortly before we met her, Sandi and her family had moved to Winnipeg from a town a few provinces away, at which point she threw out an entire deep freezer's worth of her milk since she didn't know anyone local in need. It felt like a shame to waste it, but she was able to replenish her stockpile at her new home within weeks.

Ian and I turfed a few bags of ice we'd had sitting around in our own freezer since our wedding the year before, and made some ambitious cooking plans. To make space for the breast milk, we were now defrosting a large roast as well as some organ meats for the dog. We went back to Sandi's place the next day and gathered up enough milk to completely fill our medium-sized stand-alone freezer as well as the freezer on top of our fridge.

We gave Sandi a freshly-baked pie and a spa gift certificate as a quick thank-you, but we both wondered what we could ever really do to repay her generosity.

We asked her if she minded if we shared some of her milk with friends of ours who also had a baby in need. She asked, "Oh, is it somebody with the last name Hill?"

"Yes, Nila and Lucy. They need milk for their baby, Amy."

"They called me just after you did. I told them that my milk is now spoken for. You guys got in touch first so it's all yours. Don't feel you have to share it, but if you want to that's fine with me."

We didn't just have a copious new milk supply, we had a faithful donor. Sandi made a commitment to Jacob. She intended to continue pumping for quite some time, and she wanted to make sure there was enough milk for both her baby and ours. We were astonished.

She was a dream donor in every way. She didn't drink alcohol, didn't smoke, and drank only one cup of coffee at times when she needed it badly. Before she took her maternity leave, she worked as a lab technician in the military. As a result of her training, it came naturally to her to sterilize her pumping equipment scrupulously and label milk bags with the amount pumped, the date, and the time of day on the 24-hour clock. Her house was tidy, and her kids healthy and happy. Her polite, clean-shaven husband also worked for the military.

As relieved as I was about our newly discovered treasure trove, I had an uneasy feeling, too. We'd arranged to pick up fresh milk from Sandi every Wednesday. We would need to sustain an ongoing relationship with her, and we'd probably get to know each other quite well. But I hadn't yet told her that I was trans, or that I nursed Jacob. She hadn't asked about Jacob's origin, and we hadn't volunteered the information. What if she was disapproving when she learned the truth? I was nervous, but chose for now to delay dealing with the issue.

Sandi made gallons of milk even at the very beginning when her baby was still in the hospital. Any colostrum is particularly rich in protein, fat, and antibodies, but Sandi's was especially so since she'd had a preemie. Her body knew that her baby needed a lot of help to survive.

When we first met her, Sandi was preparing to send some of this extraordinary milk to a very sick child on the west coast, in British Columbia. Since we had been through the process a few times before, we answered her questions about how to pack the milk so it would keep. The little girl receiving the shipment had Krabbe Leukodystrophy, a terminal brain disease. She was nineteen months old and was not expected to make it past her second birthday. She had developed normally until she was about four months old, and then she began to lose the abilities that her parents had joyfully watched her gain. She became blind, and her coordination deteriorated. Even worse, she lost her ability to nurse. She couldn't digest anything other than human milk, so her mother pumped for her for as long as she could. Eventually, without having a suckling baby efficiently drawing out milk and demanding more, her mother stopped producing. This frantic parent put the word out across the country that she needed milk for her sick baby. The response was overwhelmingly generous and she was able to have human milk until she passed away.

Learning about their story provided me with a beneficial reality check. We were chasing down donor milk for Jacob because we knew it was the best food for him, or any baby. We wanted everything to be perfect for him because he is our baby and we are his parents. But feeding him formula wouldn't have killed him. I'm sure I would have cried over it, and maybe he would have been fussy or had some mild indigestion or even ended up with an allergy, yet there wasn't any question of whether he would make it. Formula may have changed his life, but wouldn't have ended it in that moment.

On our trip the following week to Sandi's place for milk, Jacob barely got through the car ride without having a meltdown. I fed him right before we left, but after the half-hour ride, he was famished again. Ian went inside while I nursed Jacob in the car. I couldn't imagine walking into Sandi's house with a screaming baby and somehow managing to explain to her that I was transgender, birthed Jacob myself, and was now breastfeeding him with a supplementer. I watched the door of the house from the car, hoping that Jacob would hurry up.

Soon Sandi's toddler came in and out a few times, going no further than the end of the front steps. I knew this was bad news. He would see me feeding Jacob, and having no filter at his age, would run back inside and say to his parents, 'Trevor is letting his baby suck on his nipples!' It just had to happen.

The boy trotted down the walkway and around the corner of the house. He crossed the driveway and turned another corner, going out of sight. Seconds later, his dad came out and glanced around. He frowned. He paced quickly down the walkway towards our car. I called out the window, "He's gone around to the back of the house."

The dad, looking relieved, nodded, and went after the little boy. He hadn't noticed what I was doing, or just didn't care and didn't say anything. Jacob finished feeding and we went up to the front door just as Ian was saying goodbye and preparing to leave with the milk. No harm, I thought, in leaving my story until the next week.

I didn't grow up around babies, and didn't know anyone who had a baby until about a year before Jacob was born. Or maybe I just somehow never noticed babies until I wanted to have one myself. Unlike most people in the west, I'm pretty sure I've now witnessed more breastfeeding than bottle-feeding.

When we were pregnant, we wandered into Babies "R" Us looking for a car seat. I watched a woman there pushing her baby in a fancy stroller that had a conveniently placed cup holder containing a bottle. Other than this, I saw Simone and Elaine breastfeeding their babies, and the parents at the La Leche League meeting, and that was all.

Since Jacob's birth, I've now observed bottle-feeding twice, and both times I felt terrified at the sight of it because of the effect it seemed to have on me personally. On the first occasion, we were at Sandi's house. It struck me then how incredibly easy it looked. She was sitting on the couch, supporting her baby in her lap with one hand and holding the bottle in the other. The baby sucked the liquid back quickly and then he was done. Sandi didn't struggle to latch him on, or attempt to contain his flailing limbs while he fed, or wonder if a supplementer tube was in the right position and actually doing its job.

The seemingly quick, effortless bottle-feeding was so tempting to me it was frightening. At the time, Jacob and I were suffering through difficult nursing sessions where he'd seem hungry but get too worked up to latch on successfully. Latching a baby onto a nipple along with a feeding tube is a tricky affair. With Jacob, I often got one chance and that was it. If I failed, he would quickly get frustrated and start crying. I'd have to get up, put the milk back in the fridge, walk with him to calm him down, and then try again a few minutes later. With the supplementer, if the tube is too far past the nipple, sometimes all the baby gets in his mouth is the tube. If it is not far enough then the end of the tube gets blocked by my skin and no matter how hard he sucks, no milk comes out. For a long time, getting it right seemed to be a matter of luck.

I kept reminding myself why I was nursing him. I wanted him to get the specific antibodies that I was producing for him, even in small quantities. And I couldn't get that line from a breastfeeding book out of my head: "breastfeeding promotes normal jaw development." Who wouldn't want a normally developed jaw? I averted my gaze from Sandi's bottle-feeding like a prude trying not to stare at an uncovered breast.

The other instance of bottle-feeding that will always remain burned into my memory happened when Ian offered Jacob a bottle. Jacob was only a few months old and I had a doctor's appointment. I didn't want to be separated from the baby for long, so the whole family accompanied me. Before my physical, I told Ian, "Do whatever you need to keep Jacob happy. Bottle-feed him if you like, or stick your finger in his mouth to suck on. Anything. I just don't want to hear him crying too hard during the appointment. I would feel so bad about that." And I meant it.

Sure enough, Jacob started to fuss during my exam. Then he started to cry. Soon, he was full out bawling. The exam over, I sat up to see Ian holding the bottle up to Jacob's mouth. I felt sick to my stomach. I jumped off the examination table and grabbed Jacob, threaded the tube back through the bottle nipple, and latched him on with the supplementer. He stopped crying and started to nurse, and I felt my heart rate begin to quiet. I realized how scared I was that my body was wrong for this baby, and that if he used a bottle once, he would prefer it forever.

Jacob didn't take well to bottle-feeding, anyway. The milk came out too fast and he didn't know how to cope with it. Eventually, we learned that for the few times when I was away from him, Ian could better feed Jacob using a cup. Even newborns can successfully cupfeed, a method that is sometimes recommended over bottle-feeding if the baby isn't yet latching well in breastfeeding. Cup-feeding Jacob resulted in a soggy, milky baby shirt and bib, but he reveled in it. He would try to hold the cup himself and pull it towards his mouth and then push it away again when he wanted a break. It was a method we didn't use much though, since I rarely left Jacob during his first year.

Telling Sandi who I was reminded me of trying to come out to my parents. The longer you wait, the harder it gets. You need the reaction to your news to be good. So, you need to wait for the perfect moment.

We arrived once again at Sandi's place. This time we all went together up the walk. Immediately upon entering the house, Jacob started to fuss loudly. I went into the baby room to change him. Ian followed me and I hissed at him, "You have to go and tell Sandi right now that I'm trans and how I had Jacob. He's getting hungry and I need to be able to feed him here."

Sandi seemed to take the news well, and I sat down with great relief to feed Jacob on her living-room couch. "That's amazing that you do that every time with the supplementer," she said. We had a perfect milk donor supportive of our unique family. She had too much milk and we didn't have enough.

Years later, when our babies were preschoolers, I learned that for Sandi it had been painful and complicated to watch me breastfeed, although for reasons I wouldn't have guessed at the time. Sandi told me that as soon as Dylan had been ready to attempt a feed in the hospital without the gavage tube, she had tried to breastfeed him. For the next five months, she employed every possible trick. He latched on well enough, but he never seemed to get a full feeding at her breast, always falling asleep early and waking up famished a few minutes later. Sandi's chest easily became hard and engorged, which resulted in pain for her, and, from Dylan's perspective, an even more challenging time with latching. Sandi tried keeping him cooler to prevent him from drifting off so soon; other times she attempted to "dream nurse" him while he slept; sometimes she pumped off some milk before latching him on, since her let-down could be so forceful and difficult for a wee mouth to manage; she tested out a nipple shield to see if it might slow her let-down; and she even tried a supplementer like I used – all in an attempt to breastfeed her baby the way she had so easily with her older child. She couldn't quit second-guessing herself, wondering if she had not tried hard enough, or not yet found the right trick that would make it all fall into place. Dylan never did seem to take enough milk efficiently at the breast, and Sandi always needed to use a bottle. She told me she almost never let her husband bottle-feed Dylan because she felt so anguished to be missing the bonding that she felt came hand-in-hand with breastfeeding.

Then one day, I walked into her house and breastfed my baby using her milk. Sandi never said at the time how she ached and mourned from seeing this. Instead, she only encouraged my persistence. Just as I was anxious about what she would think of a breastfeeding, transgender guy, she worried about making a good impression on Ian and me so that we would trust the safety of her milk. While looking after her wild toddler, feeding her tiny preemie, and pumping every five hours, she also picked up toys, washed dishes, vacuumed, and did laundry in preparation for our visits.

After making space by thawing every non-breast-milk item we had, we bought a new, bigger freezer and put it in our garage. Soon that freezer, too, was full of Sandi's milk.

Our stash was now so large that we could consider traveling for a while. We'd wanted to go to Vancouver so that Jacob could meet all his grandparents, but we didn't want to feed him formula just so that he could have a visit he wouldn't even remember. We'd been living week-to-week and often even day-to-day finding milk. Now, we had enough that we could fill a large cooler, hop on an airplane, and enjoy a holiday without missing a gulp.

Around the two-month mark, Jacob hit a period where he fussed a lot. In the evenings, he'd start to whimper. I immediately responded with feeding. When that didn't work, I tried changing him, walking him, bouncing, singing, dancing, and generally making a fool of myself for his amusement. Some such distraction would calm him for a few minutes and then I'd have to change my tactic or the whimpering would start up again, threatening to move to full-blown wailing.

One testy evening we had a few friends over. Simone helped feed Jacob a bit, but she had her own kids to look after in our not-yet-childproofed house full of choking hazards and breakables. Jacob was having a particularly difficult time. I tried to feed him, but he fussed and cried. I bounced around and attempted my usual antics to no avail.

When I passed him over to Simone, he instantly latched on to her and calmed down. Soon enough though, Tim was trying to kick our dog and paint with ketchup on our furniture, while Samantha wanted somebody to get her a plate of seconds from dinner, and Simone still needed to eat, too. Simone handed Jacob back to me, and he started up fussing again. I offered him my lean chest, and he refused. He would latch on to her, but not me, his parent. Tears came to my eyes and I retreated upstairs with him, away from the party.

After a few minutes Simone followed to find me, sobbing away, trying to latch Jacob while bouncing up and down on an exercise ball and buzzing my lips for him. I frequently added this last effect to other activities in order to provide an extra distraction from whatever was so obviously unpleasant. Simone said she'd done the exact same thing for months on end with her first child.

Louise, a parent of two children now in their thirties, joined us upstairs. She had breastfed her kids when everyone told her she was stupid for doing it. She was allowed about four weeks of sick leave post partum, and no maternity leave at all. She used to breastfeed her babies up until the last minute and then rush off to work. During her hour-long lunch break she would drive twenty minutes to get home, breastfeed for twenty minutes, and then drive twenty minutes back to work, arriving seconds before she was required to be on the job. To this day, she and her husband seem to arrive at work at the last possible minute.

Her second baby had to stay in the hospital for a few days because of jaundice, and Louise doggedly went to feed him every three hours. The nurses told her she should stay home and get some sleep and look after her other child. *She would be far too tired to come in to nurse the baby – why shouldn't they just give him formula?* Determined to prove them wrong, she did up her hair and put on her makeup to look fresh for every visit. She fed her baby.

I asked how long she nursed her kids, and she said she wasn't sure.

"Sara would come in off her two-wheeler and have a couple sucks and then go back out. I guess I nursed them a while. Oh, and they used to argue over who got the 'see-side' when I nursed them both at the same time *and* they wanted to watch a cartoon on TV. I nursed them until they wanted to stop."

She and Simone proceeded to try all the tricks for Jacob that they could think of. Most new things helped for a few minutes and then he would go back to crying. Finally, out of the perfect mix of exasperation and curiosity, Louise, now sixty-something years old, lifted her shirt, brandished her breast, and tried to latch Jacob on. I swear I heard him swallow at least twice, although I suppose it could have been saliva, not milk. I had read about legendary grandmothers who relactated when there was a baby in need, decades after weaning their last child. After a minute, Jacob came off and cried again. I carried him out of the house for an evening walk and, finally, he fell asleep having tried every breast and chest around.

A woman gardening in her yard saw us go by, and called out to me, "Wow! What an amazing husband you are, giving your wife a break. I wish my man had done that even once with my kid."

When Jacob was three months old, we made our much-anticipated twelve-day trip to Vancouver. My greatest fear was that the airline would lose our enormous cooler of donor milk on the way there. Supposedly, you can bring as much liquid as needed into the cabin if it is for a travelling baby, but I'm sure a twelve-day supply of frozen breast milk is not what policymakers had in mind. We accompanied our treasure, labeled "fragile" and "time-sensitive," to the special luggage area and watched as it bumped away down the belt and through the swinging plastic doors beyond sight.

Due to a scheduling mishap, Ian and I had to take separate flights. Jacob, of course, came with me. Flying with a baby is rarely easy, but being the only adult responsible for that baby is a genuine challenge. Ahead of time I started to wonder about scenarios like answering a call of nature while holding a wriggling kiddo in one of those tiny airplane bathrooms.

Going through security screening, an officer asked to see our tickets, as per usual. Then, he looked us up and down, and said, "Who is the baby?"

What was he asking? "His name is Jacob," I responded.

"Who is *this* baby?" he asked again.

"He's my baby," I said, even more confused.

"Where's the mother?"

Ah, that's what he meant – how could a guy be traveling alone with a young infant?

"This baby has two dads," I said.

The man paused, and then, matter-of-factly said, "Oh," followed by a much louder, "Oh!" and a long stare as he thought about our situation.

Finally, he chortled, and waived us on, saying, "Ok, whatever, so long as you're the one responsible for this baby."

This was the first of many times I would hear that phrase, "Where's the mother?" Especially when I traveled alone with my child, the airline attendants, security personnel, and customs agents searched for "the mother." I always carried Jacob's birth certificate that listed me as a parent and a notarized letter of permission from Ian, but the documents and the baby comfortably nuzzled in my arms weren't enough. *How could a man care for such a young baby alone? What could be the explanation?*

Once, I explained to a security agent that I was transgender and had birthed the baby. I suppose I imagined that outlining our biological connection might provide quicker understanding, but coming out in the process led to such mocking in front of other travelers and airport staff that I've avoided it since. I now reiterate 'this baby has two dads,' and then wait.

Mostly, Jacob and I managed all right on our flight. Jacob fought sleep like his life depended on it, but we found a nice woman to talk to for a while. She asked if I had bottles or a soother with me. "Well, that's a bit complicated..." I said.

"Everybody's complicated. My family is complicated, too!"

Well, okay. She seemed decent enough. I explained about being transgender, nursing Jacob, and using donated milk. She thought it was all fantastic. Jacob got a little calmer. I nursed him to sleep, finally, and enjoyed a few pages of a book and a sandwich for myself.

When I felt the plane starting to descend, I immediately got out the supplementer. If I had only one goal on this flight, it was to nurse during takeoff and landing to help Jacob relieve the pressure in his ears. He dream-nursed in his sleep for about half of the descent. I watched the mountains become clearer through my window. It was good to be going back to Vancouver, where I was from.

Suddenly Jacob came off and started to cry, and I could not convince him to latch back on. The pilot turned on the seatbelt sign, so we were stuck. I offered him a drink of water from a cup but he only turned his head away and screamed louder. Desperate to get him to swallow, I took the tube out of the bottle of milk and tried to persuade him to suck on the plastic nipple to no avail. He started to do that horrible sobbing, gasping cry that twists my insides in knots.

"Don't you have a bottle or a soother or something for that baby?" called a female voice in front of me.

What genius! Why hadn't I thought of those things? I explained that I had tried but he wasn't willing to take anything in his mouth. She frowned and informed me that his ears were probably hurting. Yes.

We landed, and then Jacob latched on. Suck, swallow, suck, suck, swallow, hiccupping sob, suck, suck, swallow. He settled down.

The woman pushed her way past a few people to stand right in front of me.

"Why are you breastfeeding this baby?"

I couldn't quite tell if she was accusatory or just curious. I glanced around and reminded myself that I was on a crowded airplane. She couldn't do anything physically dangerous to us here. I decided to be frank with her. "I'm transgender, I birthed my baby myself, and I breastfeed him."

"Well, he needs a real boob, MAN. Come on!"

"No, I actually do make a little bit of milk for him, and the rest he gets through this." I held up the supplementer for her to see.

"You're going to wreck his ears doing this, flying with him like this. He needs an actual boob. It's about time someone told you this."

I offered to demonstrate my capabilities by squirting some milk in her face, but she declined. I could have done it; I'd only managed to latch Jacob onto one side, and my other side was relatively full.

I could see her revving up, so I added, "I hope you have a good trip. Take care."

"You, too. You know, Jesus loves you. I hope you know that."

Then we were trapped in that awful moment that happens on every flight – the time when the plane has stopped, people have stood up and retrieved their stuff, but no one can move because the door to the aircraft hasn't been opened yet. I ignored the woman as best I could and tried to chat with the guy in front of me, who rolled his eyes at my adversary.

After she left, I packed up my things and cried along with Jacob whose ears were probably still sore. I wished someone could teach me how to grow a thicker skin. I didn't know how to keep on being this parent raising this child. I was astonished, though, that it was the first time I'd been directly confronted by a stranger for nursing my baby. I'd been incredibly lucky so far, but it still hurt badly to hear someone declaring that I was failing as a parent and damaging my baby.

At the luggage belt, a man who'd sat in front of me strode over, looking stern. I braced myself.

"Don't you let anyone keep the joy of this baby from you," he said, with a hint of anger in his voice. And then, he repeated it. "Don't let anyone keep the joy of this baby from you!"

United once again with Ian, we waited nervously by the sign marked "Special Baggage" at the Vancouver International Airport only to turn around and see our cooler swirling around on the regular luggage belt behind us. Apparently our baby's food supply was not as precious as we imagined it was. To the airline, it was just another box.

When we unloaded all the milk at our friend's house in Vancouver, she burst out laughing, saying, "He's never going to eat all this!" She was right. We had carefully kept track of how much Jacob had been eating every day, and then brought twice as much as usual just in case of a growth spurt. During the time we were in Vancouver, Jacob only consumed about a quarter of what we had overzealously packed. Better to have too much than too little, we thought.

One of Ian's longtime friends in Vancouver, Lana, was a great breastfeeding supporter and wanted to contribute to our cause. She had watched on Skype as Jacob fed and grew in Winnipeg. One day she squinted at her monitor, looking at me holding one of his bottles.

Her eyes grew wide, and she asked, "Is he really going to have that much?"

She remembered occasionally pumping milk for her babies to have when she was expecting to be away. She would watch the drops come out one at a time and marvel at how this elixir alone could sustain life for months on end.

I was holding up about six ounces. "Oh yes, it's kind of wild to try to get this much donated milk for him. He does eat a lot."

"Well, I don't think I ever made that much milk."

"Did your babies grow?" asked Ian.

"Yes."

"Then you did make that much, you just never saw it coming out."

We reminded her that most babies are far more effective than machines at removing milk from a human body.

Lana decided to dust off her old breast pump and see if she could contribute something to our project. She started pumping for a few minutes each day to try to get her supply going. She was still breastfeeding her toddler at the time.

When we met up with her in Vancouver, she humbly presented us with a few laboriously produced ounces of milk in a small bag. "I don't know what happened to all my milk. I breastfed both my girls for years. I'm sorry this is all I could do for you."

She was embarrassed and apologetic. We were deeply touched that she would try so hard to help us with our goal of feeding Jacob human milk. We assured her that we had brought far more milk to Vancouver than he needed, but also thanked her profusely for her dedication and generosity.

Meanwhile, Jacob was staunchly resisting nursing in his strange new surroundings. For the first five days of our trip, he fussed and cried almost constantly. I sang to him, walked him, bobbed him up and down, rocked him, made all manner of strange noises that I imagined might somehow appeal to him, and, of course, attempted to nurse him. Much of the time he refused to latch on and simply cried. I learned that only one method of latching was successful when he woke up in a foul mood during those days: I would get up with him, holding him against my shoulder and bouncing up and down, making a zooming sound that rhythmically rose and fell in pitch.

Breastfeeding promotes normal jaw development.

With my free hand I'd get out the supplementer and place the bottle on a nearby table.

Ugh, I so want to just bottle-feed this ridiculous mess of a baby (not that that would have worked anyway). *Why I am doing this?* Then I'd swiftly move Jacob into a horizontal nursing position while continuing to bounce and zoom, and latch him on as quickly as possible.

Because breastfeeding promotes normal jaw development!

If I fumbled with the tube and took too long, he'd howl again and I'd have to bounce him in an upright position for a few more minutes before trying once more.

This will get easier. It won't always be this hard.

We did this dance many times per night and thoroughly woke up the whole house each time.

When we met Ian's parents' neighbours they were thrilled to see our new baby.

"Lovely blue eyes he's got...And, is he colicky?"

They'd heard his crying from next door, day and night.

"Oh, no! No, he's not colicky. He's normally a very happy baby."

"Oh, yes. Well, do you have *any* experience with babies?"

Well, no, we didn't. I grew up the youngest in my family and didn't have any cousins living nearby. Ian was the youngest in his family, too. We held our baby and tried to comfort him.

And then, he somehow got over whatever he was going through. He returned to his usual, cheerful self and thoroughly enjoyed all the attention being showered upon him. One warm afternoon, as Ian's dad cradled Jacob in his arms and gazed at him adoringly, Ian asked, "Dad, what changed for you? You were so angry when I came out. Now here I am years later married to a trans guy, with a baby, and it's like no problem for you."

"The alternative was intolerable," he said, without missing a beat, and quietly went back to cooing to Jacob.

Intolerance is intolerable.

We flew back to Winnipeg with more than a month's supply of breast milk as-of-yet uneaten, and an armful of new baby-soothing techniques developed by utter necessity.

When a woman in our online parenting group posted to say that she'd just had her baby six weeks early and she was having trouble making enough milk, I could hardly contain my excitement. We could offer this woman some milk from our freezer supply. With a minimal but timely donation, she'd get over her minor bump in the road, and in days her milk production would be in high gear. Who would she want to thank first? Us! And how could she best do that? By donating milk! I knew it had to work out this way.

Jesting aside, there was the matter of the baby and parent involved. I could well remember our own early days with Jacob when he seemed so vulnerable – I now shuddered at the thought of a preemie eating formula. *What would we have done if Jacob had joined us too early?* Preemies need the special nutrients and antibodies in human milk even more than healthy full-term babies do. The hospitals here have some donated breast milk available from a milk bank in the US, but it is reserved for the sickest of the sick.

Probably I'd have had Ian going up to random women on the street begging for milk. *"You don't know how to hand express? Good thing I do! Remove your shirt! Allow me! I've got a handy portable cup right here, and I have excellent aim."*

Although Jenn's baby, Chloe, was early and uncoordinated, she was not in poor enough shape to get the sanctioned stuff. Jenn had asked in her online plea if anyone could spare a few bags of milk that she could pretend were hers, since milk sharing is "not allowed" at the local hospital. She'd tell the nurses that she had pumped it at home in between hospital visits.

A few people on the forum said they'd try to pump or hand express something. Others said they would phone friends. Finally, after months of worrying and scrounging for milk for our own baby, we were in a position to help someone else. We wrote that we could spare some milk that our star donor, Sandi, had pumped. We still had a few bags of her earlier milk, the most appropriate vintage for a newborn.

Jenn accepted our offer, and the online community cheered our magnanimity. We lived only two blocks from the hospital, so Jenn came over on her way home from a visit with her baby. We gave her four full bags of milk, which would be enough to get Chloe through the next few days.

Not able to stop myself, I chatted with Jenn some about breastfeeding. Having read enough books on the subject, I was the breastfeeding dude who knew exactly which questions to ask. *How did the latch feel? Could she hear or see her baby swallowing milk? Was she pumping to keep up her supply? How often? What kind of pump?*

Jenn didn't know how to tell if her baby was swallowing milk or just sucking weakly and not getting much. I demonstrated using Jacob, pointing out the visible pause in his jaw movement each time he took a real gulp. I also showed her how to use a supplementer. Since she had to supplement, she might as well do so in a way that would support her breastfeeding efforts. I gave her a spare bottle, nipple, and tube so that she would be prepared at her next hospital visit. I was delighted to impart knowledge on my new favourite subject. Jenn left equipped with milk and information, and I was convinced that within a week she'd be drenching her bed sheets at night with a copious oversupply.

The nurses at the hospital had different plans. They told Jenn she shouldn't use the supplementer. One nurse said that it made feeding too easy for the baby, another that it just wasn't permitted in the "rules." They also limited the amount of time that Jenn was "allowed" to breastfeed because they felt that breastfeeding on demand would be too taxing for the baby. At each feeding, the infant was fed first with a tube going down her throat directly into her stomach, then breastfed, and then also bottle-fed if she hadn't consumed the amount deemed appropriate for her in the allotted time. She had to be fed every three hours and she had to eat a precise amount. Jenn had been discharged already and wasn't able to stay with her baby overnight, so for nighttime feedings Chloe received bottles.

We brought Jenn meals on a few of her scheduled breaks between nursing sessions. She mentioned that she'd love to donate milk to those in need once her own supply was going strong. *Perfect. We were reeling in a big one.* I suggested that she ask a La Leche League leader to come into the NICU to take a look at her latch and make sure everything was as it should be. She quietly admitted that she had already designated her four allowed visitors, and that they mustn't be changed once they'd been selected. She didn't want to challenge the nursing staff. They took care of her baby when Jenn wasn't around. Most important of all, the hospital got to decide when Chloe could go home.

I couldn't fathom the stress she must have been feeling. Having to leave the baby every night was miserable, but the thought of sitting around the NICU with no place to rest made her go home. Her partner only got two days off work when the baby was born, so he couldn't handle long shifts in the hospital.

"That sounds so hard," I said. "You are a very strong person."

"Well, I'm sure smoking more," she replied. "The stress is really getting to me. It's a bad habit, I know, but I can't help it right now."

My heart sank. A smoker? Our potential milk donor from heaven who would cause us to buy yet another freezer to store it all was a smoker?

Jenn's milk never did come in full blast the way she (and I) hoped. It was hard to get Chloe to breastfeed well after all the bottle-feeding she'd learned in the hospital. One day, following a supplemental feeding with Sandi's milk, Chloe had major indigestion.

Jenn's partner vetoed the use of donor milk from then on. They used some formula until, after a few months of perseverance, Jenn was able to breastfeed exclusively.

In mid-summer, Simone returned her pump to us. Her husband, Teddy, had lost his job in Winnipeg so the family was forced to move to a new one in Calgary. There would be no more pumped milk from Simone and no more wet nursing. Simone first introduced me to the possibility of breastfeeding, she told us about home birth, helped Jacob learn to breastfeed, nursed our baby, and pumped milk for us. I was losing a close friend and Jacob was losing his milk buddy.

"Trevor, why are you crying?" Simone's young son, Tim, asked me one day as the date of their departure loomed.

"Oh, I'm just very sad that you guys are leaving. We'll miss you."

"And how will baby Jacob get his milk, Trevor?"

"I don't know. That's a good question. I guess we'll need to find somebody else who can give us milk."

"I know! I will send Mommy's milk to you by UPS!"

"Perfect. Thanks, Tim. And what will I do when I need help from your Mom?"

"You can call her!"

Good advice.

Before the big move, we threw Teddy and Simone a goodbye party to which we invited all their Winnipeg allies and admirers.

Elaine and Allen were among those who came to wish them good luck. The party happened to provide the perfect backdrop from which to support Elaine in her breastfeeding efforts. There were dozens of kids and toddlers running around, all of whom had been breastfed and nearly none yet weaned.

At one point during the gathering, Allen, who preferred using formula to readily-available breast milk, found himself surrounded by four La Leche League Leaders at once, each of them expounding on the importance of breastfeeding. Simone explained that both her kids had been lean and skinny and "underweight" according to the standard charts. She emphasized that breastfed babies gain at a different pace than formula-fed ones.

Despite the crowd of persuasive, experienced, breastfeeding women talking off his ear, Allen wasn't swayed. At least Elaine relished one blissful evening where nearly everyone around her encouraged her efforts.

As we were saying goodbye that night to Ana, another La Leche League Leader and a friend of Simone, she told us she was amazed and inspired by how we were feeding Jacob. She asked if she could help. She had never pumped before but wanted to try. Her daughter was already four years old, though still nursing a few times per day – Ana knew she must have some milk. We handed her Simone's pump that was sitting by the back door, ready to be returned to the pharmacy.

We were excited to have another milk donor so eager to do her part. I waited a week and then emailed Ana to ask her how the pumping was going.

She had pumped several times without seeing a single drop of milk.

She asked her daughter, "Are you sure there's milk in there?"

"Oh, yes, mommy. Of course!"

As an LLL leader, Ana had given guidance to many parents who needed to pump their milk. She often told them that some people, but not all, respond well to the pump and use it easily. Mothers may find it helpful, she would explain, to look at a photo of their baby or think of their baby while they pump. Some, however, will always have difficulty.

At the time that Ian and I got together, Ian was sorting out affairs with his former partner. He had a lot on his mind, and often seemed preoccupied. When he was able to be fully present, our time together felt extraordinary. We finished each other's sentences and intensified one another's good energy. I wanted to continue enjoying this for each second of the rest of my life.

Once the stress of Ian's separation appeared to have lifted, other issues soon took its place. It felt hard to get through to him.

"Do you want to go out for Ethiopian, or have some of the leftover pasta from last night?"

I waited for his response. One, one thousand; two, one thousand...ten, one thousand.

"Ummm...I don't mind either way."

I would ask, "Are you okay?"

I worried that I had said something to offend him, or that I'd been inconsiderate. What was going on in his mind? When I was a kid, getting the silent treatment had been a form of punishment for wrongdoing.

"Yeah, it's just the usual stuff. Nothing new."

When Ian started having real difficulty sleeping, we both became concerned. He would wake in the early hours of the morning, unable to calm down enough to fall back asleep.

Ian saw a psychologist, a naturopath, a Chinese doctor, and several MDs. All had ideas of how to treat his problems, but nothing worked for longer than a few weeks. We had hoped that with Jacob's birth, there would be no more time for unnecessary worrying, and he would be cured. Instead, we had a newborn baby with a parent who was unable to fully enjoy him, and I had an additional being who sometimes needed me for comfort in the night.

By the time he was five months of age, nursing Jacob was like wrestling with a strong, wild little animal. His right hand would alternately pound my chest, grab at my beard, pull on my lips, and scratch my shoulder while he would kick his feet against anything they might happen to touch. With his left hand he constantly scratched my stomach or grabbed my belly fat and yanked. As he suckled, he pulled my nipple so hard I could feel the skin stretching all the way to my armpit. Then, if the wooden floor creaked, or the dog clicked her nails as she walked, or Ian turned on the TV, it was game over. Jacob had to come off and look around at what was going on. Still hungry, he'd fuss a minute later and we'd repeat the whole procedure of attempting to feed.

Worse was when Jacob's creeping little fingers discovered the supplementer tubing that snaked around his face from his mouth down to the bottle. Often he yanked it right out of his own mouth, leading to a crying fit since the food stopped coming. Sometimes he managed to pull the tube out of the bottle before I'd even latched him on.

One day I gave him an empty plastic pill bottle to hold in one hand to keep him from grabbing at the supplementer tube. *Perfect.* The bottle happened to be sitting nearby and he was easily interested in it. As he took it out of my hand, I picked up the supplementer tube and brought it to my nipple to latch him on. At the same moment, a groggy Jacob, thinking to suck his thumb, drew his hand to his face and bonked himself in the mouth with the pill bottle. He cried and, thinking I'd had a bad idea, I took the bottle out of his hand, which made him scream harder. I went back to my original method of just trying to latch him on faster than he could pull out the tubing and then using my free hand to hold his.

Yet breastfeeding him to sleep remained the highlight of my day. His sucking would go from frantic pulling to rhythmic suck-swallow-suck-swallow to a quiet, gentle caressing. He would place one hand flat against my chest, as if to declare, *you are mine and don't you go anywhere.* He was like a little suction cup, pressing as much of his skin against me as he could. Eventually the tube would move out of place and the milk would stop flowing. Jacob would respond with a soft, quick fluttering of his tongue and lips, his chin shuddering. Finally all his little twitches would settle and his whole body would relax against mine in complete trust. And then I'd do something both foolish and familiar to all parents – I'd sit there, awake, looking at his perfection and soaking up his baby smell when I could have been sleeping.

Eventually, we realized we had something like Depression mentality. We'd spent so long worrying about where we'd find each feeding for Jacob that we could hardly recognize abundance even when bags of breast milk were overflowing from all three freezers we owned. We hesitantly called up Alexa, Laura, and Tara and told them they needn't pump for us anymore. Sandi was giving us such volumes of milk every week we didn't know where to put it all, while these three women each valiantly produced a few bags once in a while.

All of them responded with some note of relief. Alexa's baby was already over a year old and her milk supply was adjusting. At best, she could express a few ounces at a time. Laura was beginning to get concerned that her own baby wasn't getting enough of her more fatty "hind" milk. She always nursed him first and then pumped for us. Since breast milk gradually becomes richer as the breast is drained, she may well have been giving her most filling, nutritious milk to Jacob. For a while, she breastfed her own baby from one breast and pumped the other, but her child didn't seem to get enough milk this way. She was happy that we'd found a new, prolific donor. Tara, too, didn't seem to have as much milk anymore as she once did. She was preparing to go back to school, and was breastfeeding less.

We still received occasional small donations from parents we met through friends, Facebook, or at La Leche League meetings. We were amazed to find out how many people happened to have a few bags of milk in the freezer that they weren't going to use. Since we'd heard from several of our donors that they had felt anguish over feeding formula for just a few days following birth, we set aside a small amount of particularly early milk in case we learned of someone in need. It happened twice over the coming months that we were able to respond to a desperate parent immediately, acting like a tiny milk bank. In those cases, it didn't take much help to avoid formula entirely before the parent's own supply became adequate.

Eventually, we decided to stop pasteurizing Sandi's milk. We'd been seeing her every week for a few months and had grown to trust her. We felt that the risk of Sandi having unknowingly contracted HIV or another STD was slim to nil. Leaving milk intact in its raw, uncooked form, even if frozen, preserves more of its delicate proteins and antibodies.

We continued to pick up fresh milk from Sandi every week. This usually lasted Jacob from around Wednesday through Sunday, and then we'd move into our sizable freezer collection for the rest of the week. Sandi continued to produce enough food for about two and a half babies.

When Jacob was five months old, we went on a road trip from Winnipeg to Calgary. We wanted to visit Simone and Teddy in their new home, take in the biggest Canadian horse show of the year at nearby Spruce Meadows, and then catch a glimpse of the Rocky Mountains in Banff before Ian had to go back to work after his summer off. I would also be interviewing for a Calgary job I'd had my eye on. Perhaps if I were offered a position we would not miss our friends for so long after all. Both Ian and I were attracted to the idea of moving to a bigger and (slightly) warmer city.

The only way we could think of to bring along enough milk for our vacation was to procure a travel freezer that we could plug into our car. We expected the 1300 km drive to take about three days since Jacob was not in love with his car seat and we couldn't bring ourselves to drive when he cried. Milk wouldn't stay frozen in a cooler with ice for that amount of time, especially with us having to open and close it frequently to take out bags to thaw. We considered shipping some in advance to Calgary, but we still would need a way to keep milk with us during the drive. Ian scoured the internet for a deal and finally decided on ordering a small, travel AC/DC switchable freezer from the US. We eagerly awaited its delivery in Winnipeg. When it arrived, we pragmatically tested it with water at first, noting how long it took to freeze. Before leaving on our trip we plugged it in for a few days in the house. Everything was set in the car with extension cords ready to go and a space left empty in front of the freezer's vents so it could work its magic.

We didn't worry about how much milk we had to pack for Calgary. After all, we had brought such excess on our flight to Vancouver that our friends and family laughed when they saw it. This time, we packed the freezer full, took a cooler of milk to thaw on the way, and that was that. It looked like plenty for twelve days. And so we set off in our small hatchback, the dog thoroughly appreciating her view from the front passenger seat next to Ian, and me in the back trying to occupy Jacob, stuck in his despised car seat, with a variety of jingly toys and silly faces. We headed west on the Trans-Canada Highway, driving past farmers' fields and rolling hills that were dotted only with cows and oil wells. We stopped for breaks along utterly shadeless, dusty side roads, ever waiting and hoping for the baby to be ready to settle into his next nap.

On night two of our trip I heard from Ian, "Gee, I hope I packed enough milk for this," and we decided to properly count what we had. Jacob had already eaten everything in the cooler bag and had just started into the freezer stuff. He had been drinking about five bags a day and, at the current rate of consumption, we realized we'd be at least three days short. We were both shocked to discover that in our carelessness we'd gotten things so wrong.

Maybe Simone could nurse Jacob plenty and give us a bit more leeway. We wondered, too, if we could make up the difference by driving back a little quicker and spending one less day in Banff. The following night, when we stayed close to Calgary, we looked up the local Human Milk 4 Human Babies Facebook site. Several people had recently posted that they had lots of milk to give away but others had also mentioned their needs. We put out a general plea and sent private messages to individual donors. We explained our travel plans and milk situation and mentioned that we were a gay couple. Never hearing back from anyone on the site, we later wondered if the milk-sharers in conservative Alberta had been scared away by our less usual partnership.

Life had changed for Simone since we had been together in Winnipeg. She was now working a full-time job. This meant she was spending far less time than before with her kids, and doing little breastfeeding. Tim had stopped nursing altogether and Samantha only had the opportunity to nurse in the evenings, nighttime, and on weekends. Over the course of a month or so, Simone's milk supply had virtually dried up.

Jacob had changed, too. Simone offered him her breast, and he mouthed around but didn't start suckling. At five months of age, he now knew the difference between my chest and anyone else's. Gratifying as it was that he would only latch onto me, his parent, I wished that Simone could still nourish him, especially now.

The next day, we went on with our plans and headed to Spruce Meadows to see the big international show jumping competition. I've had a fascination with horses ever since I was a little kid. I used to make daily excursions to feed the ponies down the street from our house. I took as many riding lessons as my parents would pay for, always hanging around the barn as long as possible. And, of course, I watched the show jumping events at Spruce Meadows on TV with fervor.

Now, I nursed Jacob in total awe amongst the huge crowds. The shared excitement was palpable and it seemed that most people were far too interested in the horses to stare at us. I juggled the nursing baby, supplementer tube, and a dog pulling every which way, while watching Eric Lamaze and his extraordinary partner, Hickstead, win their final competition before the horse's sudden and untimely death two months later from a heart attack.

Before leaving the show, we glugged up the baby again to make him full for the drive. We were near the barns where the elite horses were quarantined, as well as the bar to which the international riders were invited after the event. I needed to pee so Ian suggested I go into the bar for the bathroom. For me, restrooms house a lot of anxiety since I had to use the wrong one for the first two decades of my life. I still feel awkward going to public bathrooms, mostly because I have to use a stall to pee. I somehow imagine that everyone must know. They surely see from the direction my feet are pointing that I am sitting on the toilet, and they hear the sound, and they know. I half-expect someone to confront me about my gender when I leave the stall.

I walked by some of the famous riders still in their tight white pants and red jackets and I started to nudge past people, mumbling "excuse me." I got partway inside and felt terribly self-conscious of my roundness and curves which were not quite concealed by my baggy post-pregnancy shorts and button-down shirt that I used for nursing – here I was pushing past competitors in their sleek outfits with drinks in their hands. I imagined how I would look walking into the men's bathroom in comparison to the guys around me. I backed out as fast as I could and decided to wait.

I usually felt I could nurse in front of anyone. When Jacob is hungry, there is an imperative to feed him. He makes me feel it in my guts. I don't much care who is around or where we are as long as I think we'll be physically safe. I would rather be gawked at for being a nursing, transgender man than allow my baby to cry with hunger. But I realized that day at Spruce Meadows that without Jacob, I inevitably maintain some anxiety about my body. There was no way I could go into that washroom alongside these physically perfect athletes.

Back at Simone and Teddy's house, we came up with a plan to procure more milk. Friends in Winnipeg agreed to go into our house, pack up some bags from our overflowing freezers, and get them to the bus depot in Winnipeg that night. The bus for Calgary would leave at 10:30 a.m. the next day and arrive 24 hours later. Everything was going to be fine and our baby would be saved from the dreaded Nestlé.

The following afternoon we headed downtown so that I could attend my job interview. We didn't know how long it might last, but Ian planned to cup-feed Jacob as necessary and wait for me close by.

I was nervous, the interview went poorly, and I knew I wouldn't get the job. I soon returned to Ian and Jacob, who had done one cup feeding and wandered around the nearby museum. Jacob didn't seem to have missed me, nor did he ask to nurse, but *I* really wanted to nurse *him* after my disappointing job interview. I wanted that wonderful feeling of being needed by my little guy. I wanted to hold him close.

Jacob was happily sitting on Ian's lap and he fussed when I took him. He fussed even more when I tried to feed him. I relented, gave Ian a quick hug, and we headed back to Teddy and Simone's place.

We arrived at their house and I aimlessly wandered over to the computer, not sure what to do with myself. Ian's email was open on the laptop, and I glanced through the new messages. I clicked on an email from our friends in Winnipeg. They had sent off the milk and it would be arriving today at...5:00 p.m.? The bus company had told us the wrong arrival time for the milk. Their web site said they were open until 7:00 p.m. It was 6:38 p.m. There was no way Ian could get back downtown in time to pick up the milk. It would have to sit at the depot overnight.

I thought for a moment and called Simone's cell phone. She and Teddy and their kids were in the car already on their way home from work and daycare. She said they wouldn't make it in time to the bus depot either, and we hung up.

I told Ian, "Oh, well, it doesn't matter anyway. We had thought that the bus got in tomorrow morning and we prepared for that. The milk should be fine until then."

Simone called back a minute later, asking for the parcel tracking number. They were going to try anyway. We looked up the address of the depot and tried to give them directions in a city we didn't know and that they had just recently moved to. They missed the turnoff for the depot several times and had a fight in the car, but arrived at the terminal at 7:01 p.m. Simone was sure it would be closed – those types of places always slam their door shut on the dot. Still, she ran inside and made a frenzied dash for the counter.

Simone called us again. "Nothing here," she said. Our hearts sank. The milk was lost somewhere or the schedule was wrong. We had sent our friends on a wild errand through traffic and marital discord for something that wasn't there.

The woman said she would look again. This time she found it. "But I can't release it to you without a written statement of permission from Ian."

Of course.

Simone cited the tracking number but that was no help.

Desperate, she barked, "This is breast milk for a very, very sick baby. It will go bad if we leave it over night. Isn't there something you can do?"

The woman called Ian on his cell phone for confirmation, and then gave up the package to Simone.

We opened the cooler at the house and discovered that there had been a little too much unfilled air space inside. The milk had begun to thaw but only just, so we deemed it still safe for our purposes and got it into the freezer immediately. If we had retrieved it the next morning, the milk would have been spoiled and only fit to throw out.

That evening, Simone and Teddy's sink backed up and they spent hours with their landlord trying to clean up the mess. Then, our dog had diarrhea all over the two front seats of our car. I was going through a major post-interview low.

It was a fantastic day. We got our breast milk.

Before we had left for our trip, Ian had revisited the medical clinic, but his usual doctor was away on holiday. The stand-in saw that he had recently been placed on antidepressants, listened to his complaints about anxiety and a disturbed feeling in the pit of his stomach, and asked, "Do you mind if I run some tests?"

Ian nearly laughed, but said okay. More tests.

A few weeks later, the doctor's secretary called to say that Ian should come in for an appointment. We were excited and nervous. Finally, one of the many tests had picked something up, perhaps something diagnosable. How serious would it be?

At the clinic, the substitute doctor said simply, "You have hypot-hyroidism, meaning that your thyroid does not produce enough hormones. This is a chemical imbalance that you have, not a psychological problem."

He would have to take a thyroid medication every day for the rest of his life. His doctor would monitor his hormones through blood tests and adjust the dosage to reach an optimal level.

Ian said, "So me feeling stressed out all the time isn't just because I'm socially inept?"

"No. There's nothing wrong with your social ability to cope in difficult situations. It's simply biology, and the treatment is effective and easy."

"But how did I get this in the first place?"

"Stress can play a role in hypothyroidism. Too much of the stress hormone, cortisol, can interfere with the functioning of the thyroid and lead to an autoimmune problem where the body attacks the thyroid. Then, you can feel more and more stressed out because your thyroid isn't doing its job."

Ian was curious about how long his body might have been battling itself this way. He couldn't remember a time when he didn't have some underlying anxiety. Only several days after starting the medication, he found himself more able to focus on conversations and on Jacob's antics. Within a few months, the doctor ordered new tests and bumped up his dosage. Ian thought of the kids from his childhood happily riding ponies and paddling through the water, and wondered if he might start to enjoy those things, too, some thirty years later. He soon completed the Winnipeg Rowing Club's learn-to-row program with Jacob and me cheering him on from the docks.

We savored four beautiful days in Banff, enjoying the mountains. Jacob spent four days slurping breast milk at a phenomenal rate. The air was dry. We were drinking tons of water and our lips and throats felt sore.

Before having a baby, we reluctantly car-camped while on the road, but normally preferred to walk into backcountry sites. Having a baby eating donated milk necessitated a different approach – we required power so that we could plug in our travel freezer. In Banff, our small family car and modest hiking tent sat enveloped by great Puma Explorer 40-foot trailers that also parked in the electrical-equipped section.

We did a few short hikes, visited the hot springs, and ambled around the touristy Banff townsite. We treated ourselves to one very expensive meal of fondue at the Banff Springs Hotel. Jacob was welcomed graciously there and we were offered a high chair. For most of dinner he stood in my lap, intently exploring some vents next to where we were seated. Eventually, though, his exertions led to a full meltdown.

We hurried to the men's bathroom to check Jacob's diaper. We changed him but he was still cranky. There was nowhere to place the supplementer bottle beside me during feeding and no clean place to sit. So, standing half in and half out of the wheelchair bathroom stall, Ian held the bottle of donor milk and tube while I breastfed Jacob. The activity might have been more acceptable in the women's room, but our beards certainly would not. Ian said he felt more comfortable doing this in the bathroom than in the lavish restaurant where the wait staff and patrons were wearing more formal, gendered attire and behaving accordingly. Guys give each other privacy in bathrooms, Ian reasoned.

Unfortunately, women are often told to retreat to the restroom rather than feed an infant in public, so I guess we just did what many other nursing parents are expected to do. Jacob fell asleep while feeding and we returned to our dinner, me clutching our infant with my dress shirt still partly-unbuttoned around him.

On our second to last day in Banff, we started to worry about milk once again, despite the extra that our friends had shipped. I counted the bags in our freezer. Only 27 were left. Two days later there were only 17 bags. The day we left Banff, Jacob upped his intake yet again, this time to nine bags of milk in one 24-hour period. We didn't get far with our fussy baby and still-recovering diarrhea dog. I was in the driver's seat rolling us into Medicine Hat around 11:00 p.m. when Jacob woke up screaming in his car seat. By the time I was able to pull over, unbuckle him, and hold him in my arms, I was crying too. Everyone was tired. We decided to stop there for the night.

In the motel room I counted milk bags again. Nine left. We had enough for one more day of driving, not the two that we had planned. So it was on the morning of the next day that Ian now did the unthinkable: he went over to the pharmacy across the road and bought a jug of formula, while at home we had months' worth of breast milk waiting in our freezers. Ian got the ready-to-eat stuff so we wouldn't have to do any mixing on the road. The formula was made by a Canadian company and had decent-looking ingredients. It was the only one on the shelf that contained "skim milk" instead of the mysterious "modified milk ingredients."

Ian said to me, "You look like we're about to feed him poison."

He was close to the truth. I didn't even know if Jacob would be willing to drink the formula since he'd only ever had human milk so far. Should we mix our last few bags half and half with the formula so it wouldn't be such a shock? I just hoped that somehow we could miraculously do two days of driving in one and not need it at all. We both agreed that the priority had to be feeding the baby. If he powered through all the milk before we could get home, he'd have formula.

That morning I chatted with the kitchen lady at our motel while Ian put gas in the car. She held Jacob for a bit and asked where we were trying to go. When I told her, she replied, "Oh, that's ten or twelve hours away, isn't it? No, you can't do that in one day with a baby. They have to sit in them seats, you know."

Oh, yes, I knew very well. I smiled nervously and agreed.

For the remainder of the drive home we would pass only rural towns and smaller, conservative prairie cities where we didn't know how transgender nursing (or even gay parents, for that matter) would be received. It was another reason besides formula not to linger. We left Medicine Hat at 9:45 a.m. and drove for a few hours until Jacob woke from his nap. We stopped at the nearest town and found a small Dutch bakery full of Christian knick-knacks and posters. When we sat down to eat, the owner took Jacob from me to show him around the store. Despite her friendliness, I didn't dare to nurse Jacob in her shop. As soon as he started to look hungry, we made a run for the exit and fed him in the car.

We drove another several hundred kilometers with breaks for the baby and stopped for dinner in the city of Regina. Jacob badly needed to play and stretch and wiggle around, as well as nurse. He fussed in the restaurant so I breastfed him there almost continuously. A family sitting one table over from us stared and whispered, pointing at me. After a few minutes, the man and the woman at the table traded places, perhaps so that the one could have her turn getting a better look at us. I tried not to mind.

On our next driving break I fed Jacob and then took the dog, Quinoa, into a farmer's field to chase her ball. Time to go again, I leashed her up and looked down at her to see that she was leaving a trail of blood behind her. She had torn one of her nails almost off running in the field of roughly cut crops. We took half an hour to clean and bandage up her foot.

"Well, this accords with my general theory of pet ownership," said Ian.

"I know."

The dog was solely mine before Ian and I got together. She was my first true responsibility and a prior commitment that I would never shirk, as well as a delightful companion that I loved dearly. But no animal has ever had so many mishaps as this one. The eye infections and ulcers, the cuts on her paws requiring stitches, the hot spots on her neck and rump, the puncture wound on her face – the list goes on. Ian had only owned cats before, and imagined that caring for any other sort of animal mostly involved trips to the veterinarian. He had welcomed this dog into his life, however, and I taught him to always close the back gate, and not to throw the frisbee too close to a road. I had promised him that all these bills had been merely the result of bad luck – my parents' dogs that I grew up with never had such troubles. And now this.

Limping along at the side of the highway, I felt sorry for the dog, but thanked her that she wasn't bleeding too profusely this time around and didn't need immediate veterinary care. That kind of delay would have surely meant the end of our exclusive human milk feeding. We drove on, the formula still waiting in the back seat, unused.

Jacob was remarkably cooperative in the car that day. There was only one complete baby disaster where we couldn't pull over quickly and he and I were both in tears. By 11:00 p.m. we had made it into the province of Manitoba. We finally arrived at our house at 3:30 a.m. with only eight ounces of milk to spare, about one and a half bags. He finished that last little bit a few hours later. We had driven 965 km in one day, exclusively when Jacob was sleeping or happy enough to tolerate the car seat.

Back in the land of plenty, we called up Sandi, who said she had hoped we'd return soon because she was running out of space in her freezer for all her milk. She wanted to go to Costco again and stock up on frozen foods but would put off the trip until we could come by and clear some space for her. We were happy to oblige.

Between Jacob's fifth and sixth months, time slowed to a crawl of the inefficient, bum-scoot variety. We waited and waited, in eager anticipation, until finally, we offered him his first solid food. This would be the beginning of the end of our dependence on donated breast milk. We'd been reading about a feeding method purported to be more natural than the "bzzzzzzz here comes the airplane full of pureed peas and carrots" approach: we were going to try "baby-led solid foods." With this method, the parent waits until the baby shows true signs of readiness to eat food – the ability to pick up food, put it in his mouth, mush it around, and actually swallow it. Before that point, according to proponents of the baby-led style, an infant should not be made to eat manufactured baby cereals nor foods blended in a state-of-the-art "Baby Bullet." And the first food, preferably a nutritious whole food, may be offered at, but not before, six months of age.

The thinking behind baby-led solid foods goes something like this: infants' guts mature gradually, and some infants become ready for solid foods later than others. On the other hand, a baby can safely be nourished entirely from human milk or formula for his first year of life, with milk contributing a large proportion of total nutrition for even another year after this. During the great lengths of history before we reveled in food processors and shopping markets, it is unlikely that anyone prepared special baby food, other than perhaps to pre-chew something a little. Our ancestors probably breastfed for as long as possible due to sheer convenience and efficiency until such time as their children were able to grab, chew, and swallow their own food.

Probably, this is how our bodies were, and still are, made to develop. The reasoning seemed logical enough.

Finally, about one week shy of Jacob's six-month birthday, we couldn't help it anymore and offered him a whole banana. Ian and I were both excited to witness this new stage in his development. He grabbed the fruit enthusiastically and proceeded to mash it into his face, hair, shirt, and pants. Then, he gave what was left to the dog. We regularly offered him a variety of foods, but it ended up being another few months before he swallowed anything. We imagined his little baby intestines crying for more time: "Food under one is just for fun," or so the saying goes.

By the time Jacob was eight months old, Sandi was still producing milk, but she was no longer pumping the astonishing quantities she once was. We anxiously watched our freezers empty of human milk and slowly fill up with items such as soup stocks and all those broccoli leaves from the garden we didn't quite know what to do with. We looked online for more milk offers and soon interviewed yet another donor and her husband. This family, it seemed, had a long, dramatic backstory.

Byron explained to us that he worked on construction jobs all over the prairies. A few years ago, his wife, Katrina, had been traveling with him when she suddenly developed a terrible migraine.

Katrina said, "We went to the local clinic and they checked me out. They told me I was fine but there was something weird with how my blood was clotting."

"Then, we moved on to another town," said Byron. "She called me and said she thought it was happening again. I left my job right away and we went to the nearest hospital. They didn't know what was wrong, and she collapsed from a stroke."

"We got airlifted to Calgary, but I don't remember anything from after the stroke. For a while the only word I said was Lisa, my sister's name, over and over again."

Katrina was marooned in the hospital over Christmas that year, diagnosed with a serious blood clotting disorder. Her speech and memory returned to her, but for months after her health crisis, she needed to take a pill normally used for chemotherapy treatments. She also had to endure old-fashioned bloodlettings to help lower her platelet count. When she told her doctors that she wanted to try for a baby, they agreed to treat her with a safe, alternative medication, and she carried a healthy pregnancy.

After giving birth to a perfect baby boy, Katrina pumped as much extra milk as she could because she was worried that she might have to resume taking the chemo pill and stop breastfeeding. That didn't happen, but she ended up with about two thousand ounces of extra milk. A year later, the milk was now at its expiry date, and her freezer, as well as her Mom's and several friends' freezers, was full. We estimated that this amount would feed Jacob for about two months if we could find a place to keep it all.

I asked Simone to look up Katrina's current drug regimen in her authoritative reference book, *Medications and Mother's Milk*. In this guide, each drug is assigned a rating on a five-point scale. Both of Katrina's medications were classified as level two, meaning that they were relatively safe. Some relevant studies had been completed, and had demonstrated that these particular drugs passed into milk in minute quantities not harmful to a baby.

Sometimes it was hard to make decisions about potential donor milk. Many individuals disclosed that they were taking medications, including antibiotics, antidepressants, anticoagulants, synthetic thyroid hormones, birth control hormones, and pain killers. We considered each situation carefully, but for some drugs there was little safety information. In the case of Katrina's blood medications, we felt confident. We eagerly looked forward to receiving one more gigantic stash of human milk, especially with Jacob not showing any signs of slowing his rate of consumption.

Byron, Katrina, and their thirteen-month-old boy, David, drove in from Riverton, a small town two and a half hours away. They planned to spend the night with relatives after doing a quick milk drop-off. At 10:00 p.m., Byron called to say they'd reached the perimeter of the city. It was mid-November, and the nights were getting cold. We'd had our first snowfall of the season a few days back. While I stayed home with a sleeping Jacob, Ian got in the car and drove to the empty parking lot of the mall where they'd agreed to meet.

Byron said Ian would recognize him from his abundant tattoos – he would be wearing a muscle shirt because he was impervious to cold weather. When Byron was a child, his father died right in front of him, and his mom was left to raise him on her own. His neighbours pitched in by introducing him to bikes and organized crime. He had left gang life behind many years before we met him, but I imagined that he probably still looked like a guy you didn't want to mess with.

Ian saw the Jeep enter the deserted lot. He watched as Byron paused, driving slowly to look around, and then turned to pull up beside our little grey car.

Byron passed over the boxes of precious frozen goods. Ian imagined cops arriving right then. The police would take one look at Byron in his muscle shirt, the two parties meeting late at night in the empty lot, the transfer of product, and they'd all get hauled downtown. *It's only breast milk, I swear!*

We'd turned into milk junkies.

I was eager to meet the family the next day. Whenever possible, I try to spend time with milk donors face-to-face, especially if donations will be ongoing. Byron spoke gruffly over the phone and I imagined him to be a heavy-set, six-foot-something with a few missing teeth in addition to his much-ballyhooed tattoos.

I walked into the Women's Hospital where Katrina was having an appointment with her blood doctor. I hadn't been there since week twenty-eight of my pregnancy when I needed an injection because of my own blood issue. I am Rh negative, as about one in six people are, and a simple jab called the Win-Rho (named for Winnipeg where it was developed) would protect me and my baby from a potentially catastrophic condition where the parent's body attacks the baby due to a difference in blood type. The woman treating me at the time said she was relieved that I was transgender.

"When I saw your name, I thought you were one of those poor souls whose parents gave you a funky opposite-gender name because they'd wanted a boy, and never mind that you were actually a girl." This was a take on my situation I'd never heard before.

Now, I glanced down the hallway and saw an enormous, frowning man with a long, frizzy ponytail and endlessly billowing facial hair. He grunted something or other to his wife. *Oh, dear God*, I thought, *There he is. I cannot possibly tell that ornery, dangerous-looking former gang member that I am trans.* I instinctively lowered my eyes to avoid catching his gaze.

"Hey, Trevor, over here!"

I looked up to see that the daunting, angry-looking giant had moved on into the elevator, revealing Byron, a surprisingly little man holding a wiggling toddler. He had neat, short brown hair, dark stubble covering his jaw, and was dressed in jeans and a well-fitting button-down shirt. Upon seeing Jacob, Byron melted, his mouth forming a wide smile and his eyes softening, baby-drunk. He immediately asked to hold him and kept saying over and over again how beautiful my child was. Katrina joined us and Byron insisted that she should hold Jacob, too. I breathed a sigh of relief and had to laugh a bit at myself.

We walked outside together, and Byron suggested lunch, motioning toward KFC at the end of the block.

Fast food? I blanched at the suggestion.

Then, I replied, "Oh, yes, absolutely. Whatever you guys would like."

I was trying to be polite and easygoing. I was meeting these new milky friends for the first time and I wanted to make a good impression.

I did a quick mental calculation. *Which would be preferable? Formula, or milk from somebody who eats KFC?* It took a second, but I came down firmly in favour of the breast milk. Pretty much no matter what you eat or do, human milk is always perfect for human babies. As the lactation expert Dr. Newman has said, "Your breastmilk doesn't turn into a hamburger just because you ate it".[1]

We walked towards the smell of greasy chicken, but I couldn't help looking out for some other option. I pointed to an Indian restaurant across the road, trying to sound hopeful but not pushy.

"No, I need meat right away. I'm going to KFC," said Byron.

"Uh, we don't usually eat fast food," said Katrina. She smiled in my direction. "We don't have any fast food places where we live, so this is a treat when we make the drive to Winnipeg."

Fair enough.

Once we were sitting down with our food, I took the plunge. "So, there's a pretty interesting story about how we came to have Jacob."

"Oh, yes. I am really curious about that," said Katrina.

I felt anxious about explaining my gender history to this family. Over the phone when I had thanked Byron for agreeing to bring the milk into Winnipeg for us, he'd replied, "Sure, you guys both seem really nice. And I've never had any problem with the gays, anyway. I've known a few. There was one guy who started dressing as a woman but he was a totally decent guy. I've known him quite a while. Don't have any problem with the gays."

I wasn't sure about someone who used the term "the gays." It sounded like something a religious fundamentalist would say to describe us as a social travesty. We certainly don't refer to ourselves as "the gays" but rather as gay people, a gay couple, a trans-gay couple, or queer people.

"Well, I'm transgender. I was born female..." and off I went into my usual recitation. I watched their faces for their reaction. So far, so

---

[1] Newman, "Dr. Jack Newman" community Facebook page. https://goo.gl/7q8doj

good. Katrina was smiling, and Byron looked intent but positive.

"So, I became pregnant and gave birth to Jacob."

"Hey, then why did you say he was adopted?" Byron sounded accusatory.

"He didn't say that, hon."

"Oh, you didn't? Okay." I sensed him starting to let down his guard a little.

I told them how I could make a bit of milk, and that I used the supplementer to feed Jacob. They seemed well versed in the benefits of breastfeeding and not at all surprised that I'd want to feed Jacob at my own chest.

Their baby was starting to fuss. "Oh, you want some of my pop. That's *really* great for you," Katrina muttered under her breath.

"He can have some of my ice tea," said Byron. "That's not pop."

Katrina frowned, and rolled her eyes. "Full of sugar. Okay."

Changing the subject, I asked where the three of them were staying overnight for their Winnipeg visits.

"On the floor in my aunt's room on a crappy air mattress," said Byron.

"Well, we have an extra room at our place. Actually we have two extra rooms because there's Jacob's room and he's never in it. He sleeps with us."

"Oh, wow, that'd be great. We could actually get some sleep that way. Ugh, my aunt's, it's awful. We'll buy you a big pizza when we come." He looked at me and added quickly, "Vegetarian – you like vegetarian!"

I assured them they needn't buy us anything and they would always be welcome to stay with us. They were feeding our baby, after all. I did, however, silently resolve to cook something appealingly meaty yet healthy. Lean bison burgers on spelt buns, perhaps?

Ian was clearly pleased with himself. He had finally given away his beloved formula samples to the food bank – we sincerely had no need or want for them, and they were threatening to expire. The only evidence of formula that remains with us is the flyers we are doomed to receive in the mail in perpetuity detailing the wonderful nutrition of Nestlé and Enfamil.

Still, I delighted in regaling Ian with news of the latest baby food scandal. The maker of Ian's favourite brand, "President's Choice," found at grocery stores across the country, had just recalled some infant rice cereal because it was found to be rancid. Ian put on his best mock-scandalized frown and asked me, "But how could the President go wrong?"

I didn't know. We were continuing on with our baby-led solid food ideas, and we'd also gotten into learning about the benefits of fermented foods. We now regularly made our own kefir, a fermented cow's milk product, by mixing a kefir culture in some milk and forgetting it on our jumbled kitchen counter for a few days. With just enough neglect, the milk matured into a high quality probiotic. The bacteria in the culture fed off the lactase in the milk, making it easy to digest.

We gave Jacob a taste and he loved it. We offered some more and he downed that too. Next, we took two hippie pursuits and crunched them together: we decided to make kefir for Jacob using human milk, since, nutritionally speaking, this would be better for an infant than cow's milk kefir. We only tried it once – human milk is already perfect for human babies, and has no need to be altered.

As I became more comfortable and open to friends and acquaintances in my role as a transgender, breastfeeding parent, more people learned about our exact situation and, of course, our ongoing need for human milk. Many parents we've shared our story with have been wonderfully appreciative of our efforts. I'm sure I will always regret not being able to fully feed Jacob myself, but I am in awe of the generous community that sprung into action to help.

When Jacob was about eight months old, Dominique, a woman we vaguely knew from our local online parenting group, messaged me: "I didn't know you guys were using breast milk! I've been looking for a way to donate some. Would you like mine?"

Milk donations like these were popping up without us even looking. For the umpteenth time, I showered grudging praise on my old enemy, Facebook, for bringing us together. Dominique had pumped a modest amount of milk that she was storing in her freezer for times when she would be away from her baby. However, she had recently realized that her child was allergic to soy and dairy, even the trace amounts found in his mother's milk. She stopped consuming the allergens, but her small freezer collection was now useless to her. I asked Dominique the usual questions about her own health, and, satisfied, I gladly accepted a few days' worth of food for Jacob.

Jacob's style of feeding and our nursing relationship continued to evolve as the months rolled by. One evening, he was exhausted but terribly energetic, frantically switching between exuberant laughter and helpless crying. I decided to try a bath. We slipped into the warm water together, facing each other. I noticed his muscles starting to relax, and he was finally quiet for a few minutes. Then, he saw something in front of him that attracted all his attention.

His eyes focused, and he threw himself forward, latching onto my chest in the bathtub. I hollered to Ian to bring the supplementer, and then smoothly nursed Jacob in the water. He chose his own nursing position, one that I had never tried before but which turned out to be effortless for both of us – he sat sideways on my lap, hugging me with one arm around my back and the other over my chest. He quickly nursed to sleep. This soon became a ritual, and a nearly foolproof method of getting him to bed when he was tired yet whirling out of control.

On another occasion, we were out for a walk with the dog, and Jacob, on my front in a cloth carrier, was fighting his nap and getting frustrated. I offered to nurse him while in the carrier, without the supplementer. To my surprise, he latched on. Within minutes he was completely out, the first time since just a few days after his birth that he nursed to sleep without the irksome tube. The dog was ready to be let off her leash for a good run and I felt just as free.

An hour later, with Jacob still fast asleep, we arrived home just as a woman was approaching our front walkway. She explained that she was a provincial enumerations officer collecting voters' information on behalf of the government. I provided my details, and then she asked, "Can I get your wife's name, please?"

"Husband," I said. "I have a husband."

She stood there saying nothing for a long moment, and then asked, "So you're the wife, then?"

She *must* have heard of gay people before.

I said, "We're both husbands! We're gay men."

The enumerations officer paused again, this time looking around us. *Couldn't there be a wife, somewhere?*

Exasperated, I said, "Gay marriage has been legal in Canada for a while!"

Since 2005.

She defended herself, "This is only my second day on the job, and you're the first, uh, person like this I've had."

I frowned.

Trying again, she said, "So let me say this. Your...partner...what is his or her..."

"His!" I cried, laughing.

"Okay," she said. "His first name?"

Finally we got through Ian's information. Then, she nodded at Jacob in the carrier, and asked, "So did you adopt this little angel?"

Aha! She probably would have believed and understood we were gay, were it not for the napping baby on my chest. I said, "Nope! I'm transgender and I birthed this baby myself."

Rather than waiting for her to say anything more, I asked her if she might work later on the federal long-form census. She muttered something about how the new government had made more promises than it could keep, and then glanced at her watch and mentioned that she had better continue on to the next home on her list.

As Jacob heads into toddlerhood, he can crawl into my lap and position himself for nursing when he needs it. He rarely, if ever, refuses to nurse when hungry or tired, and I have an easy tool for comforting him after a bump on the head or for putting him down for a snooze. We're also getting into joke territory, where Jacob nurses and waves his hand about by my face, and I playfully try to grab his fingers in my mouth, chomping like Cookie Monster. He smiles up at me, still trying to hang onto his latch.

Someone once asked Ian if he felt jealous of my nursing relationship with Jacob. "You know, the closeness that they have. Do you wish you could have that, too?"

"What?! Well, I'm not exactly uninvolved," he answered.

After the initial few visits, Ian did virtually every "milk run" to Sandi's place on his own. It became tedious to pack up the baby and go on the half hour car trip every week, trying to plan around everybody's nap schedules. Ian spent plenty of time chatting with Sandi, shopping for milk storage bags, and thawing and preparing milk for Jacob. In the beginning perhaps he pursued the accumulation of milk with the fervor he did because he could see how badly I wanted it for Jacob, but before long he was just as committed to the project as I was.

"I kind of see Jacob right now as an extension of Trevor's body, and I'm helping to support that by finding donor milk and doing the necessary errands. The baby was inside Trevor for so long. Now he's outside but he's so utterly dependent. Their nursing relationship is natural – it's exactly what they need to be doing. I'm proud of it, not jealous."

And Ian has his bonding time with Jacob, too. We all sleep together in a family bed. Jacob sometimes sleeps between us, sometimes on my side of the bed. Usually for at least a few hours per night he snuggles right up against Ian. In the daytime, Ian often wears Jacob in a carrier to go out in the neighbourhood. Other times I nurse him to sleep and then hand him to Ian to hold in his lap while lounging about watching *The Daily Show* or surfing the net.

These days, when Ian returns home from a day at work, Jacob reaches out and throws himself into Ian's arms. I can already see as my son slobbers over the remote control and crawls tirelessly towards the mess of wires hooking up the computer, stereo, and TV that he will share with my husband a lifelong preoccupation with tools, gadgets, and electronics. The all-consuming nursing of infancy was brief and intense, and has been replaced with a range of parenting through nursing, snoozing, exploring, and building together.

At ten months of age, Jacob was not nearly as fragile and needy-looking as when he was first born, although I'd argue, just as cute. I'd spent the last month or so lurking on the Human Milk 4 Human Babies' sites for Ontario, Manitoba and Saskatchewan, hoping that something would turn up. With Sandi not producing nearly so much as she used to, our freezer stash was diminishing fast. Jacob, however, still had no teeth and a limited interest in solid food; he continued to guzzle donor milk at an alarmingly voracious pace.

Lately, there had been no offers whatsoever in our own province, but about half a dozen in Saskatchewan. The conversations had all gone the same way.

"Oh, Ian, I just saw a post from someone in Saskatoon so I jumped on it."

"Great!"

"Uh oh, she's asked me how old our baby is."

I'd respond, and then not hear back again after that. One donor mentioned that she was expecting to give to a newborn.

Still, it didn't hurt to ask, did it? Maybe some day down the road I'd be contacting a prospective donor, *"Lovely, your baby is four months. Mine is three."*

(Years.)

"So how about that breast milk?"

I understood why someone would want their hard-pumped milk to go to a newborn for whom it would make the most dramatic difference. I began to think that we were nearing the end of Jacob's days on human milk. It was time to get out the blender and convince the kid to eat some baby mush. Then, I saw a post from a "milk-making machine," as Ann called herself. She had a deep freezer full of milk and was starting to throw it out for wont of storage space. Again, she was in Saskatoon.

This time, I tried a new approach. I got in touch with Ann and told her about five different families in Winnipeg looking for milk for their babies – one babe in need was a newborn, there were five-month-old twins, our own Jacob, a 14-month-old girl, and another set of twins due in May whose mother wanted a small just-in-case stash. Could we divvy up Ann's stockpile in Winnipeg? I received an emphatic yes, and Ann shipped her milk in two large coolers by Greyhound the next morning. I had tapped into the sweet ir-resistibility of the "tinies," whose busy, exhausted parents were most grateful that I had done the legwork of finding a donor and arranging delivery.

Yet when I called Greyhound, the gruff shipping dude told me there was no way I could get the shipment until the day after it arrived. The bus would get in at 9:00 p.m. and the Greyhound office closed at 9:00 p.m.

I asked him, "Well, how warm is your warehouse?"

"What, you need this stuff to stay frozen or something?"

Ian decided to head to the depot that evening anyway on the off chance that he could get the milk somehow. Perhaps the bus would be a few minutes early, or the counter might stay open late.

He approached an employee and described the problem, mentioning casually, "A lot of babies would be eating tonight because of you...if only there was some way to retrieve the coolers."

The employee said there wasn't any real reason he couldn't just keep one counter open a bit later. He had to stay there anyway. The bus arrived and Ian paid for the milk. One cooler had been cracked completely open during transit, although the milk was still well frozen. Ian spent the rest of the evening on a driving tour of Winnipeg, dropping off bags of milk to the many families in need. Finally, he came home and filled our own freezers, too. Exhausted, he grinned, "Now, stay off the message boards for a little while, will you?"

I'm sitting in the rocking chair my mom gave me, iPad balanced on my lap, baby Jacob snoozing away on my chest. In his sleep, he flicks his hand up to rest his finger tips delicately against my mouth. I feel his sweaty hair on my shoulder and his rhythmic, moist breath stroking my neck. For most of his life, we've spent naps this way, but it won't last much longer.

As I take in the smell of Jacob's slightly damp skin on this hot summer day, I imagine Ian's first days. The lights of the nursery shine down in his eyes at all times. The babies next to him cry through diaper changes and heel prick tests. The stress hormones rush in Ian's veins as he is stranded, waiting. There is a clock on the wall that means nothing to him. A burning pain rises in his belly until someone comes with a bottle. Just as he begins to feel comfortable again, the stranger returns him to the bassinet and a sense of something missing, not right, unsafe.

In the midst of the interminable waiting, a pair of warm, gentle hands touches his sides. The lights of the nursery fall behind him, and one of the hands shifts to the back of his neck, the other around his trunk. Upright, he smells Ivory Soap on a soft face and feels her cotton shirt on his tiny hand. He listens to the pleased babbling of a toddler and deep-throated praises of a man with a distinct twinkle in his eye. To the amusement of his new following, Ian stretches and yawns, and then he's out.

Before Jacob was born, I thought that I would try to breastfeed him because it would be good for him – it was the healthy choice. After I started nursing, it became a way of life and my best means of responding quickly to his signals and cries, to meeting his needs.

During our pregnancy, rushing hormones made me protect my

womb at all times. In labour and just after the birth they got me through the pain and gave me thoughts and feelings only for Jacob and Ian, my little family. Breastfeeding kept the hormones flowing and taught me how to look out for a baby who could do very little for himself. No matter how exhausted I was, how sleepy, how sore, how hungry, how thirsty, how badly I had to pee, no feeling I experienced ever seemed as important and urgent as satisfying my baby.

I once asked Ian in the middle of a difficult car ride if I couldn't hold Jacob in my arms just this once. I'd keep one hand on his head and neck the whole time and hold him tucked close into my body. I couldn't imagine how anything could possibly be safer than me holding him this way. We'd been stopping and starting a lot. We'd get Jacob into the car seat, and get going, and he'd immediately start to cry so we'd stop again and I'd hold him and breastfeed him. Then I'd put him back in the seat and his face would scrunch up and he'd be crying all over. It was dark and there were bugs outside that would eat us alive. If there had been a public bus, I would have gladly taken it in order to be allowed to simply hold my baby rather than use the vile car seat, but we were on a highway in the middle of nowhere.

Thankfully Ian was in possession of a logical brain and he answered a firm "no" to my plea. I had a breastfeeding brain, which doesn't usually fail me in my parenting choices. In the age of highways and car accidents, Ian's decision was, of course, the right one. We soon learned that on longer car rides it is safest for Ian to be in the driver's seat because if Jacob does start crying, Ian can hold himself together to pull over somewhere reasonable as soon as possible.

I have read, and corroborated through personal experience, that it is the amount of suckling and not the amount of milk one produces that determines your body's hormones. Breastfeeding is known in most cases to act as an effective contraceptive for the first six months postpartum if you don't miss any nursing sessions and you don't go too long between feeds. I don't produce anything near the total amount of milk that Jacob takes in, but since he gets all of what he eats at my chest, (aside from a few solid foods nowadays) I remain menses-free at over one year postpartum. I may be using a supplemental nursing system, but I have breastfeeding hormones. I am breastfeeding. And it has changed my life. Breastfeeding made me into a highly responsive parent and I am so grateful. I am happy to take the bus.

Epilogue

October 2014

Only one of us went in. Two came out.

Ian asked, "How about Jacob and I go to Ikea and exchange the hardware for the shelving?" He was sure if he didn't get that done before the birth, it would never happen. We had moved to a 14-acre property in the country the year before, and our books were still in boxes. It was a good reason to get away and give me some space. He waited for my response.

"Um..."

He waited.

"Um..."

He looked at me.

"Isn't Ikea like forty-five minutes away?" I asked. "How about you guys just go to the library or something?"

"Google says it's only twenty."

"Okay..."

They left, and I went outside. I walked towards our forest, looking to where I'd buried my big, young puppy, Tadoo, under a tall oak tree a few months before. Next, I passed the tiny, new apple tree underneath which we'd buried the remains from our early miscarriage the previous fall. It was the only new tree that had blossomed that summer. I started out along the path that Ian had mowed all the way around the perimeter of our farm. This felt like one of the last warm autumn days before the cold set in for good, and I noticed that I was not alone. Birds chirped and flitted about in hasty preparation.

I took this rare, private moment to walk at just the speed I wanted, noticing the sensations in my abdomen, hips, and legs as I moved. Sometimes I paused to crouch low to the ground. In the back field, I was in sight of the highway traffic but it moved too quickly for me to feel anyone watching. A train went by on the other side of the path. It and its crew knew nothing of the Ikea hardware, the dog's accident, the miscarriage, the unborn, or the man in labour.

It took me a long time to get all the way around the field and back to the barn where I checked in on our goats. Velvet, my favourite, nibbled gently at my beard as I leaned against the feed stall door. She was a sweet goat, but I knew she wouldn't be much help during labour. When I cried hard over the loss of my dog, the goats jumped away from my sobs, crashing around the barn until I went somewhere else. Early labour was fine as long as it wasn't noisy and might involve treats.

I phoned Ian. "Are you heading home soon?" They were already in the car. "Bring back...nice...things. Ice cream, grapes, chocolate. Nice stuff."

I went back to the house and phoned the midwife to tell her it was starting. She agreed with me that things weren't in full swing quite yet. I didn't recognize the name of the second midwife she said would be attending when the time came. She asked if I was okay with her choice.

"I don't know," I answered. "I've never met her."

We talked about when I should call again. With Jacob's birth, I was sure in hindsight that I had called much too early. I joked that it would probably be a few more days. She warned that second babies sometimes come fast.

As we were hanging up a few minutes later, Ian and Jacob walked in the door, and I had a strong contraction. In the next couple of hours we tried to feed Jacob dinner, put away groceries, and tidy the house. I got in the shower a few times to help manage the pain. I tried to brush Jacob's teeth, but there wasn't a long enough pause between contractions to unscrew the cap of the toothpaste. I could barely recover from each wave of pain in time for the next. Suddenly, Jacob walked swiftly out of the bathroom and returned with a bucket, just in time for me to ralph. He had recognized the look on my face, familiar to him from my many months of pregnancy sickness. For the next while, I stayed on the toilet, holding the bucket in front of me.

Ian had asked me when he came home if he should get the birth pool ready. "No, not yet. I want to hold off using it until I need it, and I don't want the water to be cold by the time I get in there. Let's wait a bit."

Now, I was desperate to get into the pool. Jacob was tired and asking to be picked up and read to.

We hadn't hired a doula. Our doula from Jacob's birth had moved away, and I aimed to labor more independently this time. I wanted to find out what would feel right to me if no one made suggestions and I followed my own inclinations.

A few different friends said we could call them to help if needed. They all had varying schedules, but we hoped that between them, someone would be available if necessary, especially in case of a hospital transfer. I sent one of them a message in the afternoon as labour was beginning, but when Ian called her that evening, she said she needed to sleep for a few hours before coming over. The others didn't respond to texts.

In the next hour or so, we muddled through. I adjusted somewhat to the intensity of the pain, and the nausea subsided. Ian finished filling the pool and helped me get in, and then focused on Jacob.

I started to remember what worked for me the last time around. I allowed my muscle memory and emotional memory to guide me.

Whereas during my first labour I was excited and nervous, now I was patient. For each contraction, I went on my hands and knees and tried to centre my energy into my pelvis. I felt the pain radiate all across my belly and through my lower back. When it receded, I flipped onto my back to lean against the edge of the tub and relax my core as completely as possible. I reminded myself to pee as I recalled the troubles a full bladder could cause after birth. If I felt I had a little extra time, I took a sip of water or ginger ale from the stand Ian had set up next to me. As the tightening returned, I quickly flung myself against the tub to be on my knees again.

It is only pain, and all I can do is feel it, and get through it. Pain is just pain. Nothing more.

I had heard these words spoken by a woman at a parent blessing late in my pregnancy. They had been a total revelation. The gathering had not been in my honour, but for two friends who were due around the same time as I was. A blessing is a way to prepare for an upcoming labour and birth by surrounding oneself with support. For many, it seems to be a ceremony to embrace womanhood and powerful femininity. Some of my friends who have held mother blessings in the past have chosen not to invite me because they needed to be enveloped by a strong female energy. I would not have brought the right presence for what they needed.

Before Jacob was born, we chose a simple ritual, giving candles to our closest friends for them to light when labour started. At the moment labour began, I realized that the last thing I wanted was for people to be thinking of me being in labour. They would think about my transgender self birthing a baby. They would wonder if it had happened yet. I appreciated neither the visual nor the pressure.

After a contraction, Ian and Jacob came into the room carrying chairs. An audience had descended.

I asked, "Can you guys go put the rest of the groceries away?"

"Nah, that's okay. We already did."

"Please go read books. You have to go read books now."

They left, and Ian eventually got Jacob to sleep for the night. When he came back into the birth room, I heard him sit down in a squeaky chair behind me. He adjusted his position slightly. A miniscule piece of my awareness drifted over to his presence witnessing the work of my transgender body. My focus was suddenly magnetized to him and to the squeaking chair, and immediately the pain of the contraction became overwhelming and my muscles were consumed by tension.

I said aloud, "I don't think I can do this." I didn't quite believe the words, but I needed to say them anyway. I writhed from the pain.

When I was able, I asked Ian to leave the room. At some point I thought I heard him go downstairs. Alone, I talked myself through the sensations and I felt not exactly in control, but capable and calm.

I thought briefly about the midwife. The team had made it clear they were not comfortable attending a birth without the usual monitoring – taking my temperature and blood pressure, and recording the baby's heartbeat at least every twenty minutes. This labour seemed too intense for that. It was moving so furiously I could barely keep up with it. I thought about an epidural, but then remembered the thirty-minute drive to the hospital.

I felt the baby pummel me with its arms and legs from the inside. The baby was working hard, and was obviously vigorous. In the quiet of the room, quick thoughts flickered through my mind. *This is my body. I am the one giving birth.*

During my first pregnancy, I used "we" language – "our" pregnancy, "our" birth plan. At some point, the cumulative effect of the miscarriage, the nonstop nausea, the varicose veins (and compression stockings to treat the varicose veins, and the woman who could not wrap her head around taking measurements for a pregnant man in need of compression stockings, and who thought that "in private" meant the office next to the cash register, with the door wide open), the wider feet (and accompanying bunions), the back pain, the medical examinations – these were not happening to Ian's body. *As long as the baby is still inside of me, it is about my body.*

In the months leading up to the due date, I had tried to prepare myself mentally for anything. Birth was unpredictable. I might need a c-section. I might have another very long labour. I might have a short one. The baby could die during a home birth or during a hospital birth. I could die. As much as I had heard it said, I was not willing to simply "trust birth." Instead, I embraced that I could not and should not control it all. Going in, what I hoped was that I would know what I needed.

Alone in the birth room, I noted the different contractions. Some I felt more in my back instead of my belly, some lower or higher. The intensity and length shifted so that each coming and receding was unpredictable. After a few hours, I felt the familiar urge to push, ever so mild, at the end of one contraction. A few contractions followed without any pushing, and then, again, slight but unmistakable, the need to push. I was happy for the work.

There is no way to know how long the pushing stage took. Perhaps it was half an hour or an hour. Eventually I could feel the baby's head ready to come through, on the verge. At the end of the contraction the head slipped back up inside me, a most awful sensation. I waited for the next try, determined for this baby to finally come out. On the next contraction, I pushed the baby's head through all the way. The contraction subsided, and I waited again. I touched the head with my hand and was surprised to find it full of hair, the softest I have ever felt.

No one watched me or spoke. No one was there to gender my body or my process. I was alone with a new being partly inside me, partly out in the world. I waited. I knew that breathing would not begin until the baby's skin was exposed to air, and I was careful to keep the head fully immersed in the water even during the contractions. At the end of the next push, the rest of the baby slipped out fast. She was kicking and flailing her arms as she was born. I grabbed her out of the water and brought her up to my chest.

I screamed, "We did it! We did it, baby! IAN, COME LOOK!!!"

There was no tender, quiet moment meeting this new baby for the first time. In response to my excitement and yelling, the poor newborn started to cry loudly. Ian rushed upstairs and first glanced at Jacob, but saw he was fast asleep. He was momentarily confused, and then realized the crying was coming from the room with the birth tub. He turned around to greet us and help us out of the water.

Standing beside the tub, without thinking much at all, I brought our new, still screaming baby to my chest to latch her on but she and I were both too slippery for her to gain suction. Ian put a bathrobe over me, and one of Jacob's old receiving blankets on the baby. She latched and began to calm down.

A moment later she came off and was screaming again. I saw that we were both covered with meconium, the infamously sticky, newborn poop. Jacob woke up and came to see. He was in complete awe, but soon crawled drowsily into Ian's lap and fell asleep as Ian called the midwife.

Nursing this baby, whom we named Emily, went smoothly in the beginning. I could hear her swallowing colostrum and I knew she was latching normally. I didn't have any pain. After about 24 hours, I could tell Emily wasn't getting much and she was becoming frustrated at my chest.

Emily and I had to learn, or relearn for me, how to use the supplementer. At first, each time she felt the tube touch her mouth, she stopped suckling. All the incredible frustration from years ago came rushing back to me.

"I don't want to do this again! This is horrible," I whined.

Mercifully, what had been a two-week process with Jacob now took five minutes. Emily quickly realized she was getting milk and she became more persistent with nursing. I remembered how to position the tube for a newborn mouth, precisely at the tip of my nipple. We would be fine. Ian didn't need to help.

Once again, about four or five days after the birth, my chest became lumpy, hot, and sore as milk tried to come in and was accompanied by inflammation in my chest tissue, too. Now, I had an older child who could help move some of the milk by nursing. Jacob's bigger mouth reached different areas of my chest than did Emily's.

The tables were turned. I poked Jacob in the night to nurse.

"Want nay-nay milk? Wake up!"

He obliged. He still used a supplementer. Jacob had donor milk until he was about 17 months old, then cow's milk for half a year, and then we switched to using water.

I took ibuprofen and acetaminophen for the swelling and pain, did chest massage, and alternated using hot and cold compresses. A few days later, the areas of my chest that did not have intact milk ducts ceased producing.

I never tried to measure how much milk I made, but it was fun that Jacob could tell me about what he noticed. He would latch on for a moment and then stop nursing to exclaim, "I got some milk!" before continuing.

Ian and I maintain that it was the new baby who "sleep-trained" Jacob and reduced his nursing dramatically. In the early days after Emily arrived, nighttimes went like this:

Frantic newborn crying.

"Dada! Nay-nay milk!!!"

"I have to nurse Emily first because she is such a tiny little baby and she can't have solid food yet. She needs to nurse a lot. When I get her back to sleep, then you and me can nurse."

The reasoning was obvious to Jacob. He could see the newborn. She was not a theoretical concept we were trying to prepare him for, but a being whose crying frequently woke him up. After getting Emily down again, I would sometimes find Jacob patiently waiting for his turn, but more often than not he'd be asleep again himself.

Seeking milk for Emily was a vastly different experience from the frantic scramble we'd been through to feed Jacob. By now we knew many other parents of young children, we were familiar with Human Milk 4 Human Babies, and we already owned two deep freezers. We began collecting donor milk a few months before her due date. As before, many of our donors were moms of preterm infants that consumed pumped milk. Some gave a few ounces while others gave hundreds or thousands of ounces.

One incredible parent, Linda, provided over 3000 ounces in multiple installments for our daughter.

I asked, "Do you pump so that you have milk available for your baby when you're away?"

"No," she said. "Not really. I don't really go anywhere without my kids anyway. I like pumping, you know, to see how much I can get. It's fun."

Power pumping, the new Olympic sport. Athletes are evaluated based on velocity of spray and milk volume per minute. First, we have the Hand Expression event, followed by the Double Electric Pump-Off. Trevor MacDonald will perform a Demonstration of hand expression, despite previous male chest-contouring surgery.

Linda often asked how much Emily was taking per day, and tried to match that amount in her daily pumping. She worried about our donor milk freezer stash to the point of being stressed out. Our goal of using donor milk to at least one year of age was her goal, too.

I found it hard to take care of two children in a public space – trying to fulfill Jacob's needs drew more attention to the nursing baby and me. One day, we dropped Ian off at work and went into a nearby museum. At the first exhibit, Emily needed to nurse, so I got out her supplementer and found a place to sit down where Jacob could look at a diorama. Emily had nursed for two or three swallows when Jacob looked at me, panicked, and said, "Poop-poop!"

The baby voiced her disapproval loud and clear as I clutched her in one hand and quickly put away the supplementer, and then rushed Jacob back through the crowded museum with my shirt still half open.

During my pregnancy with Emily, I had been teaching a few students at a local music school, and I wanted to continue after she was born, but this meant more transgender nursing under the scrutiny of others. I taught up until and including the day that I went into labour. Since I knew I would take some time off when the baby arrived, I hadn't wanted to stop early. I didn't mention nursing to anyone before the birth – not the students, the parents, or the boss. They had all agreed that the baby could be with me. Under Canadian legislation, babies can be breastfed anywhere that they are allowed to be (and legally, I was female so would have been protected as a breast-feeding "mother"). I also hadn't come out at the school as transgender, but assumed that they would eventually figure it out – or not. I said only that we were expecting a baby.

Two weeks after Emily was born, I started teaching my students again. I sent out an email in advance of the lessons to say that I had chosen to feed the baby at my chest. I mentioned that it was the most effective way of keeping her happy and quiet, and asked them to let me know if they had any questions. At the same time, I wondered how I could possibly be doing this, and if I shouldn't just tell them to find another teacher.

My students' responses were generous and beautiful. Some said they had expected I'd be breastfeeding – that must have been why I wanted her with me in lessons. Others simply said it would be no problem. They all brought lovely gifts for my newborn. Lessons went well enough. I taught while holding Emily asleep in a wrap, or while nursing her. Given all this, and despite never hearing a single negative word about my choice, it seemed to take extraordinary fortitude to go into a professional setting and nurse my infant as a transgender dad. I tried to appear nonchalant, but I was exhausted from being the most visibly queer I'd ever felt in my life, never mind the sleepless nights.

I taught my students for the entire academic term, until Emily started to crawl. The following year she would be too old to be easily quieted during lessons but still too young to be away from her nursing parent. In the end, it all comes down to the baby's need to nurse, so I nurse her. She doesn't know I'm trans, but understands that when she's tired, sad, or hungry, there's no cure quite like breastfeeding. Jacob was the same. And I'm his Dada. He has never – and I'm sure never will – call me by the wrong pronoun.

———————

Bibliography

Black Mothers' Breastfeeding Association, "Open letter to Medolac Laboratories from Detroit mothers," 12 January, 2015. http://goo.gl/4lZJyg

Bonyata, Kelly, "Breastfeeding and cigarette smoking," *Kellymom.com,* http://goo.gl/DTd0kw

Bonyata, Kelly, "Average growth patterns of breastfed babies," *Kellymom.com,* http://goo.gl/LyxxFR

Cook-Daniels, Loree, "Op-ed: Trans men experience far more violence than most people assume," *Advocate,* http://goo.gl/C1m16P

Djulus, Josephine, Myla Moretti, and Gideon Koren, "Marijuana use and breastfeeding," *Motherisk.org,* http://goo.gl/FsVm3g

Gaskin, Ina May, *Ina May's Guide to Childbirth* (New York: Bantam Dell, 2003).

Special note: I met Ina May in 2014 when we spoke together on a panel at a birth conference. In 2015, Ina May signed a letter that argued against the need for gender-inclusive language in midwifery and questioned whether trans people should be included in midwives' scope of practice. The letter was published by a group calling themselves Woman-Centred Midwifery and can be viewed here: http://goo.gl/3ER7Fe

Whether Ina May likes it or not, her Guide helped this trans guy to give birth the way he wanted.

Gaskin, Ina May, *Ina May's Guide to Breastfeeding* (New York: Bantam Books, 2009).

Giles, Fiona, *Fresh Milk: The Secret Life of Breasts* (New York: Simon and Schuster, 2003).

Goldfarb, Lenore and Jack Newman, "The protocols for induced lactation: a guide for maximizing breastmilk production," *Asklenore.info,* http://goo.gl/YwTkT9

Hale, Thomas, *Medications and Mothers' Milk: A Manual of Lactational Pharmacology, 11th Edition* (Amarillo: Pharmasoft Publishing, 2004).

Health Canada, "Health Canada raises concerns about the use of unprocessed human milk," 25 November, 2010, http://goo.gl/vAZg3i

Hospital for Sick Children, "Breastfeeding without pregnancy," http://goo.gl/ortdbc

Iyengar, Geeta, Rita Keller, and Kerstin Khattub. *Iyengar Yoga for Motherhood: Safe Practice for Expectant and New Mothers* (Sterling/Penn, 2010).

MacDonald, Trevor, "Using an at-chest supplementer," *Milk Junkies Blog,* www.milkjunkies.net/2012/10/using-at-chest-supplementer.html

Midwives Alliance of North America Board of Directors, "Core Competencies," 2014, http://goo.gl/LLrNMv

Marasco, Lisa and Diana West, "How to get your milk supply off to a good start," *La Leche League International: New Beginnings,* 2005, http://goo.gl/HjrBwS

Mohrbacher, Nancy, "Why do milk storage guidelines differ?" *Breastfeeding Reporter Blog,* http://goo.gl/svhiNp

Newman, Jack, "Domperidone, getting started," *Breastfeeding Inc.,* http://goo.gl/HedqSh

Newman, "Dr. Jack Newman" community Facebook page, https://goo.gl/9WDRoH

Newman, Jack, and Teresa Pitman, *Dr. Newman's Guide to Breastfeeding* (Toronto: Harpercollins Canada, 2009).

Odent, Michel, public lecture, 13 May 2011, Winnipeg, Canada.

Palmer, Brian, "The influence of breastfeeding on the development of the oral cavity: a commentary," *Journal of Human Lactation,* 14:2, p 93-98, 1998, Sage Publications. http://goo.gl/AhEipx

Palmquist, Aunchalee, "Who is milk sharing online?" Anthrolactology blog, 5 January, 2015. http://goo.gl/wOcwzS

Pollack, Andrew, "Breast milk becomes a commodity, with mothers caught up in debate," *New York Times,* 20 March, 2015.

Rodgers, Caroline, "Questions about ultrasound and the alarming increase in autism," *Midwifery Today,* 80, 2006.

Simkin, Penny, *The Birth Partner: The Complete Guide to Childbirth for Dads, Doulas and All Other Labor Companions*, 4th Edition (USA: Harvard Common Press, 2013).

Simkin, Penny, *Pregnancy, Childbirth and the Newborn: A Complete Guide*, 4th Edition (Minnetonka: Meadowbrook Press, 2010).

Simkin, Penny and Phyliss Klaus, *When Survivors Give Birth: Understanding and Healing the Effects of Early Sexual Abuse on Childbearing Women* (Seattle: Classic Day Publishing, 2004).

Small, Meredith, *Our Babies, Ourselves: How Biology and Culture Shape the Way We Parent* (New York, Anchor Books: 1998).

US Food and Drug Administration, "Fetal keepsake videos", http://goo.gl/6z9Kms

Walker, Marsha, "Supplementation of the breastfed baby: 'just one bottle won't hurt'---or will it?" http://goo.gl/iYcre5

West, Diana, *Defining Your Own Success: Breastfeeding After Breast Reduction Surgery* (Schaumburg, La Leche League International: 2001).

Wiessinger, Diane, "Watch Your Language!" *Journal of Human Lactation*, 12:1, p1-4, 1996, Sage Publications.

Wiessinger, Diane, Diana West, and Teresa Pitman, *Womanly Art of Breastfeeding*, 8th Edition (New York, Ballantine Books: 2010).

Williams, Zoe, "Baby health crisis in Indonesia as formula companies push products," *Guardian,* 15 February, 2013. http://goo.gl/scwAo0

Yang, Sarah, "HIV in breast milk killed by flash-heating, new study finds," *UC Berkeley News,* 21 May, 2007. http://goo.gl/pEZlxd

About the Author

Trevor MacDonald started his blog, www.milkjunkies.net, to share his experiences of transitioning, becoming pregnant, and breastfeeding with the use of supplementary donated human milk. Since 2011, milkjunkies.net has received over half a million visitors.

Trevor founded the first online support group for transgender people interested in pregnancy, birth, and breast or chestfeeding. He has initiated and helped to design and carry out a study funded by the Canadian Institutes of Health Research on the experiences of trans-masculine individuals with pregnancy, birth, and infant feeding.

He received international media attention in 2013 when his application to volunteer with his local chapter of La Leche League, a worldwide breastfeeding support organization, was blocked on the grounds of his gender identity. He successfully campaigned for a change to LLL's policy in 2014.

Trevor is a Huffington Post featured blogger, and has appeared as a speaker and workshop leader at conferences such as Yonifest (with Ina May Gaskin and Michel Odent); the Philadelphia Trans Health Conference; the Canadian Professional Association for Transgender Health; the Canadian Association of Midwives; and the International Lactation Consultant Association, to name a few. He frequently presents educational sessions for church groups, university courses, LGBT youth groups, and health care workers.

Trevor lives near Winnipeg, Manitoba, Canada. This is his first book.

More: www.facebook.com/wheresthemother
Blog: www.milkjunkies.net
Please review this book on Amazon, Goodreads,
and your favourite recommendation-sharing site!

CPSIA information can be obtained
at www.ICGtesting.com
Printed in the USA
LVOW10s0925131116

512782LV00008B/657/P